CASTE AND KINSHIP
IN CENTRAL INDIA

CASTE AND KINSHIP
IN CENTRAL INDIA

A Village and its Region

by

ADRIAN C. MAYER

University of California Press

BERKELEY AND LOS ANGELES

University of California Press
Berkeley and Los Angeles
California

© Adrian C. Mayer 1960

Fifth Printing, 1973
First paperbound edition

International Standard Book Number
0–520–00835–9 (clothbound edition)
0–520–01747–1 (paperbound edition)

Library of Congress Catalog Card No. 60–2076

Printed in the United States of America

TO MY
MOTHER AND FATHER

CONTENTS

Contents

Contents

PLATES

Plates

PREFACE

THIS is a book about caste in a village of Central India and its surrounding region. The subject can be approached from any village; the problem is how to choose a settlement on which to focus study. On the one hand, the anthropologist can make a random selection of a village; on the other, he can seek a place having certain features which he wishes to study. In neither case can he be certain that he studies a 'typical' village. However, the second kind of village will have characteristics which, it is hoped, will be linked more closely to the problems of research, and will not have features clearly extraneous to them.

It is impossible to define these characteristics too closely without knowledge of the area, if not the village itself. I therefore looked only for general requirements in a village when I arrived in Indore, the capital of Madhya Bharat State, in April 1954. In the first place, I wished to stay in a settlement with a full complement of craft and other service castes, for one of my interests was the way economic interaction between castes occurred when people followed these traditional occupations. This meant that I looked for a village of good size. Second, I wished to study people living outside the orbit of a town (i.e. people who did not go to the town for daily work or trade), yet who were sufficiently in contact with the town to be influenced by recent changes in social behaviour there. This meant choosing a village fairly near a road, yet further than either the fifteen-mile 'pull' of Indore, or the half-dozen-mile 'pull' around the smaller towns of the province. In addition, I avoided a village with tribal people, not wishing to include the problem of tribal accultura-tion in my study. Finally I desired to live in a place within a newly launched Community Development Block, so that I could study the concomitants of officially sponsored programmes of change. All these conditions were best met in Ramkheri village, lying in the former territory of the Maharaja of Dewas Senior, about seven miles from the small town of Dewas. Dewas itself is known through the writing of Mr. E. M. Forster, and I was fortunate enough to have his and Sir Malcolm Darling's aid in my introduction to Dewas society.

I spent from April 1954 until June 1955 in Malwa, during nearly all of which time I lived in Ramkheri, and I was able to revisit

xiii

Dewas from June to September 1956. I went to other villages as opportunity offered, spending a few days each in half a dozen other settlements. My work was done without an interpreter, since I had had experience of fieldwork in Hindi-speaking areas. My relations with the people of the area were, I think, happy ones. After a few months of initial suspicion, almost everyone accepted my *bona fides*, and tried their best to convince visitors to the village of them. I do not claim to know each one of the nine hundred inhabitants equally well. I was forced by village sentiment to have more transitory contacts with people of the lowest castes; and I was especially intimate with those families whose members contracted ritual kin ties with my own family. In particular I was close to the men who became brothers to my wife or daughter. Such ties, impossible to refuse when offered, may have aligned me with certain sections of the village's population. I was aware of this possibility and believe that I partly avoided it and have at least made allowance for it in my evaluation of the things I was told. I think, on balance, that it was an advantage rather than the reverse; certainly, the privileges and obligations of a kinsman were most clearly illustrated when they started to apply to me! And apart from their methodological aspects, these ties rewarded me with friendships I shall not easily forget.

Ramkheri is not the real name of the village, for I promised the people that I would not use specific names if they did not wish it. Nevertheless, the village will be easy to identify for those who wish to do so, since the town of Dewas must be named in discussing the influence of the Maharaja and his government, and I was the only anthropologist working there. I have had to consider, therefore, whether to include material which might hurt people if it were published. Since I do not wish to injure any villager, I have omitted some data from this book, and have left several assertions unsupported because of this (e.g. in the passages on leadership, I have taken it as given that some men *are* leaders, and have not analysed their personal characteristics to find out why this is so; similarly, several private bases of inter-personal attitudes have been left out). I hope that nothing in what has been included is felt to be untoward.

My debt to those who have helped me write this book is great. I have already acknowledged the friendships made with the people of Ramkheri; and I must add to this my thanks for the information they and the people of other villages so unstintingly gave, however tiresome they must at times have thought me. There are also many people in Dewas whom I remember with gratitude. Above all, my wife and I recall the hospitality and many kindnesses of H.H. Sir Shahaji Chhatrapati, G.C.S.I., A.D.C., Maharaja of Kolhapur and of H.H. Krishnaji Rao Puar III, Maharaja of Dewas (Senior

Branch). To members of the staffs of both Rulers we are also grateful. The Collector, Block Development Officer, and other officials of the Madhya Bharat Government in Dewas were extremely helpful; in particular, I think of my friend Sri M. C. Pande. My relations with these officials were greatly aided by the Chief Minister of Madhya Bharat, under whose auspices I went to Dewas. Finally I am happy to acknowledge the kindness of Colonel and Srimati S. N. Bhatia towards myself and my family.

I owe a great deal to the teachers and colleagues who have contributed towards my research. I have a great obligation towards the late Professor S. F. Nadel under whose guidance this research was inaugurated. I pay tribute to his creative teaching, and know that this book would have been the richer for the help I have been so tragically denied. My thanks are due to Professor C. von Fürer-Haimendorf for his support of the research and for much useful advice. And I am glad to acknowledge the aid of those who read the manuscript and made many helpful comments: Dr. F. G. Bailey, Dr. B. S. Cohn, Dr. E. R. Leach, Sri K. S. Mathur and Dr. K. C. Rosser. My thanks also go to Professor A. L. Basham, and Dr. J. D. M. Derrett and Mr. Michael Cox. My stay in India was made possible by a Research Fellowship of the Australian National University, to whose officers I am most grateful.

Last, I record a debt to my wife which cannot easily be repaid. And I dedicate this book to my parents.

London, January 1958

NOTE ON TRANSLITERATION

I HAVE left in their English version Hindi proper names which are well known to readers outside India, and those which appear but once or twice in this book. Proper names less well known and of some importance in the book have been italicized once, and afterwards given in roman script. All Hindi terms are italicized throughout and transliterated in the Glossary. I am very grateful to Dr. F. R. Allchin and Sri G. D. Gaur for the help they have given me in this transliteration.

PART I
The Background

I

INTRODUCTION

I HAVE chosen to write about caste in this book for two reasons. One is that caste membership is still pivotal in the actions of Indian villagers; its concomitants are so pervasive that their consideration encompasses a discussion of all major group activities. This is shown in the way I can discuss the political and economic sides of village life as aspects of caste differentiation, though caste may be less important in the latter than the former. Again, an analysis of kinship is at the same time largely an analysis of the internal structure of the subcaste. Caste, then, is the most important focus for an anthropological study of this peasant society.[1]

My second reason is to fill what is at present a gap in our knowledge of the caste system. I would hesitate to add to the many general accounts of the origins of caste, or of the rules and variations in its India-wide application. Again, monographs have been written about single subcastes by such authors as Fuchs (1950) and Dumont (1957a). But no book has yet been solely concerned with the caste system as it operates in a multi-caste village and its surroundings; no account has hitherto dealt in detail with the internal and external relations of village and local caste groups. Srinivas (1952) deals with these topics largely as subsidiary to the main theme of his book, and Dube (1955) is concerned with caste and kinship as they exist in a single village. There is room, therefore, for an analysis which defines the limits of the locally effective caste and subcaste groups, and which deals with the mechanisms controlling their members in relations with each other and with people of other castes.

Furthermore, the variation in the terms used to describe the internal structure of the caste makes such an analysis necessary. This is especially so for the population of a region composed of a few dozen villages, since this is the effective unit of action in many issues of which marriage and social control are the most important. Authors like Bailey (1957) have called this a caste, others a subcaste,[2] and yet others appear to vary from one usage to another.[3] This is not

---

[1] My study deals primarily with secular matters. Sri K. S. Mathur has recently studied aspects of the religious life of a village of the area.

[2] Srinivas 1954: 158.

[3] Gough 1956. On p. 826 she writes, 'Communities of the same caste residing

3

just a terminological matter. The lack of agreement over the words to be used indicates, I think, that the problem of caste structure has not yet been fully considered. What is the relation of caste to kinship, or to patterns of residence and local demography? Such questions were not so important when villages were the foci of research. But now that the wider region is becoming more and more the object of study—for it is generally realized that the village is no longer a self-contained 'republic' if ever it was—these aspects of caste will have to be analysed and compared from province to province before we can trace the comprehensive picture.

My own data show that there are three levels of membership in a caste. The lowest is that of an effective local subcaste population, which I call the kindred of co-operation. This varies for each individual at any time, and around it there is a group which can be called the kindred of recognition. This is the population within which marriages are made and/or kin links can be traced through mutual kin. These two features tend to go together, for people will not make marriages with families about which they know nothing, and the information runs along kinship channels. The kindred of recognition forms a large and rather amorphous body, being much the same for members of a single village's subcaste group (for they are usually inter-related). The kindred of co-operation, on the other hand, varies with individual decision. The kindred of recognition is, in the instances I have recorded, a *de facto* endogamous body, for it contains enough people to satisfy the search for partners and, as I have said, people do not like to marry into the 'unknown'. This differs from the case just quoted from Gough, where the definite number of eighteen villages forms an apparently *de jure* endogamous unit,[1] and this may be a fundamental difference between types of local structure.

Beyond these two kindreds are people who are recognized as members of a subcaste which is endogamous, named and separate from other subcastes. But it usually spreads over a wide area and is therefore not an effective group. Subcastes are mostly based on provincial distinction; there will be the Malwi, the Gujarati or the Mewari subcastes, coming from the parts of India bearing these names. Occasionally, however, they have been formed through the outcasting of a group; such subcastes may be very small, no more than a dozen villages of people who were presumably the supporters of a course of action contrary to the majority opinion. Other sub-

in a given locality . . . form an endogamous *subcaste*.' But on p. 829 she continues, 'Within the sect, most of the Brahmans belong to a subcaste . . . and within this to an endogamous *division* of the subcaste comprising the Brahmans of eighteen villages within a radius of about thirty miles.' (Italics mine.)

[1] Bailey (1957: xv) also implies that this is the case in the Kondmals.

castes are sometimes formed by the issue of forbidden inter-caste unions; these may be larger in size, but will have the same sort of genesis—the contravention of subcaste rules. The provincial subcaste population is not always confined to that province; the Gujarati Weaver, for instance, is found in Malwa. But, according to my informants, a Gujarati Weaver who actually returned to Gujarat from Malwa would claim connection with the Gujarati Weavers there. At first he would not be admitted, for he would have come from a different kindred of recognition. But eventually his *bona fides* would be accepted, providing he conformed to the behaviour of the particular kindred of Gujarati Weavers with which he became associated. I do not know how far this is true in practice, for I could not make an inter-provincial study, but in theory at least the entire subcaste is thought of in this way as a group (and a potential kin-group).

Many subcastes make up a caste.[1] In some ways this is nothing but a category composed of subcastes, rather than a group in its own right. For, though the caste is endogamous, the smallest endogamous units are the subcastes. Again, the caste as a whole has no mechanism for settling disputes, for adjusting the status of members and so forth. Only in relations with other castes is the caste a significant unit. For people of other castes do not, as a rule, regard the caste as the sum of constituent subcastes, but see it as an undifferentiated group (see p. 159). The only exceptions appear to be in the cases of subcastes formed through some irregular behaviour, or when a subcaste comes from another region and has radically different habits. In these cases, people tend to vary their behaviour towards the different subcastes of that caste. On the whole, caste membership is significant for relations with other castes, and subcaste membership for activities within the caste. In turn, these activities are in fact based on the decisions of a local kindred.

This is enough to define briefly the three levels at which analysis will take place, and to start by making it clear that every man is a member of three bodies—the kindred, the subcaste and the caste. In Chapter II I describe how this membership is acquired, and then in Parts II and III detail the relations of people towards those in other castes, and towards those in the same caste respectively.

A major theme of this book emerges from this distinction between the internal and external aspects of caste. This is that the external relations mostly exist within the village, whereas the internal order of

---

[1] In some cases several subcastes make up a section which, with other sections, composes the caste (cf. Karve 1953: 8). These sections are endogamous, named units, but I would hesitate to call them subcastes since they may not have the close connection with the kindreds which, I shall suggest, is the main manifestation of the subcaste 'on the ground'.

the caste group is based to a large extent on kinship relations within the population of a number of adjacent villages. The individual's role in his village is therefore largely as a representative of his caste group, acting towards other caste groups as if they were internally undifferentiated. But in his relations with people of other villages his main role is rather as a member of the endogamous subcaste within the caste, that is, as a member of a caste which is internally differentiated. Caste groupings must be seen differently according to the spatial context of the relations studied.

A second feature follows from the fact that all castes in the village studied are internally organized along patrilineal virilocal lines, with an emphasis, though not complete insistence, on village exogamy. This means, in general, that the caste mates with whom there is most contact within the village are agnates; but outside the village, the main relations are uterine and affinal, and this is emphasized by an absence of any strong ties between men of the same clan over an area larger than the village.

The difference between the roles of an individual as a caste and a subcaste member can thus be seen as one of belonging to a village and belonging to a spatially and genealogically extended kin-group. This book will outline the size and genealogical composition of kin-groups, so as to define more closely the effective subcaste group. Kinship and residential patterns are thus added to caste as major subjects of this account.

By distinguishing between a man's roles as a member of his caste and of his subcaste, I will consider a problem which has been much discussed. This is the attempt to define the 'real' caste. The idea that 'the caste' is an endogamous unit with certain exclusive and hierarchical relations provokes the question; how should we relate the smaller and larger of the units having these properties? For both the caste and subcaste are endogamous, and have many other similar attributes.

Two approaches have been made to this question. On the one hand, there are what might be called the relativists, whose stand is shown in Ketkar's statement:[1] 'The words "caste" and "subcaste" are not absolute but comparative in signification. The larger group will be called a caste while the smaller group will be called a subcaste. A group is a caste or a subcaste in comparison with smaller or larger.'

There is no essential difference between the two terms for these writers. The groups to which they refer are distinguished only by scale, and either 'caste' or 'subcaste' can be used according to the context.

On the other side are ranged those to whom the terms 'caste' and

[1] Ketkar, S. V., quoted in Hutton 1946: 43.

'subcaste' should be used for different *kinds* of group. Blunt, for instance, maintains that there is an essential difference in the way one subcaste or one caste is discrete from another. Thus, he writes that endogamy is not a rigid enough divider of subcastes to make them the same as castes. Disputes, he says, may result in two endogamous groups emerging from a single caste; but the removal of the cause of the quarrel may mean that intermarriage takes place once again. In fact, he doubts that the attributes of the smaller and larger bodies *are* the same. And he stresses what, to him, is a more potent reason for not regarding subcastes as castes. It is that Hindu society does not treat them as such. 'An investigator is not at liberty to manipulate his material so as to make it fit his theories', [1] says Blunt— and, as we shall see, my own data indicate that by name, if nothing else, the subcaste must be placed as part of the caste, rather than as a separate entity (see p. 152).

If one agrees with the relativists, then any discussion of the two terms is mere hair-splitting over words, and indeed cannot come to any conclusion, save for very limited material. But if one follows the other side, there is a real need to agree on some consistent terminology, otherwise we shall find the same term being used for different kinds of group.

An attempt has been made to bypass the problem. Stevenson writes that the term 'caste' may of itself have created many of the illusions that exist about the caste system; and, rather than become entangled in a discussion of its precise meanings, he avoids the word (as well as the term 'subcaste'), talking instead of groups defined by their various activities (endogamous, commensal, etc).[2]

This approach is useful, for it enables the writer to concentrate on the local and interpersonal context, where one can indeed talk of a commensal group, an endogamous group and so on. But this is only half the meaning of the words 'caste' and 'subcaste'. For both are used at a higher level, for total populations. Unless we stretch the term 'group' very greatly, we can hardly see the total caste, or even the total subcaste as an endogamous group—for 'group' implies some sort of interaction, and the practical limits of endogamy are the local regions, perhaps covering only a fraction of the total subcaste. Again, to use the term 'status group' instead of 'caste' is sufficient for specific situations, but does not meet the case where the same caste or subcaste has a different status in adjacent regions.

Thus, Stevenson's solution is useful at the local level. However, here also it is partly only an analytical device, since it does not measure up to what Blunt would doubtless call the 'facts of the situation' in which the caste and subcaste are named populations.

[1] Blunt 1931: 7.   [2] Stevenson 1954: 49.

Introduction

Other anthropologists deal with the problem in various ways. Srinivas, for instance, maintains that the subcaste is the 'real'[1] unit of the system. This unit, he writes, is endogamous, and to some extent ritually and juridically autonomous. But in the rest of his account in this book, and in a paper about a Mysore village elsewhere (1955a) the caste alone is referred to. Since most of the data are about inter-caste relations, I myself would use the term 'caste' here too; but Srinivas, having dismissed the caste as not the 'real' unit, is hardly in a position to do so. In another publication he talks of the units in a village being subcastes,[2] but later says 'the village has a solidarity, even though composed of several different castes'.[3] In short, if Srinivas is using the words 'caste' and 'subcaste' to mean different things, we are nowhere told in just what ways these vary.

Another way of treating the distinction is shown by Dube. In one part of his book (1955a) he details the endogamous divisions of caste in the village he is studying. But elsewhere he treats these village caste populations as undifferentiated. For instance, there are two subcaste groups of the Golla caste living in the village, but all references are made to 'Gollas' only. Later, Dube mentions that some subcastes have separate councils, and others combine with several subcastes of their caste to have a composite council. But he does not say whether the two Golla subcaste groups in the village are separate or combine. In this treatment, subcaste divisions in the village studied are seen almost entirely as a matter of endogamy. The fact that all the subcastes of a caste behave in the same way towards other castes is not stated specifically. It is, however, an important part of the relation between caste and subcaste in the argument that follows below.

Dube is able to ignore subcaste difference because he is concentrating on a single village only. Here, save for one or two exceptions, the representatives of a caste are at the same time the representatives of a single subcaste. The two do not need to be distinguished in most contexts. But, as soon as the wider region is taken, the difference may become significant. There may be different behaviour towards different subcastes in various villages or even towards the same subcaste in different villages. At the level of the regional study, then, the subcaste may be the unit of inter- as well as intra-caste relations, though within the village inter-caste relations can be seen in terms of castes rather than subcastes. The few extensive studies to have been made concern the internal organization of a single caste, and do not treat external relations in this kind of detail.[4] This book is not based on data collected over a region. But, now that regional

1 Srinivas 1952: 24.   2 Srinivas 1955b: 24.   3 ibid.: 28.
4 E.g. Dumont 1957a, Fuchs 1950, Aiyappan 1944.

8

studies will be made, it is well to analyse the relation of caste to subcaste with the material available from one's own research.

The most fruitful starting point, I think, has been given by Ghurye when he writes: 'Stated generally, though it is the caste that is recognized by the society at large, it is the subcaste that is regarded by the particular caste and individual.'

This distinction between caste and subcaste on the basis of internal and external relations is a fundamental one. It does not, I believe, lead to Ghurye's conclusion[1] that 'There is ample reason why, to get a sociologically correct idea of the institution, we should recognize subcastes as real castes.'

The concepts 'caste' and 'subcaste' can coexist, neither being more 'real' than the other. Ghurye is penetrating, however, in so far as he considers the differences between caste and subcaste in terms of relationships held by the individual member. Viewed in this light, a man has concurrent membership of both caste and subcaste, shown in his roles in different contexts—i.e. those in which he is concerned with people outside the caste, and those in which he acts towards people within it.

The village's boundaries are something more than territorial. Broadly, they mark the difference between two kinds of relationship —that of common caste and agnatic kinship (in the village), and that of common subcaste and uterine-affinal kinship (in the region). This means both that the village is a social unit to be studied, and also that in any analysis of either caste or kinship, the data from a single village are not enough, and the influence of the wider locality must be assessed. My study builds on Srinivas' fruitful distinction of vertical ties within a settlement and horizontal links between villages[2] and will develop and modify it further. Sociologically speaking, the village is only one of several foci. It is the most easily apprehended of a series of local groupings—the ward, the village, the circle of villages, the region—all of which influence relations based on common caste and kinship, and whose study must be included in this book.

My approach is reflected in the arrangement of the material. I divide this into two parts. Part II is focussed on the village and the caste. It includes an analysis of inter-caste relations, and the way these are related to the 'unity' of the single village. Part III deals with the divisions within the caste—the subcaste, the clan, the lineage, etc., and their loci in the village and region. The village figures in both parts, for it is the meeting-place for inter- and intra-caste relations. Only the case of a single individual of a subcaste, living in a village, would most nearly avoid this overlap. For most of such a man's

[1] Ghurye 1950: 20 (for both quotations).   [2] Srinivas 1952: 31.

inter-caste relations would be within his village, and all his subcaste relationships would extend outside it. But once there is a village subcaste group, the distinction is less clearcut; relationships of both kinds exist in the village.

Turning to practical questions of research, it is clear that the village's population is the most favourable unit of study. One can gather valuable material by observing the relations between villagers and between them and the people of the region, and I think that a study of inter-caste and intra-caste relations within locally effective groups can at present be based on the data provided by villagers and the people of the region whom they entertain during the year. The problem of inter-relations between these locally effective groups demands a wider field of study. In this book, I have been content to point out that regional variations do indeed exist.

II

THE BACKGROUND

HISTORY OF MALWA

RAMKHERI is a village of 912 people, lying in that part of India which is called Malwa. This, broadly speaking, is a plateau between 1500 and 2000 feet above sea-level, stretching some 200 miles from north to south, and 150 miles from east to west. The Vindhya mountains and the river Narmada form its southern boundary, while to the west lie the Aravalli hills and the deserts of Rajasthan. Going north, the traveller descends abruptly to the plains of Bundelkhand and the Ganges valley. Only to the east is the transition less marked. Here it is hard to know just when the increasingly hilly country is Malwa no more. Indeed, the saying goes that one gate of the city of Bhopal is in Malwa, while the opposite entrance is in Gondwara.[1] Ramkheri itself would almost exactly bisect a line drawn from Bombay to Delhi.

For the most part, Malwa consists of a great plain of black, fertile soil. But Ramkheri lies in the southeast portion, in an area which is made up of long, low hills and shallow valleys. The ground is stony, poorer than that of the 'true Malwa' as the villagers call it, though this starts only a few miles to the west. The climate is moderate— the maximum daily temperature is rarely much above one hundred degrees in the hot weather (April–June), and it is usually cool at night. The wet weather (July–September) produces an average of thirty-five inches of rain, and the cold weather (November–February) is dry and warm with daily temperatures of eighty-five degrees, the nights crisp enough for warm coverings.

Malwa has had an eventful history, partly because it provides by far the best route from northern India to the Deccan and so has attracted conquerors, and partly because, when there has been peace, the fertility of the area has supported prosperous kingdoms. Much of the history of Malwa can be connected to the two cities of Ujjain and Mandu, some thirty and one hundred miles from Ramkheri respectively. Ujjain is now a bustling town of some 150,000 people, composed partly of cotton mills and shunting yards, and partly of narrow streets with mediaeval buildings, and crowded bathing steps

[1] Malcolm 1824: *I. 5.*

down to the sacred river Sipra. Mandu is a ruin of palaces and pavilions, overgrown with jungle, and set on an impregnable canyon-surrounded plateau. Ujjain is one of the seven sacred cities of antiquity, and was the centre of the important kingdom of Avanti in the Buddha's time. The city is remembered by villagers as the capital of Chandragupta II Vikramaditya (A.D. 376–414). Under his rule the region enjoyed a golden age of prosperity, and a culture whose celebrated representative was Kalidasa, author of *Sakuntala*, one of the most famous Sanskrit plays. The era which is used in Malwa (and which begins fifty-seven years before the Christian era),[1] is derived from Vikramaditya's name. Later, Ujjain flourished under the kings of the Paramara dynasty, who later moved their capital fifty miles south to Dhar. The most famous of these kings was Raja Bhoja (A.D. 1010–55) under whom Malwa again enjoyed a period of artistic and scholarly fame. After this time Ujjain and the surrounding country became the scene of wars and shifting alliances between the chiefs of Malwa and Hindu and Muslim invaders. Both Iltutmish and Ala-ud-din conquered Ujjain, the Paramara kings fled south, and Malwa finally came under the rule of the Tughluq dynasty.

At the end of the fourteenth century the Afghan governor of Malwa took on more and more the powers of an autonomous ruler. His successor proclaimed Malwa as an independent kingdom, and set up his capital at Mandu, near Dhar, in 1406. For a century and a quarter this Khilji dynasty ruled Malwa, successfully resisting the pressure of invaders from all sides. The love of the last king, Baz Bahadur, for his queen Rupmati, who poisoned herself when captured by a Moghul general, has been made into songs known all over Malwa.

Malwa was comparatively peaceful during the rule of the Moghuls, which followed Akbar's conquest in 1561, though many of the Rajput chiefs were never entirely pacified, especially during the reign of Aurangzeb. In 1703 a new force appeared, when the Marathas first raided as far north as Ujjain. From that time onwards Malwa was the scene of constant fighting as the Moghuls tried to secure their communications to the south against the Marathas. These in their turn spread northwards with ever-increasing force, being attracted by the need of money [2] as well as by the desire for dominion. Chief among the Maratha generals were Malhar Rao Holkar, Mahadji Scindia, and the chiefs of the Puar clan, descendants of those Paramara kings who had fled south under the first Muslim onslaughts

---

[1] This era, known as Vikram Samvat, has a year starting on the first day of the bright fortnight of Kartik month (October–November).
[2] Sinh 1936: 188.

and had become Marathas.[1] These leaders and their families carved States for themselves and became major rulers in Malwa. Holkar took Indore as capital, which little by little displaced Ujjain as the major city of the province, Scindia assumed power to the north in Gwalior, but also had control of the area around Ujjain, and the Puars settled in Dhar and Dewas. Two brothers founded the latter State in 1728, later dividing their realm to form the twin States of Dewas Senior Branch and Dewas Junior Branch.

The Maratha power was checked by the Afghans at Panipat (1761) and then crushed by the British, with whom all Rulers entered into treaty relations in 1818–19. The fluctuating boundaries of both Maratha and Rajput States of the area were 'frozen' from that time, and remained so until 1948, when the twenty-five States of Malwa merged to form the Indian Union State of Madhya Bharat—itself dissolved in 1956 to combine with parts of Rajasthan, Madhya Pradesh and with Bhopal in forming the new Madhya Pradesh State.

I have given this historical sketch for two reasons. First, I want to show that Malwa has its own history, which is known to the villagers of Ramkheri. They look back to the golden age of Vikra-maditya; they talk of the days of plenty under Raja Bhoja; they know of the great Muslim kings and of the palaces of Mandu, even if they have never been there. For them, Ujjain is the main ritual and cultural centre, and they compare its great twelve-yearly fair most favourably to anything occurring on the Ganges. They are, in short, conscious of being inhabitants of a specific province of India, which they consider to be superior to all others in climate and culture.

Second, the account emphasizes the political and demographic movements which have taken place throughout the history of Malwa. Both the invaders and the local chiefs waited only for the beginning of the dry weather and the campaigning season, after the Dasahra festival, to try to enlarge their realms. This, again, is well known to the villagers. It is a common saying that Malwa has such a good climate and soil that people never leave it, but on the contrary outsiders from all quarters try to settle there. The foreign origins of many subcastes are kept alive in the books of the genealogists and in the subcaste names themselves—Gujarati, Mewari, Purviya, etc. Venkatachar gives a list of fifteen castes for which there is a tradition of immigration, and only eight for which no such history exists.[2] Even now the factories of Ujjain and Indore absorb many newcomers from the south and west.

---

[1] Some writers have expressed doubt about this link (Forster 1953: 39), but the Puar genealogist has it in detail and it is believed by the present Puar Maharajas of Dewas.
[2] Venkatachar 1933: 276.

The Background

The unsettled conditions which existed until only a century ago, and which were for so long a major cause of this mobility, were graphically described by Malcolm in 1824, writing of the state of Dewas Senior in which Ramkheri is situated. 'Though their name always obtained them some respect from their more powerful Mahratta neighbours, the Puars of Dewas have suffered throughout the last thirty years the extreme of misery. They have been, in fact, the sport of every change. With territories situated in the most distracted part of Central India, and unable to maintain any force, they have alternately been plundered and oppressed, not only by the governments of Sindia and Holkar, but by . . . every freebooter of the day. A detail of their history during the last twenty-five years leaves an impression of wonder at their being in existence, or having an inhabited village in their country.' [1] Under such conditions, a village only managed to survive if it had as its headman a man strong enough to defend himself and his followers. Evidence of this is often provided by a *Gaddegal* (see p. 102), a stone monument which records a treaty with marauders who promised henceforth to leave the village alone. Many headmen, however, were unable to protect their villages, and many Dewas settlements, including Ramkheri, have a history of successive headmen. Nearby villages are not necessarily linked by long-established kin ties, nor do they often have the same caste composition, as they might have if they had continued undisturbed. This fact influences both the co-operation between the inhabitants of neighbouring villages as well as the internal organization of the various subcastes.

DESCRIPTION OF RAMKHERI VILLAGE

Ramkheri lies some seven miles from Dewas, a town of 27,879 inhabitants in 1951, which is twenty-two miles from Indore, the commercial, industrial and until recently administrative centre of Malwa. The first part of the journey from Dewas is made over the black soil plain. Fields are demarcated only by grass verges; there are few trees, and the villages are picked out by the clumps of tall mango and *pipal* trees, through which red tiles or corrugated-iron roofs can be glimpsed. Then some low hills are reached. The first of these is a landmark for Ramkheri, and is known as Harvest-Floor Grain-Heap (*kandariya*), from its resemblance to a mound of grain after winnowing. Here more trees dot the fields, which are enclosed with thick hedges of thorn branches, cut from bushes on the hills and renewed each year. About three-quarters of a mile from the village the traveller leaves the motor road, and continues along a track which

[1] Malcolm 1824: *I*. 113.

14

in the wet weather becomes a stream. This runs between six-foot banks, and hides the village until it is almost reached. Then the road opens into a kind of common, on the far side of which lies Ramkheri. The village presents a long, low line of dun-coloured mud walls, and above them a mass of dark brown roofs covering a rise in the ground. In the middle of these appears the whitewashed tower of a small temple, to one side of which there are a few higher corrugated-iron roofs.

The space in front of the village is used for manure pits—one to each family. Passing through these, the road opens out into a rough square. To the right stand two large buildings, one of which is two-storeyed. These were formerly the residence and offices of the landlord (*jagirdar*) and are now the school and the headquarters of the Village Committee sponsored by the Government. To the left there is a low platform of ground with masonry walls, and on it a small shrine to the Goddess Sakti Mata. Facing you, there is a twelve-foot whitewashed wall, and a gateway through which can be seen a courtyard and the temple whose tower was visible from the road. Built by a landlord, it is dedicated to Sri Pandharinath Maharaj, and is in charge of a Vaishnava priest.

Though this area contains the public buildings of the village, and is known as The Square or The Main Street (*cauk*), it is no more than the chief among many meeting places in Ramkheri. Save when there is a festival or a visit by an important official or a village meeting, there is no pre-eminent reason for its being the village's centre. There is no café, for example, and no club for the men which would draw people from all over the village. As I shall describe, the life of the village is largely dispersed through its wards. These are reached by streets, usually wide enough for a bullock cart to pass, but sometimes dwindling to alleys where only two can walk abreast.

Almost all houses in the village are made of 'mud'—that is, earth bound and reinforced by straw and cowdung. Only a handful of dwellings are constructed of 'country' bricks, shaped in moulds and fired by the local potter. Poorer houses have roofs of palm thatch, whilst richer people roof their houses with locally made tiles or corrugated iron. There are few windows, and these have no glass, but simply a barred frame with a wooden shutter. Houses have no chimneys, and one's impression in the morning and evening is of a village whose houses have been set on fire and left to smoulder, as the smoke oozes through the cracks in the roof.

Houses are designed on two main plans. The smaller dwelling faces on to a street, or occasionally a large courtyard-like cul-de-sac. The building is set behind an earthen veranda some four feet high and three feet wide, on which the men of the house can sit with friends and any passers-by who stop to talk and smoke with them. A few rich men have enclosed these sitting-places with a barred framework. Inside, there is a single long room, divided into compartments by tall, earthen grain-storage bins. One of these sections, which is often a separate room with a half-wall, is used for the household's livestock; another will contain the family hearth; and the central place is used for sitting and sleeping.

The second type of house is rather more elaborate. Here, the living quarters and the cattle byre are in separate buildings which face each other across a courtyard. The street runs along the back of one of these buildings, and is thus lined with a blank wall cut by a single doorway. The sitting-place is inside the courtyard. In such a house there will usually be a separate store-room, and the kitchen will be partitioned with proper walls. To indicate the size of these buildings, the poorer houses will have some five to six beams' length (there is about four feet distance between beams, which run across the ten- to twelve-foot width of the house). The larger houses may have twenty-five beams or more, including those of the byre. But there is comparatively little differentiation between rich and poor in the size and aspect of their houses. This contrasts with some other villages, where the headmen have built two-storeyed, urban-style houses. Ramkheri people attribute this to the poverty of their village; however, this is not an entirely convincing explanation, for other villages in the hillier parts contain some large houses. It must rather be seen as a village idiosyncrasy (e.g. powerful headmen of the past who were little addicted to display, or the desire of some landlord to have no houses to rival his own).

There is little privacy in a single house, and since most houses line the streets with no open ground between each other there is also little privacy in the ward. Any quarrel can be heard by neighbours right down the street, and there is nothing that is not included in the daily gossip. Villagers are involved in each other's affairs whether they like it or not.

A house cannot be built casually. Though there is no geomancy connected with its siting or the position of its rooms, building must start at an auspicious time determined from the almanacks possessed by the village priest or other qualified people. Further, the priest specifies the wall on which a red cloth and some mango leaves should be placed in a small inaugural rite. Later, the ridge pole has a similar cloth and leaves put on it in honour of the wood in the house. Finally, the moving in must take place at the appropriate time. There is a small rite performed by the priest, and this may be followed by a reading from sacred texts, or the hearth may be lit and a meal cooked for friends and relatives without further ado. Each year the house rite (*gharsari*) is performed at the start of the Raksha Bandhan festival by a male resident. The main feature is the tying of the thread of protection (*rakhi*) on the ridge pole and rafters. This is done, incidentally, during the rainy season when houses are most liable to be damaged. Major alterations to a house should also start at an auspicious time, and should be accompanied by an invocation to Ganesh.

Just as with a house, so a village cannot be started without the necessary auspicious beginning and divine protection. Here the main work is to inaugurate the proper shrines. Bheru (Bhairav), Sakti Mata and Hanuman Kherapati (Lord of the Village) must all be represented before any houses are built. Some say that Adyapal Maharaj, the guard of the roads in and out of the village, should also have a shrine. It is simple to make these shrines for all save that of Hanuman are represented simply by stones which are painted red with lead oxide each year. But they must be made at the places, and on the days, specified by the village priest. A further duty is to select a foundation stone (*thuni*). This is apparently not connected with any deity, though some people mention a general 'village god' (*ganv devata*), nor does it seem to have any other function than to symbolize that the village has, in fact, been formally founded with all due ceremony. Each village in which I enquired had a foundation stone, though not all people knew where it was (including Ramkheri residents of their own stone). This is not surprising when it is realized that there are forty-four shrines in the village, of which all but a few simply consist of red stones.

The village, then, is a nuclear habitation (for there are no houses outside the settlement), possessing divine sanctions for its foundation, and divine protection for its continuance.

HISTORY OF THE VILLAGE

We have no record of the founding of Ramkheri, nor do the villagers know of any traditional date for this event. The first headmen, it is said, were of the Tankara caste (makers of grindstones by traditional occupation). People say that the date of their coming would be noted in the books of their genealogist; but nobody knows where they went, and this information is unobtainable. After the Tankaras came headmen of the Bhambi (weaver), Khati (farmer), Brahman and finally Rajput castes; the village is not exceptional in having a history of many different headmen, as I have noted already.

The ancestor of the present senior headmen is said by the genealogist to have come 512 years ago, a headman of a different clan a century later. However, these dates are open to doubt, for it is also maintained that the change of headmen occurred when a *pipal* tree at one of the public wells was a sapling five feet high. This is now a magnificent tree, but it is not reckoned to be more than 200 years old. This date may be the more accurate one, since there is always a tendency to exaggerate antiquity (the headmen themselves claim to have been in the village anything between 1200 and 1600 years) and the genealogist may have stretched a point to satisfy his clients. The reason given for the Brahman headmen leaving the village concerns a daughter of the headman who was in Ramkheri when her husband died at Ujjain. She wished to immolate herself on her husband's funeral pyre, but her family restrained her. So she managed to burn herself in Ramkheri itself, and died cursing her relatives, saying that they would come to misfortune through their impiety and would have to relinquish the headmanship. Soon after, it is said, they left for Indore State.

The first Rajput headmen settled on the highest part of the low hill which forms the centre of the village. Later, a brother split off, going to live nearby in what was then known as The Hamlet (*khera*). Between these two habitations lay open ground, roughly fortified against the raiders of the time, and known as The Fort. On the lower ground to each side the other castes of the village were settled. The present situations of the headmen's houses tally with this account, but there is nothing to indicate when The Hamlet was founded. The first historical data I have is that Ramkheri was part of the grant (*jagir*[1]) held by the Maharani Yamuna Bai Sahiba, the wife of Raja Rukmangad Rao (1827–60). For seven years after the death of her husband the Maharani administered the State for her young adopted son, Raja Krishnaji Rao II, and some time later she again took over the administration in an effort to put right the financial difficulties into which the young Raja had entered. But in 1875 the British put the State under supervision, with an administrator of their own, and Yamuna Bai retired to Ramkheri to enjoy the peace of village life. Even when she returned to the town, her interest in the village continued, and the main buildings in the settlement—the house she used to live in, the larger temples—date from her time. Later, the village was held as *jagir* by the younger brother of Maharaja Tukoji Rao III, until in 1934 it was made a 'free' (*khalsa*) village, directly under the Maharaja's control.

[1] The Maharaja owned all the land in the State, and assessed the land tax to be paid by the landholders of each village. But this revenue could be granted to members of the royal family, or to individuals for their administrative or military service to the State. Those receiving the whole of the village revenue were known as *jagirdars*, and those who had to pay a portion of this amount to the Maharaja were called *istamurdars*. I shall call them both landlords; they existed in 17·5 per cent. of the villages in Dewas Senior at the time of the Ruler's accession to the Indian Union.

18

Though the village was to some extent atypical in being under a landlord, and though it was even more exceptional in having a royal landlord, I do not think this has set Ramkheri off from other villages of the region to any marked degree. For example, no landlord (even when royal) had any civil or criminal powers in his village. Probably the only difference resulting from the royal connection was a certain facility in gaining the ears of higher officials, a greater amount of informal arbitration in matters which did not go to the courts (for the greater prestige of the landlord would make arbitration effective), and some economic benefits (e.g. the larger buildings). In short, I do not think the material which follows deals with a village so exceptional that it is inapplicable to other villages in the area.

In 1899–1900 a famine decimated the village, causing some caste groups to die out completely, and others to leave the village in search of food. This date provides the base-line for present accounts of village affairs. It is within the memory of the oldest inhabitants, and the great changes in the village which have occurred as a result make it an obvious milestone for comparison of the present with the in-definite past. For after the famine the Maharani encouraged settlers to come to fill the gaps caused by death or emigration. Of the 257 adult men in the village, 35 are themselves newcomers, and 109 have fathers or fathers' fathers who came to Ramkheri. Most of these settlers happened to be of castes different to those of the 'old' in-habitants, and the introduction of these people has had considerable effects on the life of the village. Since they were of high caste, they have shaken the headmen's dominance of the village for they owed no traditional allegiance to them. This has of course had reper-cussions, as I shall show.

I do not know if Ramkheri and the other villages under landlords were more likely to have had such changes. The landlord was able to offer special inducements for settlers (free draught animals, grants of seed, etc.) which ordinary village headmen could not have given. This may have attracted higher-caste settlers to Ramkheri. In villages without landlords there may not have been such a rapid filling of the gaps caused by the famine, and the new people may have been either low-caste settlers or relatives of the headmen. In neither case would these settlers have caused great changes in the village.

On the other hand, there was always considerable mobility between villages quite apart from the famine period; and all villages were equally placed in this respect. For movement between villages did not stop with the restoration of law and order in Malwa in the mid-nineteenth century. It is only recently that a general rise in population and the decay of village crafts has increased the number of farmers and resulted in a scarcity of land for settlement. Before 1920 or so, there was plenty of land available, and movement was easy. A quarrel might result in a move; or a villager who could not pay his land tax might move to another State, from whence it would be difficult to extradite him. The number of States in the area—Indore, Dewas Senior, Dewas Junior and Gwalior—made for many boundaries, and a multiplicity of enclaves made it easy to move into another ruler's territory. There was no official bar to such immigration in Dewas Senior. Hence, it is possible that the changes brought about by the famine in Ramkheri were by no means exceptional, and that many other villages could point to radical changes in caste composition as a result of more casual immigration.

Besides the changes in the caste composition of the village, there has been an increase in population until the last decade or so. The table shows this, the decrease in 1921 being due to the influenza epidemic of 1919–20.

Year	Population
1901	589
1911	718
1921	499
1931	854
1941	919
1951	894
1955	912

Source: The appropriate Census records for decennial figures. The special enumeration made by the village accountant for the Five-Year Plan in 1955, checked by myself.

At present the population has levelled out around 900, which seems to be the maximum that the state of agriculture and village crafts can support; and a similar pattern exists in the three villages nearest to Ramkheri. The age distribution of the population of Ramkheri is as follows:

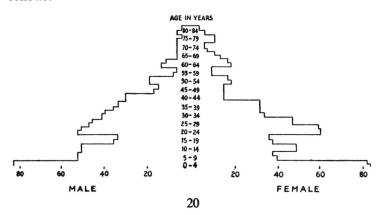

20

The Background

This pyramid is only an approximation, of course, for not all the people give their ages correct to the nearest year. The male side is fairly regular and shows two breaks—one between men of fifty-five and fifty-nine years, which can be attributed to infantile mortality during the famine: the other, of those between fifteen and nineteen years may be due to a cholera epidemic in 1943. The female side is more irregular, possibly because ages were often reported on the woman's behalf by her husband. I am unable to explain the scarcity of girls between five and nine years, but if it is general over the region it will certainly affect marriage arrangements very soon. There is an overall sex disproportion in the State,[1] which doubtless lies behind the statement that it is hard to find brides. The larger number of old women is very evident in the village, and this will enter into the analysis of household composition.

THE AGRICULTURAL CYCLE

The land belonging to Ramkheri totals 3155 acres. It is clearly marked on the map of the village accountant (*patvari*) who is responsible for assessing the crops and soils, keeping up to date the register of owners, and mapping the boundaries of fields. In most places the village boundaries can be clearly seen on the ground. These boundaries used in the past to be marked by strategically placed pillars too big to be moved by hostile villagers. Distinguishing marks were placed in them by each village, so they could be identified if there were any accusations of tampering. Though the ruins of these pillars may still be seen, the boundary is now marked by a stretch of open grassland some twenty yards wide, on each side of which lie the cultivated fields of the two villages. This ground is a constant temptation to cultivators with insufficient acreage, and many disputes have arisen over illegal ploughing of the strip. The people of the intruder's own village are often just as angry as their neighbours, for his action lessens the amount of grazing land for their livestock.

The boundary of Ramkheri is marked to the south and east with such a strip. To the west it partly runs along the crest of the hill *Kandariya*. To the north, village land runs to the top of a low line of hills which overlook the plain in which the village stands, and extend northwards for some miles. Ramkheri land is then partly delineated by artificial and partly by natural means. The average distance between its houses and those of neighbouring villages is two to three miles.

[1] In 1951 there were 519 males to 481 females in Madhya Bharat State (Census 1951*a*: 61). In Dewas District there were 500 males to 484 females (Census 1951*b*: 95).

21

Agriculture is the most important occupation in the village. Few men are wholly engaged in crafts and though Dewas is nearby, only a handful go there to work each day. The major crop is sorghum (*juar*); of the 1700 acres of land under crops, sorghum accounted for 800 acres, with a value of Rs. 21,546 in 1953–4.[1] The grain is mainly consumed in the village, providing the staple food of unleavened cakes (*roti*). Just as the earth itself is called 'mother' (*Dharti Mata*), so people never refer simply to *juar*, but always to *Juar Mata*. As I was told, 'just as our mother feeds us, so the earth feeds us; for without sorghum we could not live'. No other crop has this association, nor does any other have so many uses in the rites of the village. The main cash crop is cotton, grown on 554 acres, with a value of Rs. 16,080. The remaining crops are less important, either providing accessories to the diet, or additional income. Pulses of different kinds go to make the daily curry; they were grown on 128 acres, with a value of Rs. 2244. Less wheat is grown in Ramkheri than in villages to the west, where the soil is heavier and not so suitable for sorghum; this occupied 63 acres, and was worth Rs. 1484. Much of the wheat is consumed by the people as a luxury dish, but it is also sold for cash. Maize, paddy (unmilled rice), chillies, groundnuts and sugar cane are other minor crops, the latter two being important as cash crops.

The village is normally self-sufficient in most foods, and indeed is an exporter of some of its grain. Selling is done through the marts in Dewas, and the bulk of village purchases is also made there; the small shops in Ramkheri cater for only a fraction of imports. The main articles bought are staple foods like salt, cooking oil and refined sugar, and also cloth, kerosene, hardware (lanterns, buckets, etc.). There are a few extras, such as bicycles, watches, razors, torches, tea, and these items are growing in frequency (e.g. in 1954 only one man had a watch; in 1956 there were four in the village). The village's economic ties with the town are on a cash basis, but internally several types of payment are still made in kind. On the whole, the impression given is one of self-sufficiency, though of course considerably less so than in the days when the village produced its own cloth and oil, and there were no 'western' goods for sale.

The agricultural year starts at Akhatij (in April). On that day the orthodox will make the *tilak* mark on their bullocks, and the wives make offerings to the new agricultural year in their homes. Others may start work from that day, or they may observe some other personally auspicious time. Akhatij falls in the hottest season, when

---

[1] These and the following figures were compiled in a survey by the National Extension Service Office, Dewas. The rupee contains 16 annas (recently changed to 100 *paise*), and is worth 1*s*. 6*d*. sterling or about 21 U.S. cents.

the fields lie dusty and empty save for a few patches of irrigated sugar cane. The farmer's first task is to plough and break the soil, spreading on it the manure which is taken from the pits near the village. Towards the end of June the rains start and a period of great activity begins. Chilli seedlings which have been raised in nursery plots must be transplanted, sorghum and pulses must be sown with a drill, after the land has been harrowed yet again. Maize, peanuts, paddy and vegetables must also be planted.

By the middle of July all this has been done, and there are now two months of less constant activity, if only because many days are lost through rains which make the heavier soils uncultivable. When conditions are good, all crops must be weeded. The sorghum and other plants sown in lines are dealt with by a bullock-drawn cultivator, but crops which have been sown broadcast, like paddy, must be weeded by hand. Towards the middle of September the rains ease. Now the maize is ripening, and men live in small huts on stilts in their fields, guarding the crop from parrots and other hungry animals. At this time, too, land which has been left fallow during the first crop is ploughed and harrowed as much as opportunity offers, to be ready for the cold-weather crops. As the proverb says, 'Wheat comes from work, sorghum from the season.'

From October the harvests start. Maize is first, then the groundnuts are picked, pulses and paddy gathered, hay made on the hillsides, and finally in December the cotton is picked and the sorghum harvested. Meanwhile, the second crop is being planted. Cane, wheat and pulses are sown. These three autumn months are the busiest in the year; for there are no rains to hold up the work. These are the days when even the craftsmen desert the village for the fields, and the only men to be found in their houses are the village priest and the schoolmaster. By January, work slackens. Those with sugar cane to cut instal presses in their fields and boil the juice into crude sugar on the spot—to the joy of the small children who cluster around. In March the wheat is cut and the pulses harvested, and the village settles into a month or two of torrid respite from work, seeing to marriages and betrothals, and making visits and pilgrimages.

The cycle of public rites to some extent parallels that of the agricultural calendar. For most festivals fall between June and November. It is mainly private work, like marriages and funerary feasts, which takes place in the period when farming is not so intense.

III

CASTE MEMBERSHIP

A LREADY, in this brief survey of the village, there have been several references to the castes which have lived in Ramkheri, and the roles which these have played. Indeed, it would be impossible to discuss any major aspect of the villager's life without mentioning his caste. The manner of the rites he performs, often his occupation, the kind of social and economic relations he has with his fellow-residents, all vary with caste membership. In villages where there are only two or three castes, the importance of caste may be overshadowed by relationships within a large caste, but the reverse may also be the case—one need only think of a village with, say, two castes in serious rivalry. In villages with many castes, however, inter-caste relations must always be important, and most villages fall into this category, as this table shows for some villages near Ramkheri.

TABLE 1

Number of Castes in Village	Number of Villages
1–5	4
6–10	7
11–15	6
16–20	4
21 and over	3
Total	24

As I have already pointed out, Ramkheri is somewhat larger than the average village, and its caste composition is similarly more complex. There are no fewer than twenty-seven castes there, though some of these are small, with members who play little part in the activities of the village. Here, I shall briefly describe the basis for membership of a caste.

By far the majority of people are born to parents of the same caste.[1] In Ramkheri, for example, 252 out of 257 men over eighteen

---

[1] Their parents are also of the same subcaste, save for occasional cases where there is hypergamy or reciprocal marriage between subcastes (see p. 156). I talk of caste membership, but this is equally subcaste membership (see p. 6).

24

years were in this category. Castes are endogamous. Indeed, this endogamy is a precondition for the marriage rite (*vivah*);[1] no priest would perform a marriage for a couple belonging to different endogamous units, and no relatives would attend the wedding and perform their scarcely less necessary duties. All children born in wedlock belong to their *pater's* caste. A progenitor of different caste is not officially recognized. I know of cases, for example, where the wife of a man known to be impotent has given birth to a child, who is treated as a full member of the *pater's* caste, whether the progenitor is known or not. The fact that the *pater* is not the progenitor does not mean that his son will not inherit from him, nor be under the obligation to perform his mortuary rites.

There is patrilineal affiliation when informal unions openly occur across caste lines. Although there is no recognized marriage between people of different castes, lovers sometimes live together and produce children who then belong to their progenitor's caste. There is no recognized *pater*, since the union is neither socially nor legally sanctioned. Though a man will continue as *pater* of children covertly procreated by another man when his wife lives with him, he will have nothing to do with children openly raised by a lover. Neither is the progenitor the *pater* of such children, for they have no legal rights to his property (i.e. other legitimate children or collaterals will inherit from him).

The child of an informal union, though overtly affiliated to its progenitor's caste, is, in fact, thought of as a kind of 'second class member'. This is shown when its marriage is arranged. For it can often only with difficulty marry a poor 'full' member of the caste, and frequently ends by finding a spouse with similarly mixed ancestry. The actual status behind the façade of caste membership given to the children of these unofficial unions depends to a large extent on the stature and influence of the progenitor, as well as on the status of the caste of the woman with whom he lives. If her caste is very much lower than his own, or if he is a man of little influence and wealth, the children's membership of his caste may hardly exist in more than name. If, on the other hand, the mother's caste is nearly equal to the father's[2] and if he is respected, the children's mixed parentage will not matter so much, and people will tend to overlook it. But in either case the affiliation is with the progenitor.

The cases where a person belongs only to his mother's caste are rare. They occur when a child is born to a widow or divorced woman

---

[1] Nowadays, of course, there is legal provision for inter-caste marriage.
[2] I assume a hypergamous union, for these compose the majority of such cases. A hypogamous liaison would be badly looked on, whatever the castes of the pair.

by an unknown progenitor, or one who does not openly reside with her.[1] Of the population in Ramkheri only two persons have this status, each being born to a widow some years after the death of her husband. Such people are frequently allowed by their mother's kinsmen and fellow-villagers to act as though they were members of the mother's caste. I heard of one occasion in which a boy was born to a Brahman widow. When the question of his marriage arose, the people of a Brahman girl who had been chosen for him by his half-brothers (who had cared for him as an equal and had divided their lands with him) wondered if such an alliance was advantageous, for they had heard tales of his ancestry. The major leaders of the village thereupon sat down and ate food from his hands, signifying that in their estimation he was a true Brahman, and worthy to give them food (although it was said that the progenitor had not been a Brahman). People do not wish to penalize such men and women unnecessarily, and will help them if they are of good character.

But this aid is purely gratuitous. The mother's kin need not acknowledge the child as a fellow-caste mate; in practice, however, they are loth to take a step which would bring the person's mixed ancestry into the open and so expose their kinswoman (and themselves by extension) to shame. I know of very few cases, and so cannot say if the children can ever fully belong either to the caste of their progenitor or to that of the mother. Presumably the former could acknowledge his paternity and make them members of his caste, but I never heard of a case. I do not know to what extent an adoption by a maternal relative would strengthen the child's position in his mother's caste. It would certainly give him a *pater*, but the slur of his ancestry would perhaps remain.

There is apparently no way of formally altering the caste membership given to a man by his *pater* or his mother. For example, I could not find any ritual for changing caste, as is described by Fuchs for admission into the Bhilala caste.[2] The only exceptions are for the sectarian castes I describe below, and of course by conversion to one of the Muslim castes.[3] Nevertheless, there can be an informal change of caste and this, if it then lasts for the remainder of a man's life, is a *de facto* change of caste, and will affect the caste of his children just as surely as if there had been a formal ceremony. This change is

[1] Such cases do not involve unmarried mothers, since girls are almost always married before puberty. I heard of only one instance where an unmarried girl was found to be with child; and she was hastily married before its birth, so that the infant had a *pater* and belonged to his caste in the normal way.

[2] Fuchs 1950: 19.

[3] Here, a man or woman is converted to Islam by saying a prayer, hearing a reading of the Koran, drinking water from the same cup as other Muslims, and becoming circumcised.

made simply by living with people of a lower caste (the movement is only from higher to lower, because all are jealous of their status and would not allow movement upwards from a lower level).

One instance concerned a man of high caste who had taken as mistress a woman of the very low Tanner caste. He had gone to live in her caste's ward in the village, though not taking up the polluting task of tanning. It was generally felt that to all intents and purposes he was now a Tanner, and would be so as long as he stayed there. A village priest put it this way: 'I know of no rite to change a man's caste. What would be its use? You go and live with a different caste, and that's that. Even if you had the rite, the offspring would have no more regular a caste status [he meant that they would still be of the progenitor's caste and would bear the stigma of his history]. Thus a man lives with a Tanner woman, lives in their courtyard, he *is* a Tanner now, and his children will marry Tanners, who else would be willing? I do not think his caste would eject him, what would be the advantage?' The main points made are that the formal caste status of the mover is not altered (i.e. he is not formally ejected and could, it is said, in theory beg readmission into the caste of his birth), but that the main effect is on the status of the offspring, who take the caste of the progenitor, though it would be what we can call his *de facto* and not *de jure* status. I do not know whether the offspring could claim readmission to their progenitor's caste of birth after his death. Even if it were possible in theory, I doubt that they would do so, for people would be most unlikely to attempt to leave a caste group in which they had kin ties through their mother, however mixed might have been their ancestry, to try to brave admission into a higher group where they would meet with a great deal of opposition.

The other way to assume a different caste affiliation is to go to a place where you are not known, and assert that you belong to that caste. In theory it is easy to do this, because nobody can confirm the truth of the claim, and so must accept it; in practice, the change is a very slow process precisely because people cannot be sure of the genuineness of the status claimed. I have known immigrants from north India who have lived in a village for two generations, and of whose status the villagers were still uncertain. In one case the newcomers said they were Brahmans, but nobody would eat from them lest their claim be false.

This reluctance suggests that there may be many attempts to change caste status in this way, and that villagers are therefore on their guard, having been caught before. It may also stem from the variations in status which a caste may have in different provinces, of which the villagers are quite aware. The Potter, for example, is of much lower standing in Uttar Pradesh than he is in Malwa, and in accepting a northern Potter the villagers must be sure that the low provincial rating of his caste does not come from some custom, unknown to them, of which they would not approve. Only when they have seen over several decades that the new Potters behave like their own Potters are they prepared to give them the same status. Again, there is the general suspicion with which villagers regard those to whom they cannot trace any kin relationship. This applies to immigrants from other parts of Malwa as well as from other provinces; and in Ramkheri there are several people whose caste affiliation is not wholly accepted because they cannot establish any such common kin ties. When seen from this angle, the effective caste group coincides with a widely ramified nexus of kin ties, a point I shall elaborate later.

There is recognized admission to a caste from outside only in the case of what have been called 'sectarian castes'—the Gosain and Bairagi being main examples. These castes are founded on membership of a devotional sect (Gosains being followers of Siva and Bairagis of Vishnu) rather than on birth. People of other castes can join the sect, though it was maintained that recruits were only accepted from castes with which there were relations of equality or which were considered higher. The castes are divided into two branches; one is composed of celibate ascetics (*nihangi*), and the other of people who are married and lead ordinary lives (*sansari*— lit. worldly). The celibate branch is obviously not a caste since it is not a self-perpetuating endogamous unit, and must take outsiders to continue. But it is connected to the wordly branch, for Blunt writes that admissions from other castes were initially to the latter, after which the more serious initiation of the novice to an ascetic life followed. He mentions, however, that many of the worldly initiates never moved into the more sanctified branch.[1]

Informants in Ramkheri maintained that it was possible to join either branch permanently. A Bairagi, for example, said that his father had been a Brahman who had joined the worldly branch, his father's brother becoming a celibate. The speaker had continued in the worldly branch, and had been adopted as pupil by a celibate custodian of a shrine in Ramkheri, whose place he had taken at his death. The villagers recognized his authority, though saying that the shrine no longer had the same effectiveness under a married man. The worldly branch of these sectarian castes, then, has a certain infusion from other castes (I never heard of a woman initiated) but is otherwise as strictly endogamous as any other caste.

Caste membership is largely bilaterally acquired, the individual being of his parents' caste. Where there is mixed ancestry, the patri-

[1] Blunt 1931: 132–3.

lineal affiliation is more important, and this reflects the general weight given to agnatic descent. Rules of marriage, through endogamy, ensure that castes exist as separate social groups. But they go no further than this as a basis for the systematic differences in status which exist between one caste and another. A concurrent system of hypergamy would do so, but there is hypergamy only to a minor degree between some subcastes of the same caste. The bases for the ranking of castes in a hierarchy of status, and the pattern and operation of that hierarchy, must be set out for us to understand inter-caste relations in Ramkheri.

PART II

Inter-caste Relations

IV

CASTE AND RITUAL STATUS

THE COMMENSAL HIERARCHY

THE caste groups in Ramkheri are at the same time status groups. In some activities—e.g. political and economic—members of a caste do not always combine, and the strength of the connection between caste membership and group status varies. But this is not the case in what one may call the ritual sphere; here, caste groups form the units in what is as systematic a set of relationships as it is possible to have in a situation where other factors (demographic, economic, etc.) are also relevant. The clearest expression of ritual status is through the criterion of commensality.[1]

The commensal hierarchy is based on the theory that each caste has a certain quality of ritual purity which is lessened, or polluted, by certain commensal contacts with castes having an inferior quality. This is an application of what Stevenson (1954) has called the Hindu Pollution Concept, which lies at the root of ritual status. Commensal contacts include the cooking of food and its consumption. A superior caste will not eat from the cooking vessels nor the hands of a caste which it regards as inferior, nor will its members sit next to the inferior people in the same unbroken line (*pangat*) when eating. Drinking and smoking follow similar rules of exclusion. These are only the most general distinctions; within each there are gradations according to the type of food, the container in which it is served, etc. These need a brief summary.

Kacca food (lit. 'unripe') is food cooked in water and/or salt.[2] It includes the staple food of cakes of unleavened sorghum meal, rice and the daily run of curries and chutneys. It also includes certain foods served at feasts: a curry made from curds, for example, and unleavened balls of wheat flour roasted in ashes. Thus most major foods are *kacca*. The other category of food is called *pakka* (lit. 'ripe'), and is made with clarified butter (*ghi*) from flour, sugar, etc. Such foods are usually sweetmeats and are eaten at feasts; also included are parched grains.

---

[1] The ritual implication of occupation is better treated in the general economic discussion in the next chapter.

[2] Hutton (1946: 64–5) does not mention salt, but I was assured by villagers that this was also a controlling factor.

The difference is that *kacca* foods can only be eaten from a far more restricted number of castes than *pakka* dishes. Thus, the average daily diets make for exclusive eating. Being *pakka* food, parched grain can be accepted from a large number of castes and this is quite important, for these grains (wheat, sorghum, also peanuts and pulses) are roasted in the fields during the harvests and are offered to passers-by who stop for a chat; or they are eaten in the evening when people gather in the village after work. A man will send his son to the Grain-parcher and will share the grain with his friends.

Rules about drinking and smoking supplement those on food. Limitations on drinking water from a brass pot correspond usually to those on the eating of *pakka* food, and those governing water from a clay pot are similar to rules about *kacca* food. Men either smoke a small, stemless clay pipe or locally-made cigarettes. In neither case does the mouth come into contact with the object smoked, for smoke from the cigarette is drawn through cupped hands, and from the pipe through a cloth held in cupped hands around its base to cool the smoke. Both pipe and cigarette are passed around a group of men who are permitted to smoke together; others may use the same pipe, but must bring their own cloth; and others again cannot even use the same pipe. Smoking together is a reciprocal act, and therefore unlike most of the relations between castes over food, which involve A's eating from B, but not B from A. Permission to smoke with a caste usually exists when the two castes can eat *pakka*, if not *kacca*, food from each other.

The position of a caste on the commensal hierarchy can be assessed on the principle that eating the food cooked or served by another caste denotes equality with it, or inferiority; and that not to eat denotes equality or superiority. Those castes which are most exclusive eat from nobody else, and the lowest castes eat from nearly everyone. To put it another way, those from whom all will eat are higher than those from whom none will eat. In practice, however, the hierarchy is not so simply composed. Take, for example, two castes which do not eat from one another. In principle they are equal, but a third caste will eat from one of them but not the other, thus putting the former caste higher in terms of the general picture. In such ways one can infer the relative ranks of two castes; but such cases show that there is a certain ambiguity in the hierarchy.

Commensal relations are illustrated from the twenty-five Hindu and two Muslim castes[1] in Ramkheri. Their sizes are as follows.

---

[1] I use the word 'caste' here advisedly. For these Muslim groups are endo-gamous and have many customs quite foreign to Islam, though consistent with their caste customs before conversion. The people of these castes are conscious

TABLE 1

Caste Name		Population	% of total
Khati	Farmer	181	19·8
Rajput		118	12·9
Pinjara Muslim	Cotton-carder	102	11·3
Balai	Weaver	85	9·3
Camar	Tanner	69	7·6
Bhilala		64	7·0
Gosain		45	4·9
Teli	Oil-presser	29	3·2
Brahman		28	3·1
Ahir	Dairyman	26	2·9
Sutar	Carpenter	25	2·8
Nai	Barber	14	1·5
Nath		14	1·5
Kumavat	Tobacco-curer	14	1·5
Mali	Gardener	13	1·4
Gari	Goatherd	10	1·1
Darzi	Tailor	9	1·0
Balai Babaji		9	1·0
Kumhar	Potter	9	1·0
Bhangi	Sweeper	8	0·9
Mina		8	0·9
Lohar	Blacksmith	8	0·9
Doli	Drummer	8	0·9
Bairagi		5	0·5
Bargunda	Basket-maker*	5	0·5
Fakir Muslim		4	0·4
Bharbunjya	Grain-parcher*	2	0·2
	Total	912	100·0

* The analysis will be simplified by omitting the Basket-maker and Grain-parcher, absent for professional reasons for most of the fieldwork time.

I give the names of the castes and the occupations which are their traditional heritage. In this book I shall refer to the latter only. This is because so many Hindi names would confuse the reader, and also because there is an implied, if not actual, correspondence between caste name and traditional occupation. Not necessarily all members of the caste group do this work, but the connotations of the occupation linger and colour the status of the caste member, whatever he

of this, and distinguish themselves and other similar Muslim castes (Mewati, Naita, etc.) from those they call 'Musulman' (Sheikh, Sayyid, Moghul and Pathan). (See also Blunt 1946: 57.)

may be doing.[1] I use the Hindi caste name only where there is no clear traditional occupation, or where others may also have such an occupation. Thus, the Rajputs were at once rulers, warriors and landowners, and it would be impossible to choose a single occupation by which to designate them. Again, Brahmans are traditionally priests; but there are other castes with sacerdotal traditions—the sectarian castes of Bairagi and Gosain, the Balai Babajis (Balais converted to the Kabirpanthi and Ramanandi sects) and the Naths who are beggars-cum-shrine-keepers. Lastly, some castes have a tribal derivation (Mina[2] and Bhilala[3]) and so possess no traditional occupation, unless it was as peasants who also fought as retainers, or opponents, of the Rajputs. All these castes, then, I shall call by their proper names.

Commensal rules usually apply between whole castes; but sometimes different subcastes in a single caste will have different rules of behaviour towards some other castes. For reasons I give later, I prefer here to regard the groups in Ramkheri as representatives of the caste, not the subcaste; and I shall refer to them as caste groups in this chapter. In the account that follows, I lay out the evidence upon which I have constructed the following hierarchy, which I have made into five divisions. If the data seem too detailed, I must plead that this is the kind of information from which comparative analyses can be made. The hierarchy is as follows:

TABLE 2

Division 1	Brahman

Division 2			Division 3			
Rajput	Gosain	Tobacco-curer		Carpenter		
Barber		Potter	Gardener	Smith	Farmer	Bairagi
Oil-presser		Dairyman		Tailor		
	Goatherd					

Division 4	
	Bhilala
	Mina
	Nath
	Drummer

Division 5		
Weaver		Balai Babaji
	Tanner	
	Sweeper	

---

[1] In a previous account (Mayer 1956a) I intentionally used only the Hindi names for all castes, precisely because many do not do their traditional work. I have changed my mind about this for the reasons I give above.

[2] Russell 1916: IV. 236.   [3] Ibid.: II. 293.

First in undisputed position comes the Brahman.[1] He will only eat *kacca* food cooked by members of his own caste or, in some cases, by those of his subcaste alone. Brahmans in Ramkheri also differ over the rules for *pakka* food; some take from fellow-Brahmans alone, others eat from the top two ranks in division 2, and from the Carpenter and Blacksmith in division 3. Water from an earthen pot is treated like *pakka* food. All the Brahmans will drink from the brass pots of a larger number of castes; the stricter Brahmans include all of divisions 2 and 3 save the Oil-presser and Goatherd, and the less strict exclude the Goatherd only. Again the stricter will smoke with nobody else, the less strict with all of divisions 2 and 3 save the Goatherd. The exclusiveness of the Brahman is matched by the willingness of all castes to drink water from his earthen pots, and to eat the *kacca* food he cooks.

Below the Brahman the hierarchy divides into two more or less equal divisions. Division 2 consists of what I call the allied castes,[2] and also the Dairyman, Oil-presser and Goatherd. The former—the Rajput, Gosain, Tobacco-curer, Barber and Potter—are so called because they eat *kacca* food from one another, and sit in the same line to do so. The Barber and Potter can be seen as slightly lower because they are less exclusive; they both said, for instance, that they would eat *kacca* food from the Carpenter, when none of the other allied castes said they would do so. Again, the Barbers alone said that they ate from the Farmer, the Blacksmith and the Gardener. This would seem to contradict the general rule that castes eat only with their equals or superiors. The Rajputs explain it by saying that they must have servants, who may be slightly lower than they but who can be treated as equal because of their close contacts with their masters. The Barber is a general aide in all feasts of the Rajputs and the Potter brings the water for these occasions; it would therefore be hard to deny them a place in their eating line, say the Rajputs. Similarly, because the Barber and Potter are, to some extent, personal servants of castes in division 3, they would be more likely than the other allied castes to eat from the hearths of these castes.

There are other minor differences in the relations of allied castes with the rest of the hierarchy. All eat *pakka* food from Brahman,

---

[1] This account differs in some details from that previously given (Mayer 1956*a*), because of material gathered during my second visit. But this does not affect the rankings.

[2] Ibbetson (1916: 161–3) has already used this term, though in a rather different sense from the one I propose. He classes as castes allied to the Rajputs those with which the latter intermarry, and which in occupation and customs, etc., are really a lower class of Rajput. I will use the word for quite separate castes, which act together with Rajputs on certain occasions, but whose genealogical connection with Rajputs is purely legendary (see p. 62).

Farmer, Carpenter and Bairagi. The Potter alone refrains from the food of the Tailor and Blacksmith, the Gosain and the Potter from the food of the Oil-presser. In this context, then, the Potter appears more exclusive than the other allied castes, and so higher. It is one of the anomalies to be found in the system under which individual caste variations are permitted if they are minor. It would be a different matter, for example, if the Potter refused to eat from the Brahman. Drinking of water from earthen and brass pots, and smoking are carried on with all the castes of division 3. Only a few people do not smoke through the same cloth with an Oil-presser or a Goatherd. Again, some Rajputs are starting to smoke (though through a separate cloth) with the Nath and Bhilala of division 4.

The remaining three castes in division 2 do not belong to the allied group. For the Dairyman and Goatherd this applies especially to the subcastes resident in Ramkheri, the Goalbans and Malwi respectively. At least one of their other subcastes (the Jadavbans Dairyman and Ujle Goatherd) are counted as allied castes, making up the total of twelve castes in the 'alliance', with the addition of the Gujar, Kalota, Dakkar and Jat castes, and some Gardener subcastes (not the one residing in Ramkheri). The allied castes are the only ones with complete commensal reciprocity, and the significance of this will appear later.

The Dairymen of Ramkheri are immigrants who have only lived in the village for some forty years. They themselves eat *kacca* food from Brahmans only, and no caste save those in division 5 will eat from them. They take *pakka* food and water from all castes in divisions 2 and 3 save the Goatherd. But some of these castes would not reciprocate (e.g. the Potter and perhaps the Gosain). Dairymen are prepared to smoke with all castes in divisions 2 and 3; but again, somes castes like the Blacksmith say they do not reciprocate.

Oil-pressers accept *kacca* food from Brahmans and Rajputs only. They take *pakka* food, water and tobacco from all castes (save sometimes the Goatherd) in divisions 1–3. But we have seen that not all these castes will smoke with the Oil-presser, and no caste save those in division 5 eats *kacca* food from the Oil-presser. This places the caste below all castes hitherto mentioned, save the Dairymen, for each of these have at least one caste in divisions 1–4 eating from their hearths.

The Goatherd accepts *kacca* food from the Brahman and Rajput, but he is not as exclusive as the Oil-presser, for he also eats *kacca* food from the other allied castes in Ramkheri. There are other indications that the Oil-presser is slightly higher. The Farmers, for example, said they smoked with the Oil-presser through the same cloth, but would need a different one to smoke a Goatherd's pipe.

I turn now to division 3. All these castes eat *kacca* food from the Brahman alone; and in *pakka* food eating, too, restrictions are more severe than in division 2. Carpenters and Gardeners said they would eat only from the Brahman; Blacksmiths maintained they would eat from Rajput and Farmer as well, but not from Carpenters; Farmers said they would eat from Rajputs, Gosains, Potters and Blacksmiths, but not from Carpenters. This would seem to make Carpenters and Gardeners the most exclusive, but would also indicate that Blacksmiths and Farmers held Carpenters to be lower than Rajputs, since they eat from the latter but not the former, a fact they deny when talking generally. Further, because Farmers say they would eat *pakka* food from Blacksmiths and not from Carpenters this would imply that the latter were higher—yet Farmers, and the village generally, put Carpenters above Blacksmiths. This, again, is an inconsistency. Nevertheless, we must put Carpenters slightly above Farmers, Blacksmiths and Gardeners; they are more exclusive, and also some castes (Bhilalas, Potters) will eat *kacca* food from their hearths, but not from those of the other castes.

There are similar discrepancies about drinking water. Farmers and Gardeners will drink (in a brass pot) from the hands of all save castes of divisions 4 and 5, and possibly the Goatherd. Blacksmiths and Carpenters add to these prohibitions the Oil-pressers. The Blacksmith in addition bans the Dairyman, and the Carpenter the Tailor. Again, this seems to make the Farmers and Gardeners the least exclusive. Farmers, Gardeners and Carpenters will smoke with all those from whom they drink; Blacksmiths say they also do not smoke with Oil-pressers or Dairymen. The Tailor is exclusive to the same degree as the Carpenter; but the fact that he alone, of all the castes in division 3, has no other caste of divisions 2 or 3 eating *kacca* food from his hearth must place him slightly lower than the rest; for the Bairagi is also equal in status to the Gardener, Blacksmith, etc.

The castes of division 4 will not eat *kacca* food from each other. But the Bhilalas and Minas appear more exclusive than the Drummer and Nath. They will only eat from Brahmans, allied castes and possibly Carpenters. The Nath and the Drummer, on the other hand, eat from all castes in divisions 1–3 save for the Oil-presser, Goatherd and Dairyman. All castes of division 5 eat from the Bhilala. The Tanner and Sweeper eat from the Nath and Mina as well, and only the Drummer is banned by all. Further, the Weavers will drink water from the hands of Bhilala and Mina, but not from the Nath and Drummer.

Rules for taking *pakka* food and water are the same as for *kacca* food, being mutually restricted between the four castes, save that one Mina said he could eat *pakka* food from Bhilalas and Naths. None of the castes in divisions 1–3 smokes with these castes, though a few Rajputs said they smoked a pipe with Bhilala and Nath, though with separate cloth. Within division 4, Nath and Mina smoke together; some Bhilalas say they can smoke with these two castes, but I have not witnessed this. Nobody smokes with the Drummer.

Of the four castes in division 5, the Weaver and Balai Babaji (who eat together) eat *kacca* food from all save Nath, Mina and Drummer, and others in their own division. The Tanners eat from the Nath and Mina, as well as from the Weaver and Balai Babaji. The Sweeper maintains that he does not eat from the Tanner, though the latter contradicts this. The Sweeper is clearly the lowest of all, since he alone will eat the leavings from the plates of other castes. *Pakka* food and water follow the same rules as *kacca* food, save that the Weaver can also eat from the Mina. Each of the castes smokes alone. The Tanners eat beef, a thing the Weavers have stopped doing for a number of years, and this is considered very degrading. The four castes are collectively known as Harijans (having been called *pukari* in pre-Gandhian days), the traditional English term being 'untouchable'.

Nobody will eat either *kacca* or *pakka* food from the Muslim Fakirs or Cotton-carders. Though these are allowed to use the village well, neither water nor the pipe is accepted from them by Hindus. The Cotton-carders take *kacca* food from all castes save those in divisions 4 and 5, some also banning the Oil-presser and Goatherd. This places them in a position roughly equal to a Hindu caste at the top of division 4 or the bottom of division 2. Cotton-carders do not eat from the hearths of Fakirs, though the latter eat from them, as well as from divisions 1–3 and the Bhilala and Mina (this placing them roughly on a level with the Nath). In theory, of course, Muslims do not recognize commensal restrictions and should eat from everyone; but this is not the case in practice.

A description of the hierarchy is complex, and I have therefore confined the analysis to relations between men of the castes. Women either follow the same rules or have rather stricter versions. Some men admit this, though others fondly imagine (at least publicly) that the women do as they tell them and have the same restrictions as themselves. A Rajput woman, for example, said she would eat at the houses of the allied castes of Gosain and Tobacco-curer. But though she would eat food served to her by the Potter and Barber, she would not take food from their kitchens, though she admitted that her menfolk did so. (In this way women show more openly what I have already concluded, that the Potter and Barber are slightly lower than other allied castes.) Women are also stricter in their eating habits outside the village.

Caste and Ritual Status

THE HIERARCHY IN ACTION

I have described the hierarchy as it can be pieced together from the statements of villagers. In how far does this system reflect actual behaviour? The material suggests that, since commensality is an activity, it is influenced by factors which are not necessarily connected with the rules governing the hierarchy. The formal ranking may therefore be weakened or distorted in practice, though maintaining its essential outlines and major divisions. There may be no active disobeyal of the rules, but for various reasons these may be difficult to carry out, and so may become imprecise.

The inter-caste eating corresponded, so far as it went, with the hierarchy. Take, for example, the wedding feast of a Gosain. Eating from the hands of the Gosain cook, and at the same line were Gosains, Rajputs, Barbers, Tobacco-curers (all allied castes). In separate lines were Naths, Bhilalas, Minas and Cotton-carders. The Dairyman, Carpenter and Tailor took uncooked materials which they prepared and ate in their houses; and the castes of division 5 were fed later with cooked food which they also took home. The Sweeper moreover took the scraps from the plates of the diners. At the wedding feast of a Carpenter, there was the following alignment. Rajputs, Potters and Barbers sat in one line and were served by men of Potter and Barber castes, with food cooked by a Gosain. The Bhilalas sat separately; the Carpenters ate food cooked by one of their own caste, and were served by them alone. Farmers took raw materials to cook at home. Both feasts comprised *kacca* and *pakka* dishes, and the castes conformed to the rules for the former.

Nevertheless, some factors attenuate the eating rules. Crudely, they are the considerations which may influence the host when he asks himself 'whom shall I invite to the feast?' Several factors would usually be present, though I set them out one by one. The data come from eighteen feasts witnessed where there was inter-caste eating.

The first factor is caste size. As we have seen, this varies greatly in Ramkheri, and the proportionate numbers of castes there roughly correspond with those of the surrounding area.[1] A host from a

[1] A comparison between a few of the largest castes in the village and in Dewas Senior is as follows:

Caste	Rank in Population*	
	Dewas Senior	Ramkheri
Rajput	1	2
Weaver	2	4
Tanner	3	5
Brahman	4	9
Farmer	5	1

* Rank of all castes of over 2000 people. *Source:* Central India Census Series, Vol. IV, Pt. 1. Indore 1943.

larger caste tends to have more caste mates coming than the man from a smaller caste. Because of a greater local density, the people he invites are more likely to come (many being of the same village); and because he, in turn, has responded to many invitations of people living near, he has a greater number of obligations to invite in return than does a man belonging to a small and scattered caste. If this is so and if a certain standard of hospitality is required (and so a certain number of guests), the host of the smaller caste may more often invite fellow-villagers of other castes. We find, for instance, that in two of three Farmer weddings only Farmers were asked; whereas in all three feasts of the same nature, given by men of comparable wealth but of numerically smaller castes (Potter, Carpenter and Tobacco-curer), outside castes were invited. The point is that, other things being equal, the larger castes will be more self-contained and the smaller castes may never, in fact, have been invited by them in their own or other villages. It is possible that the rules of eating will grow dim, and the castes will end by saying that they are not on eating terms at all.

The second factor is that people of many castes live at some distance from each other. Only the very largest are represented in more than two or three wards of the dozen or so in the village. Any host reaching outside his own caste will first invite those in a ritual kin relation to him or his family; and then he will ask those with whom he has most everyday contact, usually the members of his ward. The result is that castes widely separated spatially will seldom invite each other for any but the largest, and therefore most occasional, feasts. Carpenter and Oil-presser, for example, had only invited each other once in the last decade—at a large funerary feast given by the latter. Mina and Goatherd said they had never visited each other (living at opposite ends of the village) and a member of the former caste said he did not know if he could eat from a Goatherd, the question never having arisen for him. Castes which do not invite each other may, of course, both go to the feast of a third party. In this case the question of taking cooked food is related only to the host caste. To eat in separate lines at a third person's place may then come to stand for an equal separateness, rather than a hierarchical relationship.

As a third factor, people may not be able to come when invited because of concurrent obligations. Marriages, for example, are held only during certain months, for during the rainy season the gods are said to be sleeping and—save for one day—no marriages can be held. Further, during the permitted season there are particular times when the stars are most favourable, and weddings bunch together at those periods. Often, even if a man of caste A were to invite a friend of caste B to his child's wedding, the latter would have too many obligations to be able to accept.

The economic capacity to invite is also a most important factor. A rough calculation puts marriages expenses of all kinds (e.g. clothing, ornaments, feasts and sometimes payments to the bride's father) at some six to twelve months' income. It takes a long time to save this much, and credit is not always available. Those with many children may have to be careful over their marriage expenses, spending less than average, and cutting the invitations to the bone. There is a big difference between people who invite large numbers within their caste and village, and those who invite only their nearer kin. If the latter happen to constitute the majority of the entire caste group in the village, many castes will never have been invited by it, and their commensal relations will be in the main theoretical. It is possible that this factor is responsible for the higher degree of mutual exclusion of the castes in division 5. For members are poor, and may simply not be able to invite people of castes 'near' to them in the hierarchy.

However, cold economic considerations may sometimes be overridden by other factors. For the sake of his group's or his own prestige, a man may feel that he has to spend a great deal on his feasts. The village headmen, for example, should invite many people and are criticized if they do not—though they are most able to afford this. Some castes, like the Rajputs, may set more store on display, and others, like the Farmers, may value thrift and reasonable inviting. There are instances, too, of individual inclination. A Gosain, fairly rich but with a large family, gave feasts which were large and put him heavily in debt. He and others maintained that there was no pressure on him to do so; but he said he liked to invite many people, and to be the largest feast-giver in the village. Though there is some prestige gained from giving large feasts, there is no great competition to invite the most people (lasting prestige comes in different ways) and this means that there are fewer occasions for wide inter-caste commensality.

Finally, it is clear that the membership of different factions may limit commensality. For example, the attendance at an Oil-presser's wedding was limited to a handful of Dairymen, Bhilalas and Farmers. The Rajputs and others who would normally have been invited were on the opposite side to the Oil-presser. If entire caste memberships are in factions—as may easily happen with small caste groups—the pattern of commensality may be affected for years at a time.

Caste and Ritual Status

Size of caste, economic position and spatial distribution may attenuate the hierarchy described in the first part of the chapter. The question then arises: in how far should commensal relations between castes be described in terms of hierarchy at all, or should the emphasis be placed on the equal separateness which I have said evolves from this attenuation?

A newcomer to the village, looking for signs of caste distinction, is struck by its apparent absence in everyday life. This is largely because, with few exceptions, the castes of divisions 2 and 3 can smoke together; and smoking is the main sustained inter-caste activity. For every man in the village smokes, and hardly anyone can pass a group in village or field without being asked to sit down and smoke awhile. The castes which smoke together constitute over half of the male population of the village. Again, a visitor seeing a feast is often struck as much by the number of castes eating in one line as by the gaps between castes. The former line consists of the allied castes, of course; and amongst them equality is more in evidence than the relatively minor differences which do exist, say, between Rajput and Potter.

Many writers have pointed out that the hierarchy is clear at the top and bottom, but has an imprecise form in its middle reaches. It is worth going further, and considering whether inter-caste relations are not even more different in these two instances, stemming from a real difference in outlook. Whereas castes in the lowest and highest ranks both think and say that they are higher than their neighbours, the castes in the middle may think they are higher, but say publicly that they are equal. To do this makes relatively little difference to them, for they are far less exclusive than the Brahmans or the castes of division 5 towards each other. They almost all believe that their caste originated in the same manner, from the ancient Kshatriyas in a legendary history which I relate later (see p. 62). Even where there are grounds for argument, the reasons for each side's superiority are fairly evenly balanced, so that there is usually a final agreement that there is not much to choose between them.

Take, for example, the major feature of difference between divisions 2 and 3—that of vegetarianism. Castes of division 3 eat neither meat, fish nor eggs, and do not drink liquor. Castes of division 2 eat meats like mutton, goat and wild pig as well as other game (partridge, etc.), but do not eat domestic pork, fowl or fish; and they eat eggs only when illness demands a strengthening diet. They drink liquor. (Castes of divisions 4 and 5 follow the latter rules, the Tanner eating beef and the Sweeper domestic pork too.) The vegetarians

44

base their superiority on the doctrine of non-violence which has become increasingly well known and important since Mahatma Gandhi, and they assert that Hindus have always regarded meat-eating as demeaning. They are supported in their contentions by the emergence of popular Governments since 1948 which are dominated by vegetarian castes, and they look forward to national policies which will eventually ban all animal slaughter and so bear out their superiority. The way in which vegetarianism is seen as the wave of the future is illustrated by its adoption by caste groups trying to move up in the hierarchy—the Oil-pressers of Ramkheri are an example —and by individuals who are starting to feel ashamed of their caste's old-fashioned ways and who also want to be well-regarded by the new officialdom—one of the main Rajput leaders of the village is a case, a man who has most of all to do with the Government.

The non-vegetarians, on the other hand, tend to look upon the vegetarians as weak and effeminate. Whilst never openly denying the classical merit given to vegetarianism, they point to the fact that men of action are non-vegetarians, especially their Maharaja of Dewas Senior and his nobles. Both sides thus bring in their resemblance to the authorities to support their claim. If this were all, the vegetarians would be winning, for their model is the more powerful at present. However, the non-vegetarians also have on their side the new 'western' influence of meat-eating. Rajputs, Barbers and other non-vegetarians confidently assert that they have seen people of vegetarian castes—Farmers, Carpenters, etc.—eating meat in the towns, after they had dropped their village ways. And the prestige acknowledged by vegetarians for other aspects of urban behaviour is enough to blunt their attack on this context of meat-eating, so that in arguments of this sort the disputants agree to differ. Even the numbers of the two sides are fairly equal—there are 237 vegetarians to 269 non-vegetarians among the castes in divisions 2 and 3. The fact that the vegetarian castes have a different outlook on life from the non-vegetarians is reflected in a wide variety of village matters, but in the caste hierarchy, divisions 2 and 3 can only be placed more or less equally—and separately.

We do not find this kind of attitude at the top or bottom of the scale. The Brahman asserts his superiority over everyone else from his monopoly of the performance of rites necessary in everyone's life, as well as from his commensal exclusiveness. Moreover, at the foot of the hierarchy there is no common factor about which an equal separateness might be created. A myth of common caste origin is negated by a polluting occupation; common Harijan status is fragmented by polluting differences in diet. Here the castes are separate, but wide gulfs of custom make it impossible for them to be even overtly equal.

This division is correlated with the characterization of the hierarchy as upper (*uttam*) and lower (*madhyam* = middle—or less euphemistically, *nic* = low). The general concensus of opinion puts divisions 1–3 on the upper, and divisions 4 and 5 on the lower level. There is variation only in placing the lower castes of the upper division—the Goatherd, Oil-presser and Tailor. In general, the distinction occurs where smoking relations between the upper castes end, and where the more mutually exclusive lower castes begin; that is, the villagers' division between upper and lower comes where I divide the hierarchy between 'equal' and 'hierarchical' inter-caste relations.

Further, within the upper division, allied castes form a nucleus in most villages. The relative importance of their numbers is shown for the seven villages surrounding Ramkheri:

TABLE 3[1]

Village	Allied caste		Other castes	
	No. Castes	No. Houses	No. Castes	No. Houses
A	2	13	4	18
B	5	13*	16	91
C	2	56	3	9
D	2	18*	15	86
E	2	21	6	34
F	3	20	7	56
G	3	48	11	38
Ramkheri	5	46	22	155
		(pop. 200)		(pop. 712)

* In these villages the Rajputs were of a subcaste not at present commensal with the allied castes. If a present trend towards merger succeeds, the number of allied houses in these villages would rise to 55 and 38, and the number of 'other' houses would fall to 49 and 66 respectively.

This table shows that in most villages the allied castes provide a sizable fraction of the village population, and in some cases the overwhelming majority. The most interesting cases for us are the villages with a large number of castes; for these are where the reciprocal relations of allied castes are noticeable, in contrast to the isolation of the division 3 castes. (I must stress that the allied caste

[1] The numbers in this table are approximate; for I could only find out the number of households, rather than the exact caste populations, in most villages. The actual populations in Ramkheri show that the figures are fairly accurate, though.

populations do not always include Rajputs.) Allied castes, then, provide an island of relatively 'casteless' behaviour in the middle of the already less hierarchically marked upper divisions. In these islands caste is nearer to being a mere endogamous group; the undertones of pollution-based hierarchy are to a great degree absent.

The question I asked can now be answered like this. It would not be entirely true to characterize relations between the upper castes as equal and/or separate, in distinction to hierarchical relations between lower castes; for there is something of each of these two attitudes in almost every inter-caste relation. The problem is to decide just what the proportions of these ingredients are in any given relation, whether there is more feeling that one's own caste is higher as well as separate, or whether there is a feeling of separation overlaid by a certain common feeling discernible, for example, among the allied castes. I do not pretend to be able to interpret the innermost feelings of the villagers about this—and one would have to do so to be certain of striking the right balance. But it is in these terms that inter-caste relations may profitably be discussed, and be seen on a continuum tending towards the hierarchical at one end, and the equal and separate at the other.[1]

FLEXIBILITY OF THE HIERARCHY

In a hierarchy in which there are anomalies of rank, there is room for alteration, for a certain fluidity. Sometimes this occurs between individuals; for there can be differences of opinion about rules among members of a caste. Thus, some Farmers said they could drink water from a Goatherd, though others denied it. But this latitude extends only to relations with 'nearby' castes, and action would be taken if disputable relations were with a caste fairly 'distant' in the hierarchy, or if these relations were demonstrated publicly. Allegations may also be made by the caste as a group about its position in relation to the one or two castes above it.

Details of the hierarchy I have drawn up would be disputed by many castes. Oil-pressers, for example, say they are equal to Farmers because they do not eat from them; the Bhilalas say they are above the Oil-pressers and Farmers, also because they do not eat from them, but eat from the Rajputs and so are identified with them. The Weavers give the same reason of not interdining to maintain that they are, in fact, equal to the Nath and Mina. Even the Sweeper, acknowledged to be the lowest of all, says he is above the Tanner since he does not eat beef. Each of these castes tries to place itself

---

[1] Cf. Bouglé (1908) for the difference between this formulation and one based on hierarchy and repulsion, rather than separation.

one or two places up the hierarchy which can be abstracted from statements and observations of who eats from whom. The loophole often provided is the fact that so many castes do not eat from each other; and there are always citable instances where castes are said to have interdined, often in unspecified villages and at vague times. (Indeed, such variations do exist between villages, as I shall indicate.) This desire to have a higher rank frequently makes people conveniently vague when talking about commensal rules. Many of my enquiries were met with such statements as 'There are Brahmans, and then no high or lower' or 'it is Madhya Bharat now, there is no caste left' (a reference to recent legislation against inter-caste discrimination).

One must distinguish these informal efforts to claim a status within the *existing* hierarchy from attempts to change position (i.e. change the hierarchy itself) with the overt acknowledgement of all castes, through the adaptation of their own rules to the change. The latter attempts seem to occur most in castes which are on the verge of moving from one division to another. The castes at the bottom of the division apparently do not think agitation worthwhile, whereas castes at the top see a big difference to be gained—even the transition from lower to upper. In the four cases which I know about the Oil-pressers and Goatherds tried to become allied castes, and thereby firm instead of doubtful members of division 2, the Bhilalas tried to enter division 2 from division 4—e.g. from lower to upper—and the Weavers to move from the Harijan category to division 4.

The two ways of trying to improve rank may be described as overt and covert. The former consists in making demands, or in taking action which clearly shows one's pretensions. Thus, the Oil-pressers asked to be allowed to sit at the same line as the allied castes;[1] this was refused, and when a Rajput touched the food of an Oil-presser one day, the latter would not eat it, thereby indicating that he thought he was of higher or at least equal and separate status. Covert policies are those which improve the caste's prestige, in the hope that sooner or later it will be recognized as having risen. Thus, the Weavers stopped eating beef, the Bhilalas decided to build a temple on the river Sipra in the same way as other castes, and to call themselves 'Bhilala Rajputs'.[2] Covert also is the factor of wealth or political influence. I do not think that any caste has moved up

[1] This appears inconsistent with their adoption of vegetarianism. I did not question the Oil-pressers about this; perhaps they played both vegetarian and non-vegetarian horses in the hope of winning on one.

[2] Neither overt nor covert efforts have so far gained these castes any great change. The Oil-pressers' demand was rejected by the allied castes, the Weavers have registered no change, and only the fact that a few Rajputs now smoke with some Bhilalas may be connected with the latter's efforts to rise.

ostensibly because it has become rich; but this fact has undoubtedly added weight to its claims, which are cast in the form of discoveries of historical/legendary proofs of higher status, or the adoption of 'higher' customs like the banning of widow remarriage.[1] One must note that a rich individual, or one who has influence with officials or politicians cannot change his rank alone. The entire caste group must change with him; this is partly because the new status is for the most part shown at gatherings where others of his caste group are present. Hence, the village caste population must be seen as a group, acting as a unit in the hierarchy, and bearing the same rank in external matters for all members, however important or however poor they may be.

Nevertheless, this is only a *village-wide* unit; for the commensal rules may vary considerably in different villages, quite apart from the standards now admissible in towns like Dewas. There is a general principle that, within limits, visitors should follow the customs of the places to which they have been invited. As one man said, 'We accept the customs of the villages where we are guests, except when these concern the lower (*madhyam*) castes. We can eat from all those from whose hands we take water, if they have not previously associated with lower castes. But if they have joined with these lower castes, we cannot eat with them; they can do what they wish in their own village, it is nothing to do with us. For instance, suppose the Rajput and Farmer of Ramkheri go together on a wedding party (*barat*), to a village where Rajputs and Farmers eat in one line [this, it may be recalled, is forbidden to Ramkheri people]. We shall also eat in one line; and it will not be a matter for our Ramkheri caste councils, because it is the custom of that village.'

An important feature of this statement is that variation is only within the limits of the upper castes. It would, in any case, be hard to find any village where upper caste hosts would eat with castes of divisions 4 and 5. The variation is between castes of roughly similar status, whose members are likely to feel equal. The other point is the degree to which villages are seen as separate hierarchical systems. The village boundary seems to insulate villages against the need for their commensal rules to be consistent, and so allows variation. Similarly, a man going across the boundary to another village automatically sheds his status as a resident of his own village and can conform to the rules of the host village, which, were he to follow them in his own village, would mean disciplinary action against him. Commensally speaking, then, the village is very much a reality.

---

[1] I leave the subject of the content and changes in a caste's religious customs to Sri K. S. Mathur, who has made a special study of this in another Malwa village. I do not therefore think it appropriate to consider the 'Sanskritization' of castes.

These differences between villages are of long-standing and are universally recognized. In contrast, there are the recent changes brought about by urban influences and Government policy. The centre of this kind of variation is the restaurant in the town. Here all castes must be served, under pain of fine. For the new laws against discrimination can be enforced in public places, in contrast to the village where the refusal to eat with certain people can be made a purely personal matter of inclination. Most men of Ramkheri go to restaurants when in town, where they drink tea or have light refreshments (i.e. *pakka* food). Only the stricter souls forswear this pleasure, together with those of the lower castes who are afraid of meeting upper caste villagers. A Sweeper, for example, said he would never go inside a hotel; if he met a Ramkheri man he would have to leave, and might be penalized in the village for his presumption. But Sweepers of the town eat in the Dewas restaurants, he said, for they did not fear such recognition. Ramkheri men admit this, and say that it is impossible to know either who is serving you, or which caste has just used your cup and plate. This is the 'new air' (*nayi hava*), they say, and it is of no consequence to most men. Only the handful of elders and a few more orthodox younger men abstain. This difference between village and town works both ways, of course, for townsmen may become more orthodox when they go to the country. One day a Dairyman working in an Indore mill arrived to see his kin. He and I were sitting at a Muslim Cotton-carder's shop, and the proprietor offered us tea. The townsman refused. 'I would willingly drink in Indore, but I must be careful not to offend anyone here', he said, and the shopkeeper made no demur.

Ramkheri men eat *kacca* food together in the town much less frequently. Nevertheless, people estimated that 10–15 per cent. of men had at one time or another eaten *kacca* food with otherwise forbidden castes. I know of cases where Rajputs and Farmers have eaten together, or Rajputs and Cotton-carders, or Oil-pressers and Farmers. Sometimes this has happened in the town, sometimes on informal occasions outside the village (e.g. at a meal cooked on the roadside, or at Government gatherings). Such instances show that the lines between divisions 2 and 3 are crossed, but I have no instance of inter-dining between Ramkheri's upper and lower castes.

This eating of *kacca* food is subject to one proviso—that there are no men present from Ramkheri who do not agree to it; for these would report the incident, and it would then be a disciplinary matter. Though the orthodox in Ramkheri know that the rules are being broken outside, they are content not to investigate, so long as the matter is not given open recognition. An instance of this attitude occurred when a training camp for development workers was held in

Ramkheri by the Government. Townsmen and villagers of many castes were present. Their food was cooked by a Brahman, but they all sat in the same line. There were two men from Ramkheri, a Rajput and a Farmer, and these observed the proper routine. They sat apart from the others, and separate from each other, too. And they placed themselves nearest to the kitchen, so that they would receive the food before it had been distributed to such a hetero-geneous line. As one of them put it, 'We could not sit with them here; but they, being away from their villages, were able to sit next to Muslims and even Harijans.'

Not all people accede to this new freedom, of course. At another Government camp, food was also cooked by Brahmans. But Barbers and Potters went into the kitchen, and a Brahman and Farmer of Ramkheri, who were of orthodox bent, were unable to eat there. The Rajputs present did not mind the Potter and Barber, of course, but they were most uneasy at having Weavers in the same place, though there was a two-foot gap between the two lines (for castes of division 5 should eat separately when all have finished, or at home). The problem was solved, as one man put it, 'For God sent two dogs to fight and knock over the plates of the Weavers. They left, and the upper castes were together; and afterwards the Weavers ate separately.'

There are thus different degrees to which people are willing to over-step the restrictions current in their own village. Some are prepared to eat food cooked by 'prohibited castes'; others will eat only from those whom they accept in Ramkheri, but will sit in the same line as 'prohibited castes'. The strictness is not correlated with hierarchical position, save as it appears that the castes of middle range are the least conservative. This may be connected with their greater edu-cation, as well as their greater traditional freedom, in the case of allied castes.

The situation is one in which breaches outside the village are not acknowledged so long as they are not made public. This is different from the dual standard based on separate village traditions—that what is right in village A can be wrong in village B, and yet a man can follow both sets in the appropriate village. But it has a similar effect, in that it isolates behaviour within the village from that which is possible elsewhere. The village boundaries distinguish two standards of behaviour, that accepted by the public of one's settlement, and that which follows one's private feelings about what constitutes correct behaviour.

I have said that village standards are maintained by the orthodox men, but one must not ignore the part played by women, too. For women, we have seen, are stricter in their interpretations of commensal rules than men. And they have fewer opportunities to relax their behaviour outside the village. They seldom go to the town, and would never visit a restaurant; they do not go on marriage parties, as a rule, and many of their visits are to their natal villages. Women, therefore, think far more that the rules of their conjugal village are the correct ones, and keep their men to these as much as they can. As one man said, 'I will eat anywhere with any caste; but not in my home, of course.' This would explain why many men see nothing wrong in relaxing the rules in town, but do not risk infringements within the village.

The wall between action inside and outside the village helps to explain the relatively unchanging nature of the commensal hierarchy in Ramkheri. Yet the influence of the town and of official policies make people look at commensal rules with an increasing awareness that they are often strictly illogical, and this may one day lead to changes which would bring the village in line with the town. As one man said, 'It is hard to keep the purity of food nowadays. Look at X- [a Brahman woman]. If she touches anyone of lower caste, she will go and wash. Yet, when her daughter married, the wedding party came bearing eatables, and had them on their arrival. But the bus in which they had come from Ujjain was driven by a Muslim, and so the food should have been spoilt.'

OTHER ASPECTS OF RITUAL STATUS

The commensal hierarchy is not the only manifestation of differences in status between castes. There are other criteria, based on pollution and ritual status. But these do not give as intricate a system of inter-caste relations as the commensal; they tend to divide castes into two or three categories, often distinguishing only the 'clean' castes and the Harijans. But they resemble the commensal hierarchy as far as they go.

For instance, water for domestic use is drawn from a large well at the main entrance to the village. It is used by all castes of divisions 1–4, and also the Muslims. Though some of the wealthier houses have their own wells in the back garden, their women usually come to the common well for the gossip it provides. Harijan castes have each their own wells; the Weavers, Tanners and Sweepers draw water at places in or near the wards in which they reside.

This separation of the Harijan castes is taken for granted in Ramkheri, and there have been no efforts by Harijans to change it. A few Weavers commented on it to me once, but a higher caste man reminded them that if the 'new ways' were adopted, they would have to drink from the same well as the Sweeper, and they were not prepared to do this. Yet this separation seems to be mutable from village to village. I was told of places where Harijans (at least Weavers and Tanners, if not Sweepers) drank from the village well—though the proviso was made that they should draw water in brass, rather than earthen, pots. In one village, a Harijan well had run dry, and the Harijans had only been able to get water by asking higher caste women to fill their pitchers from the high caste jars. They were now demanding permission to draw water, too. A Ramkheri man who heard this advised immediate construction of a Harijan well, as good as if not better than the common village well. This would silence such demands. And, indeed, the Weaver well in Ramkheri has been completely rebuilt, and work is to start on the Sweeper well. The principle of 'equal but separate facilities' does not belong to the Deep South of the U.S.A. alone. Today, of course, it must to some extent fit into the official programme for improvement of Harijan conditions. Thus, because improvements to the Weaver well were made with money from a Government which officially opposed such discrimination, the fiction was maintained that the Weaver well was for the entire village's use—it was a voluntary matter if only a portion of the village used it.

Outside the village there is a stream, which flows quite rapidly in the rainy season, and then with increasing sluggishness until it dries up completely for the last month or two of the hot weather. Most of the village's clothes are washed here, especially those of the women, for women are not allowed to wash or bathe in the field irrigation wells. They must take water from such wells and bathe at a little distance, and many therefore prefer the stream which is more handy though less private. There are no men of the Washerman caste in Ramkheri,[1] and all clothes, including menstrual cloths, are washed by the women of the house. Clothes after childbirth are at first washed by the Weaver midwife—also in the stream—and after a few days by the women of the house. There is no discernible rule whereby upper castes wash upstream from the lower castes; only, as usual, the Harijans keep separate and wash near their ward, which is also downstream. This is ideally held to be unnecessary, for running water purifies itself. In some villages, for example, where there is no well, the entire populace draws water from a stream, and both upper and Harijan castes are said to use the same place. I have not seen this, and cannot say whether here again there is some sort of distinction which marks off the Harijans.

[1] Very few villages have a washerman, in contrast to northern India. He is accounted low, about the equal of the Drummer. It is not thought to be degrading to wash one's own soiled clothes in Malwa, though it would be to wash anyone else's (cf. Hocart 1950: 2).

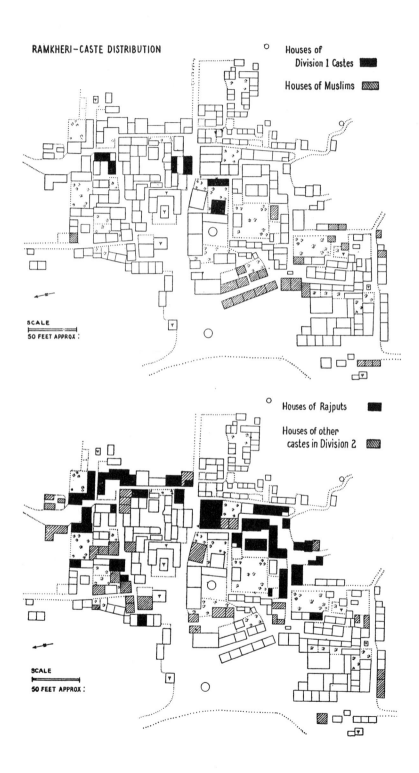

RAMKHERI–CASTE DISTRIBUTION

o Houses of
  Division 1 Castes ▮

  Houses of Muslims ▨

SCALE
50 FEET APPROX :

o Houses of Rajputs ▮

  Houses of other
  castes in Division 2 ▨

SCALE
50 FEET APPROX :

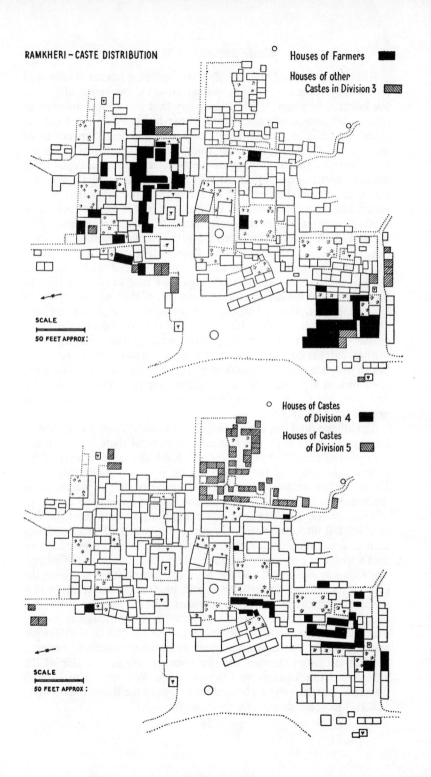

RAMKHERI – CASTE DISTRIBUTION

○   Houses of Farmers ■

Houses of other
Castes in Division 3 ▨

SCALE
50 FEET APPROX:

○   Houses of Castes
of Division 4 ■

Houses of Castes
of Division 5 ▨

SCALE
50 FEET APPROX:

Ritual status also dictates rules about entering houses. These vary for different rooms, with that most barred to visitors being, of course, the kitchen. In general, it is true to say that this room can only be entered by people of castes from whose hands *kacca* food can be eaten. In addition, some people said that the sectarian castes of Bairagi and Gosain could enter since they are keepers of shrines—but I imagine that the latter, as meat-eaters, would be kept out of many kitchens of division 3 castes. The kitchen is seldom a separate room, it will be recalled, but rather part of the large living-room which has been separated off by storage bins. A larger number of castes can enter this main room. Rajputs, for example, said they allowed in all castes of divisions 2 and 3 save the doubtful members (e.g. Oil-presser, Dairyman, etc.). If any other castes should enter, the room should be washed and freshly plastered with cowdung; but not more than a quarter of people are said to observe this. In fact, few castes would enter this room unless they were of more or less equal status, if only because they would have no reason to come. (The only exception might be the entry of the Weaver midwife.) The cowshed may be part of the large room, or a separate building. If the former, entry is bound by the same restrictions as for the large room; but in practice this is overlooked if entry can be made directly from the street. A separate cowshed, and the courtyard and veranda of a house are open to a large number of castes, depending on the strictness of the householder.

The village does not have streets whose entry is restricted, even in the wards occupied by the Harijans. In general there is a tendency for castes of roughly equal status to inhabit the same locality of the village. The maps of the settlement on pp. 54–5 make this clear. There are two main areas of Rajput habitation, in the places where the headmen first settled. Around the Rajput houses are dwellings of allied castes. The Farmer centres are, first, on the site of the fort —which fell into disuse with the end of the unsettled times and was used as a common until after the famine; the second centre is in an area which was previously garden land on the outskirts of the village. The castes of division 4, and the Muslims, live on what was once the edge of the village, though the rise in population has resulted in a varied settlement of castes in divisions 2 and 3 beyond them. All over, there is a certain amount of intermingling, though it is clear which caste provides the nucleus in any ward. But in the Harijan wards there is clear separation, both from other castes and between the Harijan castes themselves. The Sweepers are to one side of the village and the Tanners to the other. The Weavers form a more dispersed pattern, ranging behind the houses of the Rajputs who were, and still to some extent are, their masters.

Everyone, including Harijans, can walk freely through all parts of the village. But people should go to the Tanner and Sweeper wards only on business, it is said; and some added that they should wash their feet afterwards, though these people are the first to admit that this injunction is rarely obeyed. The Tanner ward is off the beaten track, and few people would go there for casual conversation in any case. It is also a naturally uncongenial place, for cow and buffalo hides hang drying between the houses, and there is a tanning pit in the middle of the houses which gives off an unpleasant smell.

Most public places are to some extent barred to the Harijans. The most strictly closed is the main village temple. This is maintained by a Brahman, who does not allow Harijans even within the temple wall, let alone on to the platform on which stands the actual shrine. Clean castes gather on this platform to hear sacred readings. Besides this, there is one other large platform which extends around the shrine of the Sakti Goddess, and is maintained by a Gosain. Harijans are not ordinarily allowed here, but when the Smallpox Goddess was worshipped by the entire village even the Sweeper was allowed to go to her shrine on the platform.[1]

Secular public places include the school and the village hall. Harijan boys go to school and sit in the same line as other castes; previously they were admitted to the building but had to sit apart. But Harijans are to varying extents separate at the village hall. The Balai Babaji member of the Village Committee sits with other upper caste Committee members on the carpet spread for them, and may go into the inner room; Weavers may come to hear the deliberations, but would never sit with upper caste people near the Committee, going to the back on the edge of the veranda; Tanners and Sweepers cannot sit at all, but stand near the veranda—neither do they sit with others at such informal meeting places as the barber's veranda or the shop.

This is a good place to discuss untouchability in general, since only those castes which are untouchable have these disabilities. In principle, untouchability is only a more severe form of the concept of pollution which runs right through ritual regulations. To pollute by mere external contact, the polluting agent must clearly be stronger than one whose ritual status only pollutes 'internally' through the consumption of food or water. Even stronger, of course, is the pollution projected from a distance by an 'unapproachable' or an 'unseeable'. Neither of these categories exists, or has ever apparently

[1] This is similar to the great Gokulashtami celebrations in Dewas (Forster 1953: 100 seq.) where the Maharaja sings hymns in the temple of Krishna and can be garlanded by all castes, including the Sweeper, since these are allowed in the temple during the eight days of the rites.

existed, in Ramkheri or its environs, where such extended forms of pollution seem to be weak.[1]

The prohibition on touching castes of division 5 is not uniform. Most people say that no harm is done if a Weaver is touched, and only the most orthodox would deem it necessary to wash their hands afterwards. Touching a Tanner is a more generally acknowledged matter for purification (one is said to wash the hands, and to sprinkle a few drops of water over the head in lieu of taking a complete bath) though it is admitted that many people would not do anything if they were not seen to touch, and some youths maintained that both Weavers and Tanners could be touched with impunity. The touch of the Sweeper appears to be the only matter over which it is agreed that action *should* be taken and that action *is* taken. Most said that only the orthodox would bathe completely, but that the rest would wash the part of the body which had been in contact and sprinkle water over themselves as a general purification.

The severeness with which touch is dealt with is in inverse ratio to the opportunities there are for touching. The Weavers, as village messengers and servants have relations with headmen and others; again, as contract labourers for farmers, they have more contact with other castes than do the Tanners (most of whom are craftsmen) and Sweepers (who are not asked to do farm work, and indeed say that they are unsuited to it). When a farmer and his labourer hold the handles of a cultivator, or one holds the seed drill and the other drops the seed into the funnel, there is frequent occasion for physical contact. Again, many Rajputs have their Weaver servants drive them to marriages and other festivals, so that they can take care of the bullocks whilst their masters enjoy the festivities. Only one who has ridden in a small country cart can wonder how people could expect to avoid touching each other in such cramped conditions. I do not know whether there was more care taken when the Weavers were still beef-eaters; but at present they can hardly be classified as untouchables. This may, I suspect, be the case in other villages where there are 'untouchable' castes of fair size, having occupations which take them into contact with other castes and being without polluting diet or occupation. In such cases, touch should not be the main criterion of the separation. The denial of the right of entry to the temple, of water from the common well,[2] and of services of the village barber, potter,

---

[1] For example, it is only among one or two of the highest castes that the custom exists of eating food privately, lest it be polluted through the looks of lower castes. Though Harijans do not come too near where food is being prepared, even the Sweeper looks on (from a distance) when Rajputs and allied castes, for instance, eat in public at feasts.

[2] There is, of course, legislation prohibiting such discrimination.

priest, etc. (to be discussed below) are far more constant and important. I would thus prefer to call these castes Harijans or, as was at one time official usage, 'exterior' castes rather than untouchables. The former is the word locally used, but 'exterior' describes the essential feature linking these castes—for they are outside many common village activities.

The lowest caste in division 4, the Drummer, to some extent overlaps with these Harijan castes. For example, no Harijan eats from the Drummer, the only caste so distinguished. Again, whilst cremations of Harijans go on at the common village ground (the Sweepers bury their dead), those of the Drummer must take place in the fields on the village boundary. Finally, not all the village craftsmen (e.g. the barber) serve him; and he is the only craftsman to serve Harijans without distinction. Yet the Drummer draws water from the common village well, lives among the other castes of division 4, and has the services of the other craftsmen. When pressed, people say that he is not a Harijan, but rather an *adivasi* (an aboriginal or tribesman, low in status but outside the hierarchy and so able to fill an anomalous position). This appears to be a rationalization, for the Drummer is as much a caste as the Weaver, for example. Srinivas has well characterized the difficulties in making a hierarchy under these conditions.[1] He points out that one caste has a particular set of disabilities, whereas another which would be below it according to the same standards, has itself other features setting it off as higher. Thus, the few disadvantages of the Drummer caste are far less than those which make the Harijans truly exterior, and it is best to include it in division 4.

The ranking of castes is nowhere more clearly seen than in the commensal rules of eating, drinking and smoking. The analysis of this hierarchy has shown us several features of wide significance in the lives of the villagers. For example, it shows that village caste populations act as groups. All people conform in their relations with other castes, and any movement up in the hierarchy is also as a group. Further, we have seen that these groups are coterminous with the village; for different rules can exist in other settlements, and the people of Ramkheri can conform to these as well as following different norms of behaviour in the town, without prejudicing their standing in the village.

Commensal and other ritual restrictions do not weigh equally heavily on all castes. I have suggested a broad distinction between the upper and the lower castes. The upper are bound by certain ties

[1] Srinivas 1955a: 25, Stevenson (1954: 61) also discusses the problem of defining untouchability.

(e.g. a common legendary origin, the daily act of smoking together) and, save for the Brahman at the top of the scale, the hierarchy does not seem to be as important as for the lower castes. For the latter are more separate and more jealous of their status.

Already, the general characteristics of the principal castes in Ramkheri start to emerge. We see the Rajputs, relatively liberal in their non-vegetarianism and their contacts with allied castes, by this attitude providing the lower castes with the hope of becoming allied to them, and so being the caste which these lower orders try to emulate. We see the Farmers, the largest caste in division 3, restricted in their vegetarianism, isolated in their commensal habits and thereby more indrawn and exclusive, being able to sustain their main occasions for eating together with invitations within the caste. Again, we see the Oil-pressers, aspiring to higher status in the face of opposition, especially from the Rajputs, with whom they wish to eat. These features are confirmed by the pictures which are to follow of the economic and political sides of village life.

V

ECONOMIC ASPECTS OF CASTE

I HAVE said that there is not the same specificity of caste group
status in the economic sphere as there is in commensal activities.
The nearest approach lies in the ritual values of various traditional occupations which clearly grade those caste groups still doing
this work; but, in fact, most people in the village have ritually
'neutral' occupations. Again, there is some correspondence of caste
status and wealth, but this is general and is supported by none of
the sanctions attending commensal relations.

The problem to be considered is therefore: how is caste related to
the economic pattern in the village? To what extent are the castes
now occupational groups; in how far is the economy based on these
groups, and to what extent on individuals of a caste following
different occupations? What influence does the traditional value of
an occupation now have? Again, is economic power held by one or
two castes, or is there a more diffuse spread of influence? Also, we
shall investigate in the economic sphere the degree to which the
village is an isolable unit.

TRADITIONAL BASES OF OCCUPATION

Caste is very closely linked to occupation. For each caste has a
traditional occupation; not only do villagers say that its members did
this work in the past, if not in the present, but their doing so pro-
claims their caste membership. This is clearly shown in the myth
which explains, on the one hand, the very existence of many castes,
and on the other hand their connection with a specific occupation.

There are several versions in the village of the myth I was told, but
they all contain certain salient points and refer to the period before
the creation of a multitude of castes. At that time there were only
the four divisions (*varn*)—Brahman, Kshatriya, Vaisya and Sudra,
formed from the head, arms, thighs and feet respectively of Brahma,
and making up the priestly, military, mercantile and servile sections
of society.[1] As one informant told me, there was once a sage called

[1] For classical bases of this fundamental Hindu division see, for instance,
Manu I. 31 and *Vasishtha Dharmasastra* IV. 2 (Bühler 1886 and 1882 respectively).
I have put forward some comments elsewhere on the present structural signi-
ficance of the *varn* (Mayer 1956a: 136–43).

Jamadagni, a Brahman. His wife's sister was to marry a Kshatriya called Sahasrarjun. As the latter came to Jamadagni's house for the wedding, he thought, 'Jamadagni is only a sage, there will not be any good food in his house for the wedding feast.' Jamadagni had the power to know other people's thoughts, and when he heard this, called to Indra to provide for him. His prayer was answered, for Indra sent the miraculous cow Kapila, from whom issued all the food required for the wedding. As Sahasrarjun was leaving after the ceremonies, Jamadagni asked him what he would like as a present. Kapila was demanded, but she had already gone back to heaven. Sahasrarjun was very angry at this and, assaulting Jamadagni, killed him. Then Renuka, Jamadagni's wife, beat her breasts twenty-one times. At this Parasurama, Jamadagni's son, returned from his travels, and when he saw what had happened, he vowed vengeance on the Kshatriyas twenty-one times.[1]

When it became known that Parasurama was scouring the country, looking for Kshatriyas to slay, many of these considered how they would hide their affiliation, and decided to disemble their occupation. Thus, Parasurama would come across a man pressing oil. 'Are you a Kshatriya?' he would ask. 'How can I be a Kshatriya?' the man would reply, 'Look, I am pressing oil.' 'All right, you are an Oil-presser [Teli—from *tel* = oil], you can go safely.' In this way do the Ramkheri Gardeners, Oil-pressers, Farmers, Tobacco-curers, Barbers, Potters, Tailors, Goatherds and Dairymen explain their origin and occupation. Even when there is no apparent etymological connection between the occupation and the caste name—e.g. nobody can suggest how tobacco-curing is related to the caste name Kumavat—the same myth is said to validate the caste's origin.[2]

Some people, indeed, lay *all* occupational distinctions to these events, saying that Tanners, Weavers, etc., originated in this way from Kshatriyas who disgraced themselves by taking up polluting work and diet. Most, however, maintain that these castes stem from the Sudra *varn*, and reserve a Kshatriya origin to castes in divisions 2 and 3 of the commensal hierarchy. There is a tendency to see the castes of division 3 as non-Kshatriyas (e.g. Farmers, Gardeners and Tailors), since they are vegetarians and so opposed to the meat-eating Kshatriya tradition. This is aided by some castes of division 3 whose members say openly that they do not stem from Parasurama's time, and are not ex-Kshatriyas (and are then called ex-Vaisyas for

[1] The story of Parasurama (the sixth reincarnation of Vishnu) is of great antiquity (see, for example, *Anugita* XIV in Telang, 1882), though varying in details given by written and oral sources.
[2] Nobody is able to say who was, for example, pressing oil *before* some of the Kshatriyas started to do the work.

want of a better category). The Carpenters, for example, claim descent from Visvakarma, the divine architect and artisan of the gods.

The Rajputs, of course, are the prime Kshatriya caste. Some maintain that they are descendants of the only people who did not deny their true Kshatriya status and managed to escape from Parasurama; others say that they changed their name to Rajput to deceive Parasurama, but alone of the Kshatriyas kept on with their martial occupation. They appear in any case to have the strongest claim to Kshatriya status. This gives them a direct connection with traditional origins possessed by few other castes (e.g. the Brahman is another), and is a major factor in their leadership of many ex-Kshatriya and now allied castes, and their pre-eminent position as the caste to be emulated.

Because each caste is said to have some link between its occupation and divine decisions and actions, occupation is not only traditionally, but also religiously linked with caste. It is a man's fate to be born a Teli, and it is this same fate (*karam*, or more colloquially, *dana-pani*) that means he is an oil-presser. I do not wish to discuss the degree to which Ramkheri people see their caste and occupational positions as results of actions in a previous existence; it is enough to say that there is a belief in the doctrine of reincarnation. My main point is that one's traditional occupation is also one's religious duty and one's debt to the past.

To what extent is this concept of traditional occupation significant in inter-caste relations in Ramkheri? In answering this, we must see how many people still follow the traditional occupation, and what their status is as a result.

OCCUPATIONS IN THE VILLAGE

People of Ramkheri distinguish three classes of occupation. There are those for which payment is at least partly given in kind on an annual basis—most of these are crafts, and those who follow them are called *kamin*. Second, there are occupations followed by the *mangat*—the word in Hindi means literally 'beggar', but as I shall show, this is inadequate to describe these people, and I will call them ascetics, or alms-takers. Last, there are all the other occupations, for which there is no generic name; these include crafts for which piecework payments are made, usually in cash.

The following *kamin* occupations exist in Ramkheri: those of the barber, carpenter, blacksmith, potter, tanner-shoemaker, drummer and sweeper.

The barber shaves his clients about once a week, and cuts their hair. He had no particular place to do this; his clients will often assemble on the veranda of his house, but he may equally well go to their dwellings, or even meet them at their work in the fields if it is a busy season. Besides this, he acts as general factotum at the rites of his clients, being paid separately in cash for this service. It is largely his duty to run errands and to see that necessary materials are ready at major ceremonies (some of which, like leaf plates for a feast, he makes himself, and others of which—betel, areca nuts, camphor— are purchased and must be checked before the rite starts). He also has specific duties—he carries the umbrella in the procession of a bride- groom, for instance, and he bears the trays of clothes presented at a wedding by the bride's or groom's mother's brother and his relatives, which are taken in display through the village. The barber's wife has similar ritual duties; she may rub the bride with purificatory turmeric paste, or may help to grind spices for the feast—though more often these jobs are done by the women of the house and their guests. The barber issues all invitations (save those for a funeral feast), sometimes going to quite distant villages to do so, though more often telling people by word of mouth at market day in Dewas.[1] He also makes the announcements of meetings held by the headmen or Village Committee. In previous times the barber used to act as matchmaker, having unrivalled knowledge of personalities and families from his travels; but nowadays people arrange marriages among themselves.

The barber serves all castes save Harijans, where one or two men in each caste will act as barbers for their fellow-members. He will rub the Drummer groom with turmeric if required, for turmeric is a purifying agent, but will not shave him or issue his invitations. He shaves the Muslim Cotton-carders and may also run errands at their rites; but he does not help serve their food, reserving this for the castes at whose hands he can eat. In some cases the Fakir issues the Cotton-carders' invitations, rather than the barber. The barber's work lasts throughout the year, but is more concentrated at times propitious for weddings (i.e. mainly in the dry-weather months).

The carpenter constructs and maintains all the wood implements of his farmer clients (plough, seed drill, harrow, sickle, bullock goad, etc.). The materials are provided by the farmer, unless he prefers the carpenter to get them, when he pays for their cost. The making of bullock carts and anything to do with houses are outside the carpenter's annual duties, and are done for cash; running repairs to a client's bullock cart is, however, done free, unless it requires major work. Each carpenter works in his own shed, which is a favourite gathering place for clients and others. Carpenters serve all farmers, including Harijans. Non-farmers rarely have any work that needs

[1] Many people now deliver invitations themselves, to save money; and a few rich people will call on the village priest, rather than the barber.

carpentry, and this is done on a cash basis. The carpenter has a few minor ritual duties—at a wedding, for example, he makes the wooden model of a parrot (*manikum*) which is placed under the wedding booth, and also the parrots which, placed on a triangular wooden frame (*toran*), are struck by the bridegroom's sword when he arrives at the bride's house. The main times for work are just before the periods of peak farming activity, when repairs need to be made. But a carpenter's general work is constant; if he is not repairing, he is making a new plough or a cart. So the carpenter's workshop is rarely silent, and the passer-by will see him squatting among his chips and odd pieces of wood, whittling down a tree-trunk to a perfect rectangular block as he holds the wood with his feet, and at the same time talking with the group of people who sit smoking and watching him.

The blacksmith's annual obligations are similar to the carpenter's. He must maintain all iron equipment—the tip of the bullock goad, the blade of the cultivator, the iron tip of the plough. The client supplies the material, but the blacksmith fits it and provides the charcoal for the forge. He serves all farmers, of whatever caste. The time of major activity is before the farming season starts (from March to June) and during the monsoon months; at other times the forge may lie cool for days at a time.

The potter works in a shed near his house. He brings suitable clay from a spot about four miles off, and throws it on a hand-operated wheel. While the pots are still damp he thins the clay, and so enlarges them, by beating the surface with a wooden paddle, and this is a familiar sound in the village. He must supply a certain number of pots at fixed times to his annual clients. Thus, one potter listed his commitment as: one jar at the hot-weather harrowing (April), two in the sorghum harvest-field and two at the sorghum threshing-floor (October–November), three at the sugar-cane pressing (March), one at the pulse harvest (February–March). He has also to furnish pots at certain rites; thus, at the *phera* ceremony of the wedding, the four corners of the space where the rite takes place are marked by towers of four pots of diminishing size. Such pots are provided for cash; the only one given free is that used for washing a corpse, this being later broken.

Most potters also make tiles and bricks, forming them in molds and firing them in crude kilns; these are sold for cash in the village and at markets. The potter sells to all castes, but his annual clients are non-Harijans. Clients having few metal pots may need more earthen containers than are provided under the annual contract, for the breakage rate is fairly high with this fragile material; and they then have to buy the extra requirements. At weddings and other major gatherings the potter brings drinking and washing water to the houses of those clients who can drink from his hands (in Ramkheri this means to all but the stricter Brahmans). This can be a very onerous task; if there are several hundred guests, the potter can be seen at any hour of the day or night filling his pots at the well and bringing them to the house on the backs of his donkeys. These he alone of the villagers breeds to carry his wares.

The tanner serves all those having cloven-footed livestock (e.g. cattle, buffaloes and goats). When any of his clients' animals dies, he drags it to the tanner's ward. There he skins the carcase and tans the hide, the meat being eaten by his family and others among whom there are reciprocal arrangements for distribution. The skin is acquired free of charge, and the shoes which the tanner and his womenfolk then make from it are sold for cash to the client. Only repairs are made for an annual payment in kind. Tanners play no part in the client's rites, though they have a small part in some village festivals. They sell their shoes in markets too, and also sell leather irrigation buckets to their clients, repairing them under the annual contract.

The drummer's work is performed on a large, iron-barrelled drum, some three feet long and two feet in diameter. The goatskin at either end has a different pitch, and different rhythms are played at the same time. Any rite or public gathering, even those of the most modest nature, needs an accompaniment of drumming, and the drummer works for all castes including Harijans. At the height of the marriage season he is a very busy man. He must, for example, precede the daily procession of the bride or groom round the village for five or seven days before the wedding. And when there are half a dozen occurring simultaneously, he goes from one house to another without pause. Again, the occasions for drumming at a wedding occur at intervals throughout the day and night. Perhaps this is why the drummers work together, alternating in the peak periods of work. Besides being paid for these specific occasions, the drummers also receive annual payments from farmers, and collect flour, grain, salt, etc., from the villagers on the full- and new-moon days of the month (*punam* and *amavasya* respectively). These are not regarded as alms, however, but as payment for services to the village as a whole—for the drummer must work at all village assemblies, ritual or secular.

The sweeper is seen by some as a *kamin*, and by others as a *mangat*. His duties are to remove any carcase of an animal which does not divide the hoof (e.g. horse, cat, dog, etc.) and to clear away nightsoil from any latrines that may be in the village. He should also sweep the ground at public places when a meeting is to be held—the barber sweeps the inside of public buildings. This is all work for the village as a whole, and in return he begs food daily; he is never given uncooked stores, but rather cooked food and the leavings from plates. He is also given a small amount of grain by the farmers at harvests. The sweeper has few duties connected with individual households. He is sent by some castes to invite people for a funerary feast (*nukta*), for which he is paid in cash; and he takes the shroud at the time of a cremation, and any money thrown by the relatives in front of the bier. In the old days the sweeper shaved a man to purify him after he had killed a cow, but this duty appears to have lapsed in Ramkheri. The sweeper rarely works on the land; some men raise pigs, others play in bands at weddings.

Most of the *kamin* castes have work in village festivals. The barber, for example, is required to attend the headmen when they worship the village shrines at Naumi, on behalf of the village population; and at the Holi festival he goes round the village with the wives of the headmen. The potter goes to each of the forty-four village shrines during the Naumi festival and washes them with water, before lead oxide is put on them. The drummer is in constant demand, as I have said. The tanner provides the skin of a calf on the day after Divali, which is then used in the cow-baiting; the headman gives the tanner two annas as nominal payment from the village. Only the carpenter and smith have no such duties towards the village.

The annual payments given by clients vary; they are calculated 'per plough' (*saman*)—but only six men have enough land to justify the upkeep of two ploughs.

TABLE 1

Item* (*Approximate Weights*)	Carpenter Blacksmith	Kamin Occupation Barber	Tanner	Potter Drummer
Sorghum (harvest)—sheaves	2	2	2	2
Sorghum (threshing)—sheaves	4	4	4	2
Sorghum (clean grain)—lb.	50	20†	20	10
Unrefined sugar—lb.	10	10	3	3
Peanuts (unshelled)—lb.	20	20	20	10
Maize—cobs	50	30	30	20
Wheat (clean grain)—lb. (at sowing time)	10	5	5	5
Wheat (threshing)—lb.	10	5	5	5
Pulse harvest—lb.	10	5	5	5

* If a farmer is not growing a particular crop, the *kamin* do not get an extra allowance of other crops to make up for it. Cotton is a cash crop only, and no share is given to *kamin*.

† This is the rate for each man over about twelve years in the client's house (i.e. who needs a shave).

The payments are related to the service given. The blacksmith and carpenter are highly skilled, the latter doing rather more work. The barber is less skilled and his ministrations, though constant, do not take as long as, say, making a plough or harrow. The tanner is perhaps paid rather highly for his inconsiderable services; one might see this as a high payment to the only person who will undertake the polluting work of disposal of carcases. Both potter and drummer have light duties. There is no fixed payment made to the sweeper; he is given two sheaves of sorghum at harvest field and threshing-floor, but any further amounts (of wheat, sugar, etc.) depend on the generosity of the landowner.

The *kamin* sometimes had duties towards visiting officials; usually they were paid in cash or kind, but if they waited in attendance on the Maharaja they were given rent-free land (*inam*) as payment. In former times, all larger villages contained men who had duties towards the Ruler, and the system of rent-free land was common. But with the improvement of transport, the Maharaja more and more visited villages on daily journeys from his capital, and it was thus unlikely that he would need the services of the barber to shave him, or the carpenter for his carriage, or the sweeper, etc. Hence the rent-free grants were abolished in many villages, and maintained only where the Maharaja frequently visited, or a landlord specifically requested it for his own benefit. Because of connections with the Royal family the Ramkheri *kamin* kept their grants up to the present time, but the system was abolished a year or two ago, and the lands placed on a normal tenure. The gradations of amount of land given followed the caste's status and the work performed. Thus, the barber had a grant of 5·54 acres, the potter 5·34 acres, whereas the drummer had only 2·42 acres and the sweeper 1·63 acres.

How do people become clients of the *kamin*, and what kind of relation do client and craftsman have? In a few cases there is no question of choice, for only one household of craftsmen exists in the village—e.g. the blacksmith, sweeper, drummer have no competitors. Clients also seldom choose their tanner, who is thereby 'inherited' (conversely, tanners divide their clients when a joint household splits, etc.). This is because there is little contact between client and craftsman. The main item of exchange, the slippers, are sold for cash and can be bought from any tanner, so there is no need to have a good craftsman attached to one's family.

But in the case of the barber, carpenter and to a lesser extent potter, there is a close relation, and several factors go to make this an unstable one. An understanding is reached at the start of the agricultural year for the services throughout that year—in practice, there is no formal act, and the relationship is taken for granted unless the client or craftsman specifically says that he wishes to end it. This he may do for any of several reasons. The craftsman may live too far away (e.g. when a new carpenter started work in the northern part of the village several neighbours changed to him); or there may be disputes over the quality of the work; or the client may complain that he is never served quickly enough in emergencies; or the craftsman may break the tie if there are disputes over his wages. Again, features of the client's or craftsman's private life may affect the bond, and competition between craftsmen may also change their clienteles. This competition is exemplified by the potter who refused to teach his younger brother the art. The latter learned at his mother's brother's house, and then came back to Ramkheri and managed to get almost one third of the village as clientele; needless to say, the two brothers are not on speaking terms.

All this makes for changes, sometimes very frequent,[1] and perhaps even cyclical, as a barber maintained. 'People come to me for a few years,' he said, 'then they start to give me bad grain as payment, and there is a quarrel, so they go to another barber. But, later, they will try to pay him in the same way, and they will return to me.' The client might tell a similar tale, only substituting bad work for bad payment. An illustration of the changes that can occur is shown for the Ramkheri barbers:

TABLE 2

| Barber | Number of Clients* | |
	1955–6	1956–7
A	80	19
B	12	41
C	40	72
Total	132	132

* I do not have details for all of the 211 non-Harijan clients; but these figures undoubtedly represent the position.

The most important reasons for these big changes are personal. A- was helped by an old kinsman, who died in 1956; though A- could have carried on without him, he became involved in a lawsuit, losing interest in his work and disputing with clients, so that these complained that they never knew how or when they were to be shaved. B- had been almost completely boycotted by villagers because of a scandal in his household; but he is now starting to collect the clients that his skill in barbering and conscientiousness in attending to rites

[1] This contrasts with the very stable relations described by Dube, for example (1955: 60), which sometimes last for generations.

deserve. C- is an average craftsman, by all accounts, who has at present cashed in on A-'s eclipse. But none of these men take the present situation for granted; and we shall see that this degree of change is duplicated in a similar system of contract farm labour.

Interdependencies between individual craftsmen and their patrons may be changeable; their inter-relations as village occupational groups are more stable. For many village craftsmen have the right (*hak*) to work in Ramkheri, and if there is nobody to carry on, will call on a kinsman to come to the village.[1] The strength of these rights varies from craft to craft. It finds its clearest expression amongst sweepers, where the rights to work and its perquisites in a village are exclusive and can be bought and sold. Other people (e.g. potter, drummer, barber) say that they would resist the attempt by anyone else to come and work in the village, but would not have a case to lay before a caste council unless the newcomer had inveigled clients away from them in the middle of the annual contract period. Their strength would rather lie in the fact that such competition would exist only among fellow-caste mates, and so would be tempered by the desire of both parties to avoid quarrels which might spread to other spheres (e.g. a reputation for quarrelsomeness might affect the supply of spouses for a disputant's children). In these cases, then, changes in clientele are generally made by agreement. But these rights are not the 'property' of the incumbent, as for the sweeper.

In contrast, carpentry is an example of a craft which is now open to many castes, and here the word 'rights' is almost too strong. Carpenters now come from Blacksmith, Nayak and other castes besides the traditional Carpenter, and these people have no compunction in trying to build up a clientele, nor do they lose any reputation in this competition. If anyone tries to take custom away from a carpenter, his only protection is the excellence of his work and the support of his fellow-villagers against an outsider. Only to the extent that he receives this support can he speak of his work as a right.

The village is the unit of operation for craft groups—and also, we shall see, for the priest and alms-seekers. For *kamin* do not recognize some of the decisions of their fellows in other villages. Thus, a man was boycotted by the whole of Ramkheri, after various disputes, and the village's craftsmen, priest, etc., refused him their services. But he was able to go to carpenters and others in nearby settlements to get

[1] The villagers do not, it seems, have a corresponding right to the work of the craftsman group. For a villager boycotted on some matter will also be denied the craft services; and there are instances where craftsmen have left a village which became an uneconomic proposition, the villagers having to 'share' the craftsmen of a neighbouring settlement, the latter then having rights in that village, as if they were residents there.

his work done; these maintained that they had nothing to do with the quarrels of their caste mates in another village. Only if he had been boycotted for a serious ritual offence (e.g. cow-killing) would the outside craftsmen have followed suit, more for the sake of their own purity than from solidarity with the boycotting village. The 'right' of the *kamin* to a client lapses, then, if he himself is not willing to exercise it.

Kamin are paid partly in cash and partly in kind. The former services are performed for every villager according to his requirements. Services for payments in kind, on the other hand, are partly performed for the cultivators, and are partly village service (e.g. one can see the drummer's sorghum sheaves as representing payment for his work at village festivals).[1] In this way, then, the cultivators pay for the whole village population—and in principle this is reasonable, for these are usually the richer men of the village. One could thus say that the *kamin* are more the servants of the cultivators (i.e. those with ploughs) than of other villagers. This does not mean that they are necessarily indebted pre-eminently to the most powerful and wealthy caste—in this case the Rajputs. Though, as we shall see, Rajputs own more land per plough than anyone else, the Farmers have as many ploughs—the figure is, in fact, forty-six Rajputs' to forty-five Farmers' ploughs. The *kamin* thus get an equal amount of their income from either caste, not to mention payments by all other cultivators.

I have indicated that the name of people in the second category of occupations, *mangat*, should not be translated literally by the term 'beggar'. This is because all these people are more or less priests, and the alms given them are in some way a return for services rendered to the village and also bring the donor general merit. The village priest (*parsai*) is the clearest example of this. He is termed a *mangat* and on the full- and new-moon days he goes round the village and is given grain and other uncooked foodstuffs; again, at harvest he claims two sheaves of sorghum and other gifts on the same scale as the potter. But these presents can be seen to supplement the payments he gets for performing such rites as marriage, sacred readings, etc., and until recently mortuary rites.[2] Besides this, the priest conducts village rites. He and the headmen worship, for example, at the three main village shrines during the festival of Naumi. There is only one village priest in Ramkheri. Without him, life could not be conducted properly, and he is as necessary as the carpenter, etc., and has rights of service in the village in the same way.

[1] For a slightly different classification see Dube 1955: 59.
[2] Formerly, the priest did not object to performing funerary rites, but now he says that they are defiling and refuses to do them.

The other *mangat* castes are also paid for services to the common welfare. The Naths tend the shrine of Hanuman who is Lord of the Village and so important for everyone. The Gosains are in charge of the shrines to Bholanath (Siva) and Kali Mata; the Bairagi takes care of the shrine to Narsingh (Vishnu). The Balai Babaji has a small personal shrine only, but performs minor rites and gives sacred readings for the Weavers. Finally, the Fakir has no shrine, but has the duty of building a *taziya* at the Moharram festival.

All these people collect small payments of grain and cash whenever people worship at their shrines. At one time in 1955 there was a threat of locusts, and many people made vows to Hanuman. When their fields were spared, they performed thanksgivings at the shrine, and the Naths received some sorghum grain, a few annas, and sometimes a piece of cloth. Besides this, the *mangat* are entitled to seek alms in the village where their rights exist. The poorer members (Nath, Balai Babaji and Fakir) collect on the new- and full-moon days, and are also given cooked food daily by certain sympathetic Farmer and Rajput families (they can beg cooked food from any householders from whose hands they can eat). In addition, the Naths beg food and clothes at the Maka Sankrant festival (the winter solstice) which they treat as their special privilege. The Bairagi and Gosain do not beg, though they could, if they wished to, take uncooked foodstuffs; but they consider it demeaning.

Like the *kamin*, the *mangat* receive aid from the State. The village priest had a block of rent-free land. The remainder held land only by being officiants at the shrines in whose name the land was registered. That is, they were connected to the shrines, whereas the village priest ministered directly to the village.

There is no generic name for occupations which are not in the *kamin* or *mangat* categories. Some are crafts, but are not carried out on annual contracts. This would include: the tailor, who has regular clients but is paid in cash for each garment; the tobacco-curer, who buys additional leaf from farmers, cures and sells it; and the cotton-carder, who charges a cash rate for fixed amounts of cotton which he cleans and cards. Then there are those occupations which are not connected with crafts at all. The goatherd, the dairyman, the market gardener and the farmer—these occupations depend on the facilities given by the craftsmen, but their main economic focus is in the towns, where the products are sold.

There are two main stores in the village, and one or two men, like the tailor, stock small amounts of goods as a sideline. The occupation of trader is partly that of a storekeeper and partly that of a minor grain broker, for about three-quarters of purchases are paid for in kind, mostly in sorghum grain. The storekeeper calculates the price

72

of his articles on the current price of grain, thereby making his profit as if payment were in cash; and he then tries to sell the grain in the town and reap a second profit from this transaction. The risk run is that he often will not be able to wait until prices are high in the town, being forced to sell his accumulations of grain to buy further stocks of cigarettes, kerosene, salt and other commodities. Ramkheri is near the main road to Dewas, and most people with carts shop in the town. For prices there are slightly lower, and there is a wider selection of goods. Hence, the village stores mostly cater for the poorer people, who have no way of bringing back their purchases from Dewas, and who are too poor to buy large quantities at a time. Storekeeping in more remote villages may well be a more rewarding and prestigeful occupation than it is in Ramkheri.

This chapter is an appropriate place to mention the offices held in the village, though these are different from the occupations there, being positions of authority held under the State. The headman (*patel*) has the duty of collecting land revenue, of maintaining law and order and reporting any serious crime to the Police, and of acting as a liaison officer to visiting officials. He has under his orders the village watchmen (*caukidar*) who patrol the village each night, and make a weekly report to the Police on the state of the village. The village servant must run errands for the headman, and must also be on hand for any services required by visiting officials. Recently the posts of chairman (*sarpanc*) of the elected Village Committee and councillors (*panc*) have been set up to deal with village development and self-government.

All these people live in the village, in contrast to the village accountant (*patvari*). He must maintain a map of village lands and a record of the crops grown and the yields. He is therefore the centre of all disputes over land, since he is the authority on boundaries, qualities of soil, etc., and the assessment of land revenue is largely based on his reports. The State Government made it a policy not to have village accountants working in their own villages, holding that they would be more impartial elsewhere. The accountants have always been paid in cash salaries, but the other positions have had rent-free lands. The three headmen of Ramkheri had an average of 22 acres each, the two village watchmen had 16 acres each, and the six village servants (of whom two serve each year on a rotation system) had an average of 3 acres. Like the rent-free grants to the craftsmen, these are now abolished, the headmen being paid a commission of the land revenue they collect, and the other village officials having cash salaries.

Although in theory these administrative offices are not caste-linked, in practice the headman and village accountant are from higher castes, and the watchman and servant from lower ranks. Of 28 headmen in nearby villages, no less than 19 were from Rajput and allied castes (7 Rajputs, 4 Kalota, 2 Dakkar, 2 Gujar, 1 Tobacco-curer, and 3 Dairymen). Of the rest 2 were Brahmans, 4 Farmers and 3 were Muslims. Only Weavers occasionally represented castes of divisions 4 and 5 in the commensal hierarchy.[1] I do not have as detailed figures for the accountants; there are not many Rajputs or allied castes here, and most would be from Farmers, Gardeners and Oil-pressers (of the castes living in Ramkheri) and Kayasthas. The same would, I believe, apply to schoolmasters, who are also Government servants. Of the watchmen in 21 villages, 10 were Bhilalas. One Ramkheri resident of that caste told me how the Bhilalas had come from the West to the kingdom of Dhar. From there a contingent had settled in Dewas (the Maharajas of Dhar and Dewas are collaterals), and had been given the rights of watchmen in all the villages of the State by the Ruler. Of the rest, 3 were Weavers, and others were from castes in division 4 (Drummer, Nayak, Bagri, etc.). The lowest castes, such as the Tanner and Sweeper, are not represented. The village servants are always Weavers, in my experience. This caste is in every village, and the term for village servant is, indeed, *ganv Balai* (village Balai).

Besides these official posts, general labour, mostly agricultural but also in such work as well-digging, house repair, etc., is also not limited to any caste, though here again there is some identification with caste rank, as I shall show shortly.

THE HIERARCHY OF OCCUPATIONS

Occupations are regarded as having different value, in some cases being ritually distinguished, and in others varying in the general prestige attached to them.

The clearest division sets off four occupations as lowest. Any work which is connected with dead things or bodily emissions pollutes seriously. Hence the tanner and sweeper are the bottom of the scale —the sweeper is a little lower because he handles human excrement and receives a dead person's shroud. The drummer's work demeans him because he plays at the rites of Harijan castes. Drumming itself is not forbidden to others, for anybody can play the hand drums

---

[1] It is interesting that a Harijan can be headman at all. The villages of which I know were settled by Weavers, and a member of the caste was made headman. When other castes moved in, notably Farmers, they tried to get the headmanship transferred; but the Maharaja ruled that the Weavers had done their work loyally, and refused to penalize them because of their caste status.

(*tabla*); but nobody would think of playing the big village drum (*dhol*) which is the drummer's badge of office.[1] Higher still is the barber's work; for though it involves handling hair and nail parings which are impure things, the barber who works for the higher castes does not also serve the Harijans.

Second, there are some jobs which are regarded as messy, or as rather ridiculous, rather than actually polluting. Oil-pressing makes a man greasy and somewhat odiferous. The goatherd spends his time among animals which are regarded as mainly useful for meat and in any case inferior to cattle. The word for donkey can be used for uncouth behaviour and stupidity, and the potter, who breeds these animals, is thus the constant butt of jokes. His work may also be low because the donkey in India can be a foul-feeding animal.

The value of the remainder of occupations is well summed up in the widely quoted proverb, 'highest is agriculture, in the middle is trade, next is service, most worthless is begging'. This illustrates both the regard in which independence is held, and the way in which the cultivators, who constitute the largest occupational group, have put themselves at the top of the scale, a position which most people admit, albeit sometimes grudgingly. The best work, say many, is that of a cultivating landowner, for his time is his own and he takes orders from nobody. Tenants paying rent or receiving a share of the crop are less fortunate; they are left to themselves in the daily work on the land, but are not really free to decide what is to be sown. Lastly, of course, labourers have no independence, save when they are unemployed.

Both the trader and the craftsman depend on farmers for their livelihood and so, say the latter, their work is inferior. The craftsmen deny this, especially the carpenter, whose work is perhaps the best-regarded of the crafts (for the blacksmith's is hot and messy). Without their skill, they hold, the farmer would have no tools to cultivate the land. And some craftsmen can be independent if they wish; a carpenter can switch to making only carts and houses, and so get paid in cash for each job. But the farmers are in the majority and their view is more widely accepted.

The alms-takers also depend on the farmer. But though beggary is regarded with scorn, and all who can afford it take up some other work, there is an ambivalent feeling towards the *mangat*, because of their religious duties. The village priest must be put in the highest category, with the farmers. For though some may say he is just the servant of the public, the importance of his work for village welfare, together with the easy life he leads and the comfortable income he

[1] Hocart (1950: 9) deals with the difference between ceremonial and secular drumming.

gets from his ritual payments and fortnightly alms-round, makes his work of the first rank. The others must be put lower down. For one thing, the shrines they tend can be approached without their mediation, and for another, they are to some extent judged by their secular occupation. Most of the Gosains are landowners, but the Naths and Balai Babajis are tenants or labourers.

The position of 'white collar' occupations is well to the top. The schoolmaster is respected in the ancient tradition of the *guru* and would be held to be equal to the landowner; the village accountant would come a little below this, for though he may take an exalted view of his work and the influence it brings him, the farmers resent this and say that tender hands do not necessarily mean higher status. One could make a rough diagram to represent the status of different occupations as follows:

TABLE 3

Kamin	Mangat	Other
	Village Priest	Headman Master Landowner Trader Accountant
Blacksmith Carpenter	Ascetic (uncooked food)	Tailor Tenant-Farmer
Barber Potter	Ascetic (cooked food)	Watchman Goatherd Labourer
		Oil-presser
Drummer Tanner		
Sweeper		

A few traditional occupations are no longer followed by castes in Ramkheri (e.g. warfare and weaving). A great many others engage only a part of the village caste group. Table 4 shows the number of men who are mainly and secondarily occupied traditionally. 'Secondarily' means that some other work takes precedence in time and income; 'mainly', that an alternative occupation, if any, is not sufficient to maintain the man's dependants.

The figures indicate that only slightly more than half the populace are carrying on their traditional caste occupations, either part- or full-time. There is variation in the degree to which these are retained by the occupational categories, as shown in Table 5.

This difference can be explained by the nature of the occupation. There is, for example, no substitute for the craftsman on the spot. People cannot go into town to be shaved; often their implements need

Economic Aspects of Caste

TABLE 4

Caste and Traditional Work*	Adult Males Occupied		
	Mainly	Secondarily	Not at all
Farmer	49	—	4
Cotton-carder	—	3	27
Weaver	—	—	23
Tanner	11	7	—
Gosain	—	2	8
Oil-presser	—	1	7
Village priest	1	—	6
Dairyman	—	—	9
Carpenter	7	—	—
Barber	4	—	1
Nath	4	1	1
Tobacco-curer	—	2	2
Gardener	1	—	2
Goatherd	1	2	—
Tailor	2	—	—
Balai Babaji	2	—	—
Potter	2	—	—
Sweeper	2	—	—
Blacksmith	1	2	—
Drummer	2	1	—
Bairagi	—	1	—
Fakir	1	—	—
Total	90	22	90

* I omit the Rajput, Bhilala and Mina, because it is impossible to say what their traditional work is.

TABLE 5

Occupational Category	Mainly	Secondarily	Not at all
Kamin	27	10	1
Mangat	10	4	15
Others	53	8	74
Total	90	22	90

to be repaired at short notice; and when an animal dies, it must be cleared away quickly. Hence, there is a good representation of *kamin* castes in every village,[1] which are engaged in their traditional work. Representatives of all seven castes were present in 7 out of 18 nearby villages, and 4 or more existed in a further 6 villages. Those most frequently absent were the Sweeper and the Drummer. The latter does

[1] Villages without a particular craftsman are served from neighbouring settlements, as I have pointed out.

not do work of an emergency nature; and since there are few latrines, or horses and donkeys to be removed, neither does the former. With the *mangat* castes it is the poorer people who continue to depend on charity. Gosains who had become farmers laughed when I suggested that they might seek alms; they said that they could do so, but would consider it rather a ridiculous thing to do.

Within the 'general' category, there are few occupations still important to keep up. Tailoring is one, goatherding another; but cotton-carding, oil-pressing, weaving and tobacco-curing have more or less been taken over by industrial processes. In this category there are more men divorced from their caste work than there are those following it. (This does not mean that their traditional occupation is forgotten in the general assessment of their status, though.) The main castes traditionally occupied are those connected with agriculture.

Seventeen men have moved into trade, industry, etc. Of these, some spend most of their time away, though all are based on Ramkheri.[1] But hitherto agriculture has been the main outlet for the unemployed and those who wish to leave less highly regarded traditional work. The overwhelming influence of agriculture is shown by the fact that the total number of men of traditionally agricultural castes (Farmer, Gardener, etc.) is only 69, whereas there are 162 men who are primarily or secondarily farmers. Moreover, of the 40 men I class as non-agriculturists, some have interests in land which they lease to others. Let us therefore look at the agricultural system, to see how caste operates therein.

THE AGRICULTURAL SYSTEM

There are three classes of farmer: the landowner, the tenant and the labourer. In former times all land was owned by the Maharaja, who had the power to grant or withold permission to cultivate it. In 1921 proprietary rights were made purchasable on payment of five times the annual land tax. About three-quarters of the State was converted in this way. The remainder of the land was retained by the Maharaja on the old basis, but by 1954 most had been made over to individual freeholds.

The landowner is known as the *pattedar* (*patta* meaning the certificate of ownership); *pakka krsak* is the legal term, but is not

[1] These comprise 2 Schoolmasters, 6 Village accountants, 3 High school or college students, 2 Traders, 1 Army, 1 Police, 2 Factory workers. Their castes were 4 Oil-pressers, 2 Gardeners, 4 Farmers, 2 Dairymen, and one each of Mina, Cotton-carder, Brahman, Gosain and Barber. There were no Rajputs amongst them, these having land and so need less to get other work.

ordinarily used. There are certain restrictions on what he can do with the land. He cannot mortgage it, for no private person can foreclose on land, only the Government being able to auction it for arrears of tax. Again, it is forbidden to gift land to another, or to bequeath it. Since 1948 the only way to transfer land is to sell it, even if the sale is a fictitious cover for a gift. Sale, too, is restricted. No inherited land can be sold, for it is part of the ancestral property and its alienation needs prior consent of the heirs. Even if this is obtained, or if the land is self-acquired and so freely disposable, there are limits on the size of plots saleable and purchasable. For land cannot be sold if a balance of less than 15 acres of ordinary land or seven acres of irrigated land is left in the owner's name. Again, it cannot be bought by someone who would then have more than 50 acres in his possession; and this purchaser must be a *bona fide* cultivator, too (i.e. he must have his own bullocks, etc., and cultivate through his own or through labourers', not tenants', work). All this limits the powers a man has over his land. The measures are designed to protect people from moneylenders, and to see that holdings are neither too large nor are uneconomically small. Within these laws, the owner has absolute rights over the land.

Tenants are of two kinds. There is the *sikmi* tenancy, where a fixed sum in cash or kind is paid annually as rent. And there is the *batai* tenancy, where the tenant and owner divide the crop (the tenant here is known either as *sikmi* or *bantedar*). Tenancies in Ramkheri are all of *bantedars*, save for two men farming land belonging to courtiers in Dewas. The proportions in which the crop is divided vary. For an equal division, the owner contributes the land tax and half the seed; the tenant gives half the seed, the bullocks, equipment and his labour. To receive two-thirds of the crop, the owner must give the land tax, two-thirds of the seeds, and the bullocks and equipment. And if the owner gives everything save the actual labour, he receives three-quarters of the crop. The present Government's policy is to abolish non-cultivating landowners, and various measures have recently been passed to prohibit these tenancies. So they must now be made informally, and appear on the surface to be a working of land through labourers, with the owner giving daily supervision.

Two types of labourer exist. Every year at the start of the agricultural season in March–April, some landowners arrange to have a labourer for the rest of that year. Payment is made partly in cash and partly in the proceeds of each harvest. This labourer (*naukar*) is distinct from the man who is hired on a daily wage and is called *majdur*. The former is always at his master's command, and some men condemn the loss of independence and what are often longer hours. The advantages are a year's security at a rate of pay more or less equal to what a day labourer might expect to earn.[1]

Agriculture in Ramkheri is in general the preserve of small and medium owner-cultivators. The largest area held by one man is 70 acres, and the average owner will have between 10 and 20 acres. By far the major part of the land is self-farmed, and tenancies exist largely when the plot is so small as to make it not worth while for the owner to keep draught animals and equipment, or when the owner is out of Ramkheri (there are a few men working outside, and some land belonging to the Maharaja's courtiers). It is, by and large, a system without the glaring inequalities seen in some other parts of India.[2]

TABLE 6

Area held by Owners		*Area held per head of Caste*	
Caste	Acres	Caste	Areas
Rajput	24·40	Rajput	21·76
Gosain	15·60	Gosain	14·06
Farmer	11·30	Farmer	10·07
Gardener	11·25	Fakir	9·99
Brahman	10·86	Brahman	9·51
Fakir	9·99	Gardener	7·50
Goatherd	8·81	Oil-presser	7·30
Tobacco-curer	7·54	Goatherd	5·87
Oil-presser	7·34	Tobacco-curer	5·39
Cotton-carder	6·93	Cotton-carder	4·55
Bhilala	5·94	Dairyman	4·11
Dairyman	5·88	Barber	3·58
Potter	5·34	Bhilala	3·14
Barber	4·18	Weaver	3·05
Weaver	4·13	Tailor	2·98
Balai Babaji	3·36	Mina	2·76
Tailor	2·98	Bairagi	2·69
Mina	2·76	Potter	2·67
Bairagi	2·69	Balai Babaji	1·68
Nath	2·48	Drummer	1·12
Sweeper	1·63	Carpenter	1·11
Carpenter	1·55	Nath	0·83
Tanner	1·20	Sweeper	0·82
Drummer	1·12	Blacksmith	0·73
Blacksmith	0·73	Tanner	0·20

[1] The annual rate between 1954 and 1956 was around Rs. 200. To this must be added some perquisites of hay, grazing, etc. A day labourer makes Re. 1, but cannot expect to be employed all through the year.

[2] For instance, the large holdings hitherto owned by non-cultivating landlords in parts of Malabar (Mayer 1952: 84).

Within this system, caste status is significant. In general, of course, it is the higher castes which own land, and the lower which provide the landless labourers and tenants. This is shown by the previous table. The first column shows the average area held by owners of each caste (these include both men and women,[1] both cultivating and non-cultivating owners). The second column shows the average area of land per head of the adult male caste population. In some cases there is little difference between the two, e.g. where most men of the caste are also owners. But where there are only a few owners, and many landless people who are labourers or craftsmen, the difference may be great—e.g. the figures for the Tanner or Bhilala.

To make the correspondence of landholding with caste clearer; if one takes caste status as it is represented by the commensal hierarchy, the land held per head by men in the five divisions is:

TABLE 7

Division	Acres per head
1	9·51
2	13·00
3	8·15
4	2·30
5	1·75

Table 6, of course, shows only an over-all statistical distinction between castes. It does not tell us how many Rajputs are landless, or on the other hand that a Weaver has 31 acres. Caste does not give agricultural status, as it does traditional occupational or commensal status. Nevertheless, it is clear that the allied castes are prominent as landowners. Not only is this due to the large holdings of the Rajputs, but even the allied craft castes have more land than their opposite numbers in division 3, e.g. the Barber and Potter have more than the Carpenter and Smith.

In former times, this supremacy of the allied castes must also have been marked. As I have already said, it was only after the 1900 famine that Farmers started to move in, though these now operate as many ploughs as do the Rajputs. In the old days many castes had land—even the Tanners—but their attachment to it was slender. Partly because there was so much vacant land, and partly because prices were so low as to make economic farming difficult, there was a great deal of movement, of relinquishment of land by men who would work a few years as labourers, and then take up some land

---

[1] Included are three women owners with no grown sons working their land. Land held by Ramkheri people outside the village is said to be small, and unlikely to vary these figures greatly.

again. The Rajputs, however, did not move; they were the headmen of the village, and they were well enough off to be fairly unswayed by changing prices. Thus the continuing core of landholders was Rajput. Nowadays, in contrast, land is more evenly distributed, and is keenly sought by every caste, including even the craft castes. The people who managed to get land in the 1930s when it was available have not moved from the village. But any trend towards greater holding by non-Rajput castes is countered by the fact that Rajputs are themselves major buyers of land (few of them having more than the 50-acre limit for holdings). In the last year or two most of the Dewas courtiers with land in Ramkheri have been selling it, anticipating their expropriation as absentee landowners. And of the 13 buyers, 6 have been Rajputs and 5 Farmers.

Landholding is only one aspect of agriculture; let us now look at the relation of caste to tenancies and to contract labour. In the 1955–6 season I recorded 41 owners with 52 tenants. The castes of the owners were as follows:

Brahman	2	Cotton-carder	3
Rajput	9	Fakir	1
Gosain	2	Bhilala	1
Farmer	4	Nath	1
Gardener	1	Drummer	1
Carpenter	2	Weaver	2
Tobacco-curer	1	Sweeper	1
Barber	2	Outsider	5
Dairyman	1		—
Tailor	2	Total	41

The castes of the tenants were as follows:

Brahman	1	Bhilala	4
Rajput	11	Nath	1
Farmer	9	Weaver	6
Gardener	1	Tanner	5
Tobacco-curer	2		—
Oil-presser	3	Total	52
Cotton-carder	9		—

In eleven instances the owner and tenant were of the same caste. My figures show there was a tendency for the owner to be of upper status (26 of the 36 Ramkheri owners were from divisions 1 to 3). Many poorer landowners (of whatever caste) lease their holdings, not having the capital or equipment needed to farm them. Tenants, on the other hand, came from a wider spread of castes (only 27 out of 52 were from divisions 1 to 3). Some were upper caste men without sufficient land of their own to occupy themselves full-time. On one occasion, for instance, a Drummer leased his land to a Rajput. But there were also 11 Harijan tenants.

In 1956–7 the following men were contract labourers:

Brahman	1
Rajput	2
Farmer	3
Dairyman	1
Tobacco-curer	1
Cotton-carder	4
Bhilala	1
Nath	1
Drummer	1
Weaver	6
Tanner	3
Total	24

The castes of their masters were as follows:

Rajput	11
Gosain	2
Farmer	3
Dairyman	1
Oil-presser	3
Cotton-carder	2
Total	22*

* 2 labourers were under contract to the Maharaja, who has a small private holding in the village.

This follows the same pattern as for owner and tenant. The employers come from a fairly small number of upper castes, dominated by the Rajputs, as the main landholding caste. The labourers show a much wider spread of castes; though a slight majority are of lower status, they include representatives of the economically powerful Rajputs (though these are not from the kinsfolk of the headmen, it must be admitted).

There is a rapid turnover in tenants and contract labourers. For example, of the 13 contracts in the 1955–6 season, only 5 involved the same labourer as in the season before. In some cases, a man was said to have signed a written understanding to stay with his master, on the security of his house. But, in fact, he could leave earlier if there was a quarrel between the two men—over wage payments, quality of work, etc. It is in the landowner's interest to keep the labourer for the first half of the agricultural year, when the major work must be done, for at that time it is hard to replace him. But after the first harvest and the sowing of the second crop, some labourers cancel their contracts and look after their own affairs. And, of course, there is the tendency to seek a new master when the next year's arrangements are made. Here is the history of a Rajput who had been a labourer and tenant for most of his working life:

> 10 years contract labour for a Rajput master*
> 6 years contract labour for a Farmer master*
> 1 year day labourer
> 6 years work on own land (later lost it in lawsuit)
> 1 year day labourer
> 2 years tenant of a Dairyman master
> 2 years tenant of a different Dairyman master
> 1 year day labourer
> 1 year tenant of a Dewas courtier
> 2 years tenant of another Dewas courtier
> 1 year day labourer
> 3 years contract labour for a Rajput master

* The first two periods are probably shorter; the informant was 46 years old, and could not have been working more than 30 years or so; hence, the 36 years shown here should be shortened by about 5 years.

In twelve other cases the labourer remained with his master for an average of just over 4 years, the shortest being 1 year, the longest 14 years. Hence, these ties do not have a great deal of stability. Nor could any informant recall a time when families of contract labourers or tenants remained with their masters for decades or even generations. Interdependence in agriculture (as well as in crafts) is therefore only between castes in general, and is not reinforced by specific, long-established relations between individuals. People change their masters easily and frequently, and the only hold that masters seem to have at present is that there is insufficient land to go round. Otherwise, the present high agricultural prices might tempt many *kamin* to become farmers, leaving nobody to provide the services essential to agricultural and social activities. Some of the Carpenters and Blacksmiths have, indeed, bought land and are trying to turn into at least part-time farmers; but this is impossible for most.

TRADE AND MONEYLENDING

There is not much to add in the economic sphere to the analysis of the agricultural and craft systems. Trade, as I have noted, is a minor occupation in Ramkheri, most purchases being made in Dewas. The market for farm products is also there, and the commission agents (*dalal*) who sell the grains and other produce for the farmers are all Dewas men. One or two villages try to trade in other commodities; thus, one man rents tamarind trees, has the fruit picked and sells it in Dewas; another, on the occasion of the village's corporate worship of the Smallpox Goddess, contracted to collect and deliver the hides of the hundreds of goats killed at that time. Much of the movement of milch cattle is through gifts by kin at certain rites (e.g. the mother's brother may give a cow at the wedding of his niece). Since people both give girls to and receive girls from the same villages, the flow of cattle between the kin of any two settlements is roughly equal after several years of match-making. Actual livestock trading—the buying of bullocks for farmwork, etc.—is more often done at the weekly cattle market in Dewas, though there may occasionally be cattle traders in the villages, as well as people who buy goats to take to Dewas to the butchers. But this is all very small-beer, and these people do not become very rich from this trade, though it gives them a certain prestige born of contacts with important merchants in the towns.

A remaining economic activity is moneylending. Loans can be made from private sources, or from the Government. It was estimated that in 1956 some three-quarters of the village was in debt. People were said to have borrowed about Rs. 20,000 from the State (of which at least half was said to be for agricultural improvements) and some Rs. 6000 from private lenders. This reflects the declining influence of the private moneylender. Watched by the authorities to see that he does not charge too much interest, unable to foreclose on land for bad debts, even the larger moneylenders in Dewas are less enthusiastic about investing their money in this way. Moreover, moneylending is regarded by the villagers themselves as a tiresome and sometimes foolish business. If one lends to fellow-villagers it is almost impossible to get repayment unless they are to some extent willing to co-operate. For a court case leads in the last resort to eviction of the debtor from his house (since movables can be foreclosed upon)—but this would be a shameful thing which nobody would wish to do. Some villagers have therefore had to write off quite large sums lent in the past, and this has taught everyone a lesson. Another objection is that if one lends to one fellow-villager, one may cause offence by not lending to another—that one does not have the money to do so is rarely believed; therefore, many people now lend to nobody.

At present there is only one even moderate moneylender, the village priest, and he has only advanced sums totalling between Rs. 2000 and Rs. 4000 (the largest single loan being Rs. 1000 to a

Rajput headman). None of the Rajputs lend comparable sums, though several would, I think, be rich enough to do so. After that, there are half a dozen or so who have each lent out around Rs. 600–800 to perhaps ten people, the loans never exceeding about Rs. 100. These men include two or three Farmers and two or three Oil-pressers. Below this comes a whole network of tiny loans between villagers, involving numbers of those with a little spare cash or some surplus grain to lend as seed or food. The interest on loans runs between 12 and 26 per cent. for money, and one and a half and twice the grain borrowed for loans in kind.

As an example of the pattern of small loans, I give the affairs of an old Rajput widow; the various loans were brought for settlement after her death, and in this case alone I am fairly satisfied that I obtained the full extent of a person's financial affairs.[1] The woman had lent Rs. 50 to a Gosain, Rs. 25 to a leading Rajput, Rs. 20 to a Farmer who had re-loaned it at higher interest, Rs. 15 to an indigent Cotton-carder, Rs. 10 to a Tanner, Rs. 7 to a poorer Rajput, Rs. 5 to a Weaver, Rs. 4 to one of the wealthiest Rajputs, and loans of grain to Tanners, Weavers, a Cotton-carder and a Bairagi. This was a moderate set of petty loans, totalling some Rs. 150.

Another type of loan is that made within the kin-group. People borrow in particular from their mother's brother, or from their wife's father or brother. These are loans made without interest. They link people of different villages for the most part (loans between agnates of the same village are very rare); and I shall indicate their social significance in the discussion of kinship.

It is difficult to relate this pattern of moneylending to caste in anything but the broadest terms. In the first place, few rich people lend money; and so we cannot say that the Rajputs, as the richest caste group (for wealth is closely related to landholding in this farming community), are also the main moneylenders. Indeed, it is the men of moderate means who lend most; they do not have the security of property behind them, and so are ready to take a chance on lending money to increase their wealth. This is why we find Farmers and Oil-pressers mainly in the field of medium loans; these are the newer castes in the village, of upper status but as yet moderate wealth (the few rich Farmers do not appear to lend, like the Rajputs).

Second, we cannot simply say that the upper castes lend and the lower castes borrow. In terms of the number of loans, this may be

---

[1] In general, people are most reluctant to tell of their savings and borrowings. One of the disadvantages of dividing a joint family was said to be that financial matters would be made public. People do not like to display their wealth too much—a man refused to buy a pedigree bull because, he said, it would show he was rich and attract thieves. My figures and financial estimates are therefore very tentative.

true; for lower castes are more in need of money or grain, and make small loans where they can. But upper castes also borrow, and their loans are the largest, as we have seen in the example of the Rajput widow. Again the upper castes also contain a few poor members, whose borrowing is on a par with that of the lower castes. It appears though, that the Rajputs do not borrow much from the Farmer and Oil-presser moneylenders. They either get money from equal or higher castes (e.g. from fellow-Rajputs or from the Brahman) or from Dewas. We can then broadly say that the middle castes are at the head of the system of smaller loans, and that the upper castes have their own ways of getting loans.

It is interesting that the Rajputs, who are the centre of so many other activities, are not at the head of these moneylending networks. It illustrates, I think, the great importance paid to money, and the deep disputes which can occur over it. Rajputs, with their reputations as leaders in so many other fields, do not find it worth the risk to lend money inside the village. And this decision makes money of secondary importance in inter-caste relations, though it is primary in inter-personal relations. This adds to our picture of a lack of any great wealth in Ramkheri.

Although the general attitude towards wealth is the same in all castes—that it should be guarded carefully and its extent never revealed—there are some interesting differences in expense patterns between castes. These stem partly from the differences between vegetarian and non-vegetarian standards. Some feasts have a vegetarian diet irrespective of caste—weddings are an example. But at others—the informal dinner after an engagement (*sagai*) is made—the non-vegetarians have considerably greater expenses. For they must give meat and liquor to their guests, and these items are not cheap, especially the latter under the Government's present policy of prohibition by price. The vegetarians, on the other hand, give feasts of more or less the daily diet, with the addition of other vegetables and clarified butter as cooking medium.

Variations in custom may make non-vegetarians spend more. The Farmers, for example, have the final funerary feast (*nukta*) at the same time as the purificatory rites twelve days after a death; the Rajputs, on the other hand, hold the *nukta* separately, at anything from a few weeks to a few years afterwards. In the Farmer's case, there is rarely a large gathering—people do not have much time to assemble, for one thing, and the purification is a matter for nearer kin only, in any case. The *nukta* of a Rajput, on the other hand, is as large an affair as relatives can make it; even if a man holds back, his *amour propre* demands that he make more expense than he would were he in a caste with no such ideal. It is held at a time of year when people have the leisure to come, and I estimated around one thousand people at a *nukta* I attended; it was for a headman, but was not considered anything exceptional. Again, the difference between the expenses of Farmers and Rajputs was noticeable at the village Smallpox Goddess worship. Rajput guests were more numerous, they came earlier and stayed later than Farmer guests, and as I have said, their diet was more expensive to provide. The Rajputs set the tone for the allied castes, and together these give the lead for the non-vegetarian castes of divisions 4 and 5. So this difference in attitude and expense is more than of internal caste importance. Allied castes scoff at the Farmer's prudence (some might even say meanness); and in return they are given compliments on their own improvidence (some might even say foolishness).

CASTE AND OCCUPATION

I can now attempt answers to the questions at the beginning of the chapter. The first concerned the relation of caste to the village economy and asked: are caste groups seen as units in the economy, or are roles filled rather by individual caste members? If economic roles stress the individual rather than the caste group, what is now the influence of the traditional link of occupation with caste membership? The answer is clear when there is correspondence between the entire caste group's present and its traditional occupation, and where this occupation is exclusive to the caste. For here the caste group is the unit. Further, these traditional occupations are hierarchically ranged. This applies mainly to the *kamin*, and to a lesser extent to the *mangat*. Everybody knows that carpentry is higher than tanning, and by following these occupations as entire caste groups the Carpenter and Tanner castes are distinguished by both activity and status in their part in the village economy.

The connection of economic activity with the caste group is less clearcut where an occupation is not followed exclusively by one caste. But even here, traditional caste status is important. Take farming; on the whole, the upper castes own the land and the lower castes help to cultivate it as tenants or labourers. But these positions in the agricultural system are themselves partly reflexes of the castes' traditional occupational positions. For many men now farming were previously weavers, oil-pressers, etc. As these occupations started to decay, the men coming into agriculture were at first able to get land of their own, for it is only for the last twenty years or so that there has been a shortage in Ramkheri. The Weavers, for example, farmed quite a lot of land at that time. But on the whole the lower castes do not seem to have kept land for any time, even under these favourable conditions, and it reverted to upper caste owners.

One reason, one can suppose, was that the Rajputs and other higher castes disliked the prospect of seeing as landowners caste members who were ritually inferior to them, and had previously been occupationally inferior too, and so forced them out of their holdings. Another reason may well have been that these caste members did not have the experience and skill needed to farm, even when given aid by the landlord. Even now, when a Tanner tenant's crop was not as good as it might have been, the owner gave as a reason that Tanners did not know how to farm. Many of the lower castes were probably only expected to become labourers, and may themselves have held no more than this prospect. Thus, traditional occupational rank has to some extent influenced a caste's place in the agricultural system which, with its available land, until recently provided freedom of opportunity to all. Agriculture has always been a safety valve when the other occupations became overcrowded; but within agricultural work, too, caste distinctions have persisted.

As long as the caste name calls to mind a particular occupation, so long will it influence the position of the individual who goes into other work.[1] A Sweeper who owned shares in a bus line was a Sweeper, not a financier. A certain respect was shown to him as a man of means, but he was also mocked because of his low traditional status in comparison to his present economic position and (what is more important in this context) villagers refused to believe that he was a capable businessman. Only for those whose traditional calling is relatively neutral (e.g. the farming castes, and upper craft castes) is this not really significant. Otherwise, it is a factor which varies with the size of the gap between the traditional and the actual occupation. Thus, not much comment would be made if a Tanner became a day labourer, but there would be considerable influence from his traditional occupation if he went into Government service.

Because the traditional occupation, through legendary history and through the doctrine of *karma*, lies at the basis of caste distinctions, one can say that this occupation is a group attribute, whatever the actual occupation followed by the group's members. In terms of these actual occupations many castes are obviously not groups in the economy in the sense that their members perform and have rights to certain work, with the possibility of appeal if rules are contravened, like the craft castes. But there is a distinction made between different castes in a single occupation; this is the case even in agriculture. People will say that only Farmers, Gardeners and

[1] I am talking about the situation in the village, of course; this may not be true in towns.

other agricultural castes like Kurmis can *really* get the best out of the land; others are seen as amateurs, and until agriculture is a legitimate first occupation for them instead of secondary work, this distinction will remain.

The classic answer for a caste with two primary occupations is to divide into two endogamous subcastes—say, farming Carpenters and carpentering Carpenters. This tendency to split on the basis of occupation shows, conversely, that when the split has *not* taken place the traditional occupation does indeed to some extent influence the status of all in the caste group, even if it is only as outsiders think of it. Occupation may make for separate groups just as commensality does, and indeed the two are closely connected; for the traditional status of the occupation may be a factor in the caste's commensal position (e.g. a caste having a polluting occupation could not have a high commensal status), and in return, the overflow from his caste's commensal status follows a caste member, whatever his present occupation. An example of this is provided by castes which have polluting occupations and at the same time lower commensal status. When such castes wish to change their status, they first try to dissociate themselves from their traditional occupation. This is easier than a change of commensal position, because it does not involve any reciprocal action by other castes (as would a change in, say, smoking relations), and because there are many neutral occupations (farming, etc.) which it can take up. Only when this has been done do the caste members claim a higher commensal rank, and partly back up the demand with evidence of their new occupational status.

The second problem mentioned at the beginning of the chapter concerned the economic power held by the various castes. In a farming community, ownership of land is the main source of wealth and command over the services of others. There are several castes, nearly all of whose members own land. The Rajputs have the greatest area per head, but Farmers, Oil-pressers, Dairymen, Brahmans and Gosains are also mainly landowners. In terms of benefit to the craftsmen, etc., all caste members stand equal, for all pay their craftsmen per plough. In terms of quantity of money paid, the Farmers and Rajputs are equal; but the Rajputs have greater power over labour, having more land which they work through labourers. There is no clear picture of which caste has most power over tenants, since Rajputs are often themselves the tenants of lower castes (though the land involved in such cases is negligible).

The Rajputs would have greater economic influence in the village if they lent money as extensively as they could. But lending is risky and only people who are sufficiently educated to be able to handle their accounts, or who wish to risk having disputes in order to make money, will do it. Here the middle castes are in front (many village accountants lend money) but with no great volume of loans.

In social expenses the Rajputs emerge at the head of the village. Their positions as rich men, and their standards of hospitality as non-vegetarians and members of a caste of headmen having close contact with the Maharaja and his open-handed court demand this. And so they invite more fellow-villagers to their feasts, and pay more to the Barber, Potter, etc., for their services at these feasts than do other castes. But even Rajputs do not completely outclass others, and this supports the view of Ramkheri as a rather poor village with small gradations of wealth.

Major economic relations are with the town—for the really powerful figures in the economy (the commission agents, the big private moneylenders, the Government officials with power to make loans) are in Dewas.[1] Though the village is not a separate economic unit, its ties with other villages are in certain fields only. Loans between kin, and the gifts of cattle, ornaments and houseware constitute the main ingredients in what becomes a roughly reciprocal exchange between the subcaste populations of different villages. Trade in crops and livestock, and the purchase of consumer goods, on the other hand, are almost entirely with the town. Inter-village economic contacts, then, are along kinship lines, and this supports my contention that inter-village activity is mainly within the subcaste.

[1] This is not always the case, for I know of important moneylenders living in other villages. The reason for the lack of contact with other settlements may lie partly in the fact that Ramkheri was bounded by Gwalior territory to one side, and many nearby villages in other directions were in Dewas Junior. Customs posts between these States prevented trade. I do not know how far this makes Ramkheri atypical, but I suspect that all villages tended to have economic ties with the town rather than nearby settlements.

VI

CASTE AND VILLAGE LEADERSHIP

THOUGH there is no caste head and shoulders above all others in the economic affairs of the village, the Rajputs have whatever priority exists. The position is very different when we turn to leadership in the village—for here the Rajputs are clearly dominant, both in positions of statutory political authority and also in the informal and traditional contexts of inter-caste village activity. People of other castes play parts on these occasions; but even when they themselves are influential, their caste group as a whole does not have the weight of the Rajput group (nor, very often, the interest in village matters possessed by Rajputs as a whole).

Much of this Rajput dominance comes from the fact that the headmen of Ramkheri are Rajputs. They are the representatives of the state political organization, and have certain statutory powers; it is therefore not surprising that there should have been an overflow from this context of authority to other informal situations. But that is not the entire story; for in previous chapters we have seen that the Rajputs are the objects of emulation for a majority of the village's population, for reasons other than this political power—because of their diet, because of their relatively liberal commensal habits which hold out the promise of equality to lower castes, because of their position as major landholders in a farming community. We must take all these aspects of inter-caste relations into account in our picture of Rajput dominance. And there are three questions to be considered by description and analysis in this chapter.

The first is, simply, what are the contexts for village leadership (as distinct from leadership within the caste), and what sanctions do the leaders possess? The second is, in how far are these leaders acting as individuals, and in how far do they represent caste groups? This question raises the whole problem of the extent to which the Rajput caste dominates the village's political activities, dispute-settling machinery, and any corporate village activities. The last question is, what activities are *not* covered in the village? Those which are confined to the subcaste will be considered in another chapter. Here, I only want to show in how far village leaders operate outside the village, either as influential men *vis-à-vis* officials in the town, or with the leaders of other villages in associations embracing

92

a larger area. The question carries a step further our consideration of the village as a discrete social unit.

The main position of authority has been that of the village headman; only within the last few years has the start of an officially sponsored Village Committee weakened his pre-eminence. The headman is a hereditary office-holder, the chief representative of Government in the village, and until now the leader of the village in its dealings with officialdom. Traditionally, Ramkheri had four headmen. It is rare to find more than two headmen in a Malwi village, and I was never able to discover a satisfactory reason for this number. A village in which there is much revenue to be collected may have two headmen; and two may be created in places where there are two powerful caste groups in rivalry. It is possible that headmen were created from each of the two major Rajput clan groups by the Maharaja, these then informally dividing their offices when their households split. At all events, two headmen are now from the Chauhan and one from the Solanki clan (or 'branch') groups of Rajputs, one Solanki headmanship having lapsed.

Succession to the office was patrilineal, passing to sons of a marriage or to adopted offspring. Children of a remarriage were not acceptable, since this institution was not well regarded. Occasionally there were complications of succession; thus, the fourth headmanship was ended when a headman died issueless, and his adopted son also died before marriage. Attempts were made to have a collateral installed, but the authorities declared the position void, feeling perhaps that three headmen were enough for the village.

There is no hierarchy among the headmen; all have equal authority and perform the same duties. Nevertheless, at any time there are differences in the personalities and inclinations of the office-holders which make them more or less influential. At present, the eldest headman (a Chauhan) is one of the most respected men in the village. He does his job towards the inhabitants, but does not make any great efforts for outsiders. It is said that he 'escapes to the fields' when he hears of the approach of an official; and he himself admits that he grudges the time spent on entertaining visitors. The youngest headman (Solanki) is unassertive and does not count for a great deal. And so it is left to the remaining Chauhan headman to be the chief player in the waning role of hereditary leader of the village. He has sufficient wealth to be able to entertain visitors, has servants to carry out essential work so that he can spend time on official business, and has wisdom and experience enough to use his authority correctly—and these are the criteria cited for a successful head-man.

The present situation, in which one of the headmen is more or less given the lead by his colleagues, has not necessarily been common in the past. There are stories of rivalry between headmen of strong personality (see p. 239). But in those days the power attached to the post was worth quarrelling about. At present, as I shall show, the importance of the headmanship is diminishing, and the headmen grow less and less interested in it, seeing only the time they spend away from their work or relaxation with little compensating power. Nowadays, then, there is little content for rivalry between headmen, nor profit for villagers to manipulate the relations between headmen for their own ends. The new Village Committee is now the place to look for such matters, and indeed it has in its short life already experienced one severe split amongst its leaders (see p. 116).

Headmen have now no formal badge or token of office (*sanad*), and there is no investiture of a new headman. When one of the Ramkheri headmen grew old, his son started to fill his place. The latter maintained that the authorities in Dewas would presumably have entered his name on the register of headmen when they saw his signature on the land tax returns, instead of his father's. But there has been no public handing over of power and this is not surprising, since the headman is not distinguished from other people by trap-pings of office, or difference in ritual status.

A major duty of the headman is the collection of the tax on land holdings. This is assessed by the Government, and periodically revised to suit crop values, etc., the amounts due being calculated by the village accountant. It is collected after each harvest. In 1955, several weeks before time for payment to the Treasury in Dewas, the headmen started telling villagers to get their money together. A week later they installed themselves on the veranda of the school house and started work. Rent-owing passers-by were summoned then and there, and the village watchmen were sent to fetch other cultivators. There was a general reluctance to pay, even if a man had the money with him. If there was the slightest queue of men waiting to pay and receive their receipts, the people at the back would melt away, not returning until summoned. This was in marked contrast to the usual inclination to sit and smoke wherever a crowd collects, and it was as if the cultivators hoped that something would happen in the mean-time which would absolve them from payment! The total tax from Ramkheri is in the neighbourhood of Rs. 6000. Each headman is supposed to collect one-third of this, though the village is not divided for this purpose. In fact, the three headmen sat together during the days of collection. Formerly, there was no commission on tax collected, for the headman had rent-free land in payment. Since this was abolished, they now receive 6 per cent. on taxes paid before a certain date.

A second most important duty of the headman is the preservation of law and order. In the 'olden days' (some forty years ago, I judge), stocks stood in the village square, and it is said that headmen had the power to punish people for minor misdeeds by incarcerating them for a day or two. The central authorities are said to have left many such matters to the headmen. Ramkheri people tell, for example, of the time they caught a bandit who had been thieving in the neighbourhood. When they turned him over to the Police, the latter scolded them 'why bring him to us, you should have dealt with him yourselves'. But in the more recent past the headmen have had no such power. They use their influence to prevent fights; but if serious affrays occur, they must report them to the Police in Dewas. And when people known to the villagers as thieves or outlaws are caught, they are tried in court, with a much greater chance of acquittal than in the former days of rougher justice. The headmen supervise the village watchmen, who guard the village at night, and countersign their weekly reports to the Police. (One such report reads 'This week there were no disturbances, nor any lost or straying livestock. All was peaceful.') The headmen must also report the presence of any strangers in the village (showing the degree to which the government looks on the village as a distinct social as well as administrative unit).

Besides these major duties, the headman acts as the channel for much other official business, though this task is now devolving increasingly on to the Village Committee. In the days of compulsory labour (*begar*) it was his job to provide manpower for the Government (as beaters for hunting expeditions, to repair public buildings, etc.). He has to look after officials who visit the village, and make their orders known to the people. And there are many other small orders given to him. An instance recently concerned a school sports organized in a nearby village. The authorities sent word to the headmen to procure enough bullock carts to take the children there from Ramkheri.

Conversely, the headmen is the main link for communication upwards, from villagers to Government. There are, for example, histories of boundary disputes with nearby villages, in which Ramkheri headmen defended the interests of the village and enlisted the help of any officials and nobles whom they could contact, up to the Maharaja himself. Sometimes the headman would be helped in such matters by other influential villagers who had contacts in the Court (e.g. the tenant of a courtier-landowner, the bailiff of a landlord);

there were two such men in Ramkheri in recent years, both Rajputs.

Before 1948, the headman's place as a Government official was strengthened by his personal attachment to the Maharaja. This was renewed each year in the court held at the Dasahra festival. The Maharaja sat on his throne, surrounded by his personal retinue. Down the hall in long lines stood his nobles, in descending order of rank. And at the back were gathered the village headmen, dressed in their court clothes. One by one the members of the assembly paid homage to their ruler, and renewed their loyalty to the State. The headman was thus in a very real sense the 'Government's man' in his village.

In most settlements the headman was the only man having such a personal link with the Maharaja. But in one-fifth of Dewas Senior villages there was a landlord. As I have already said, this man was a noble who had been given the revenue of the village for services to the Maharaja. It is worth repeating that he did not have any power over the villagers beyond that given by his wealth and rank. He did not assess the land tax, nor did his bailiff collect it. He had no statutory judicial powers, though he might if interested use his influence as an arbitrator. The position of the landlord thus depended greatly on his inclination. He could easily be the head of the village in all but name—or he could be a mere absentee beneficiary. In Ramkheri, the Royal landlords took an interest in the village; besides improving the buildings there, they lent their good offices to settling disputes, and sponsored the major village festivals. Nevertheless, the headmen's positions do not appear to have been weakened by this, but even strengthened, since the landlord worked through them. The landlord's bailiff was entirely concerned with his master's property. He was influential in that he controlled a large labour force, and also held quite a lot of land himself, as a gift from his master. He sometimes had influence at court through contacts with friends of his master. There might thus be rivalry between the State officials and the landlord's staff. In the years after 1934 the village reverted to 'free' (*khalsa*) status, both landlord and bailiff disappeared, and the headman became the only person with close contacts with the administration.

The headmen had a position of power in the village which ultimately rested on the State's statutory backing (e.g. fines for those who did not pay their land tax when ordered to do so). But they were nevertheless not despots, largely because of caste divisions in the village. Firstly, their status was in a sense shared by their caste group; for the division of the village into so many castes meant that, for outsiders, all men in a given caste group were to some extent

96

identified. Thus, headmen were members of the Rajput caste group, and conversely, all Rajputs tended to have something of the ruler about them, and to arrogate this to themselves. (The *'patel'* with which *all* Rajputs in Ramkheri are addressed is not entirely a form of courtesy, but represents this status.)

Secondly, between headman and villagers stood the leaders of each of the larger caste groups. Because these castes had different statuses, and because there were no ties of real kinship between them, the headman's authority tended to be more tenuous than it would have been had he been at once headman and senior member of a pervasive village kin-group. His decisions were enforced, of course; but the data indicate that he relayed decisions through the leaders of major castes, rather than gave orders directly. A headman would consider it beneath his dignity to enter the Harijan ward; instead, he sent for the Harijan leaders and told them what was wanted. And in dealing with large castes of higher status (e.g. Farmers) it was felt to be more honourable on both sides to proceed indirectly. In cases where there were clear decisions to be transmitted, the commands went through unchanged. But where there were discussions on what was to be done (e.g. how to meet the requirements of a Government demand for labour) the headman would, in fact, consult with the major upper caste leaders. In those days, it is said, affairs in Ramkheri 'were run by five men', meaning such influential villagers. These men did not constitute any formal body, nor were they limited by anything more concrete than their own abilities and influence. As many men as liked could join in a discussion, and be equally free to offer their opinions, though these would be considered with different degrees of seriousness. I call this way of deciding matters the 'headman's council'.

In the statutory sphere, then, the village has been ruled by three hereditary leaders, assisted to some extent by other men of their caste as well as influential villagers of upper castes. In fact, the pattern of village authority was fairly simple in recent years. The old days when the headman had great powers as the protectors of the village had passed. Law and order were increasingly concerns of the authorities; public works were ordered from above, and supervised by the Government too, and the villagers did not see any need to do more. Most matters were thus carried through on outside supervision, and the headman was largely a go-between, rather than an initiator of policy.

THE HEADMAN—UNOFFICIAL DUTIES: SECULAR

The headman has a more varied role in non-official affairs. For one thing, he tends to be called in to arbitrate disputes of other castes.

A common occasion is the fixing of compensation payable by a woman's second husband to her first husband, in cases where she has deserted the latter. The two husbands do not meet, but their supporters gather at the village of the second husband. Often the discussions take place in a very tense atmosphere, and could easily break down or lead to fights; and so the headman may be called to lend his prestige to a peaceful settlement. This occurs in the lower castes; for upper castes (e.g. Farmers), though allowing remarriage and compensation, think it a rather demeaning custom and would not call in outsiders to help wash their dirty linen (amongst Rajputs themselves, no compensation should even be demanded).

Another frequent type of quarrel is that between a landowner and his tenant. This usually breaks out at harvest time, when the division of the crop puts the relation under its greatest strain. A Carpenter, for example, recently bought a small plot of land. Having no draught animals, he let the land out on a 50 per cent. crop-sharing basis to a household of Cotton-carders. These men also gave him a loan of Rs. 200 to help to pay for the purchase of the plot. For a year all went well. The second harvest came at the same time as the Carpenter was due to give interest on his loan. He refused to do so, alleging that the Cotton-carders had not sown all the wheat seed he had given them, but had secretly sold some. The Cotton-carders thereupon called on him to repay the principal of the loan too, and the dispute was heard before two 'neutrals'. One was the mother's brother of the Cotton-carders, who wanted to make peace to avoid the cost of litigation for his nephews, and so was not held to be biased. The other was a Rajput, not a headman or even very influential in his caste; he had been passing when the discussion started, and he stayed and more or less took over the role of principal arbitrator. The upshot of an afternoon's discussion was that the Carpenter undertook to repay the loan, the question of the seed was more or less dropped (everyone doubtless realizing that this was a mere counter-attack by the Carpenter) and the two sides agreed to sever the tenure relation. When at the start of the agricultural season the Carpenter had not yet repaid the money, the Cotton-carders simply went ahead with cultivation of his land. The Carpenter accused them of doing so forcibly, and the matter was taken to the Rajput chairman of the Village Committee for settlement; no decision had been reached when I left. This kind of case is common, and my data show that Rajputs are usually involved in arbitration; the more serious cases would tend to go to the headmen or the chairman of the Village Committee; other affairs might be settled by other Rajputs or perhaps influential men of other caste groups.

The headman also takes the lead in certain rites held on a village-wide basis. It is worth describing these in some detail, because we see in them the headman's unofficial influence and duties towards the village, the changing position of the headman and his caste group, and the degree to which there are corporate, exclusively village rites.

THE HEADMAN—UNOFFICIAL DUTIES AT NAUMI

The first nine nights of the bright half of Kuar (Asvina) month (September–October) are devoted to the worship of the Nine Goddesses (*Naudurga*). The period is known to villagers as Nine Women (*Nauauraten*).[1] For us, a major significance of this period is the worship by the unilineal descent group (see Chapter IX). The main village festival is on the ninth day, and the people refer to it as Naumi (ninth), to distinguish it from other festivals during the period.[2]

The Naumi day is divided into two parts. The first occupies the afternoon, and is taken up with a procession of men possessed by gods. This is the climax of the nine days during which the mediums of the village have been active. There are two principal mediums (*panda*), one a Weaver, the other a Carpenter. The former has the Mother Goddess (*Mata*) as his tutelary,[3] the latter is visited by Ram Deoji Maharaj, the spirit of a Marwari incarnation of Vishnu,[4] who is now venerated in Malwa. Both men have histories of mediumship in their families, and the quality of possession is seen by people to have a tendency to adhere to the agnatic line. Of the two mediums in Ramkheri, the Weaver operates more elaborately. For the Nine Nights he fasts, living in a small hut with an image of the Goddess, five baskets of sprouting wheat and other ritual objects. During this time he is frequently possessed, and answers questions put to him in consultation. These appear to be purely personal, and I have no data of disputes settled through a medium's arbitration. A Rajput woman came, for example, to ask what she should do for pains in

[1] The traditional name of the occasion is Nine Nights (*Navaratri*). The local name may stem from the linguistic similarity between this name and the word for the nine goddesses worshipped on these nights. This is not a normal development, but seems to be an example of village etymology. Marriott cites the instance of *Navaratri* being changed into *Naurtha*, which his informants held to be the name of one of the nine goddesses (Marriott 1955a: 201).

[2] The tenth day (Dasahra) was marked by a big procession in Dewas, and the homage paid by headmen and nobles to the Maharaja. The present Maharaja still maintained his Dasahra court in 1955, though it had a social rather than a political significance, of course.

[3] Some said that this was Sakti Mata, others said it might be one of the many goddesses respected by Ramkheri people.

[4] Carstairs 1957: 103.

the back. She was given some grains of sorghum to eat, and told to make an offering to the Goddess.

The Carpenter is a practising craftsman and cannot, he says, afford to neglect his work for nine days. He fasts, but is not secluded, and does not plant the wheat seedlings to be 'cooled' on the Naumi. But he also has sessions for people who wish to consult him. These clients tend to be of upper caste, and he is particularly supported by a headman whose requests for a son were answered by Ram Deoji Maharaj. This headman gives all the grain, oil, etc., necessary for the sessions.

On the afternoon of the Naumi both mediums have rites in their houses; the Carpenter's tutelary has offerings of *ghi* and grain, that of the Weaver has a goat sacrificed, and liquor offered. As the mediums go to a central meeting-place the crowds gather, attracted by the noise and the constant drumming. Most simply follow the procession, but some stop the mediums as they pass their houses, and receive sorghum grain which they eat for their ailments; once, a sickly baby was placed in the street to allow the Carpenter to step over it. The main aim of the procession is to take the seedlings and 'cool' them by sinking them in a well near the village. In the year of my stay a Nath conjurer had come from outside, and he entertained the crowd with tricks, and also made the mediums perform. The Weaver medium, for example, became very excited at the sight of a lime (for the Goddess is accompanied by limes), and would lunge and writhe if the conjurer made as if to throw juice over him. Large crowds followed the procession, which took about three hours; I reckoned that the gathering which formed in the main village square contained at least 80 per cent. of the village's population. It was this spectacle that people wished to see, for only the attendants of the mediums accompanied them to the well to complete the performance, and to bring the mediums out of their possession.

The Naumi procession is an established feature in Ramkheri, for 'there has always been a medium' as people say. It may not occur in all villages, though the rites with the wheat seedlings appear to be widespread,[1] and this period is known to be a time when tutelary spirits are especially active.[2] The headmen have no specific duties in the procession, but have the general responsibility for controlling the crowds and seeing that there are no quarrels. One occasion, for

[1] Fuchs 1950: 321–3.

[2] Another period is the nine days of Vaisakh (April–May) month before the Birthday of Rama (Ram Naumi), and there are also isolated occasions when possession of a medium is expected (e.g. Divali). Ram Naumi is not generally observed by Ramkheri people, though some with urgent business might have a session with the Carpenter medium. It appears to be more popular in north India, whereas in Malwa more stress is placed on Krishna's birthday.

example, saw a dispute between followers of the two mediums over their precedence, and the headmen had to move quickly to prevent a fight. The second part of the Naumi activities, on the other hand, features the headmen in leading roles. It consists in sacrifices and homage paid to the shrines within the village boundaries.

The work starts in the evening, at dusk. The main part consists in having a fire rite at three shrines—those of the Sakti Mata, Hanuman Kherapati and Heja Mata. When the service is over the fire is kept alight, and people pass their possessions through the flame, to ensure their well-being in the coming year. Thus cowbells, butter churns, swords and staves are passed through. The tailor put his scissors through, and I was advised to do the same with my pen and camera. Amulets and medicines are also brought to these fires. After, a goat is killed at each shrine, beheaded by the village watchman with a single stroke of his sword. Previously, a goat was also sacrificed to the State flag; but now nothing is done at Naumi, and a coconut is broken on August 15. As well as these three main rites, homage is paid to all shrines in the village. They are washed with water, painted with lead oxide, and a coconut broken and some of its meat left there, the rest being distributed to bystanders.

The group performing this work is not large. The population has dispersed after the procession of the afternoon, and the excitements of the conjurer and mediums. People are busy milking their cows and cooking the evening meal; later, they sit on their verandas and watch the headmen pass on their duties. With the latter are all the village servants holding rent-free land for precisely such services. The village priest performs the rite, the barber must be there to run errands, the potter washes the shrines, the Weaver village servants bring the goats and take away their bodies, the Bhilala watchman kills them, and the drummer plays at all important moments. Only the tanner, sweeper and carpenter are absent.

The lack of a general village attendance does not alter the fact that the rites are done on behalf of the whole village, and are made at both public shrines and those which may 'belong' to a single unilineal descent group—e.g. to a particular descent group's Bheru or Sati.[1] The list of shrines, forty-four in all, gives an idea of the way *all* sacred places are treated as the concern of the entire village, and their propitiation made a prerequisite for its welfare during the coming year. The shrines are as follows, in order of worship:

Sakti Mata—Mother Goddess
Sitala Mata—Smallpox Goddess
Pandharinath Maharaj—Vaishnavite Temple

---

[1] See Chapter IX.

101

Ambika Mata—Mother Goddess
Adyapal Maharaj—Lord of the Village Gates (south)
Bholanath—Sivaite Temple
Goya—Local godling (goya 'road')
Bheru—Nath caste
Gaddegal—Place of treaty with marauders
Dewaldi Mata—? Local name for Mother Goddess
Bheru—Brahman caste
Narsingh Maharaj—Vaishnavite Temple
Gal Maharaj—Lord of the Holi Swing
Sati Mata—Brahman caste memorial
Heja or Mari Mata—Cholera Goddess
Koka Mata—? Fertility Goddess
Chamunda Mata—Mother Goddess
Hanuman Kherapati—Lord of the Village
Sati Mata—Not known of which caste
Adyapal Maharaj—Lord of the Village Gates (east)
Bheru—Unknown
Bheru—Drummer caste
Ram Deoji Maharaj—Rajasthani saint (aids lepers)
Thuni—Village Foundation Stone
Bheru—Sargara caste
Bheru—Weaver caste
Bheru—Gosain caste
Bheru—Weaver caste
Bheru—Balai Babaji caste
Paliya—Memorial to violent death (Carpenter)
Chira—Stone dividing Ramkheri from Khera hamlet
Bheru—Tanner caste
Ganesh—Patron of the blacksmithy
Adyapal Maharaj—Lord of the Village Gates (west)
Ishwar Maharaj—Unspecified god
Hardar Lala—Local godling
Palit Maharaj—? Local godling
Phutli Mata—Smallpox Goddess
Sati Mata—Memorial of Weaver caste
Bheru—Barber caste
Bheru—Rajput caste
Bheru—Rajput caste
Bisesa Maharaj—Lord of Village Boundary (north)
Udeyrao Maharaj—Lord of Village Boundary (southeast)

It is the headman's duty to lead these rites, but he has no special ritual status because of this. If the headmen were all ill or absent, it was said, another person could take their place. But the headman is seen as the 'natural' person to do such a rite, and he thereby represents the village to the spiritual as well as the temporal world outside it.

A further link between the rites and the population of the village was the distribution of the meat of the sacrificed goats to each house in Ramkheri. This, of course, was only a token amount (I was not able to see a distribution, so do not know if the amount varied with the status of the caste). People of vegetarian castes used either to bury the meat in honour of the Goddess, or give it to meat-eating neighbours. The goats themselves were donated by the Goatherd, in return for free grazing rights on uncultivated lands.

In 1955, meat was not distributed for the first time, nor were goats given but instead were purchased by the headmen. This change illustrates three significant trends in the village. One of these is that vegetarians, though not increasing their numbers, have a growing influence. I have already mentioned that this is now the custom of many powerful men in Dewas and Madhya Bharat, these having displaced the mainly meat-eating entourage of the Maharajas; consequently, one mark of status is repugnance to meat. An influential Rajput in Ramkheri (not a headman) is a vegetarian, and he pulled me away from the sacrifice of the goat to the Weaver medium, saying that this was 'dirty' work, and should really not be allowed. Under such influences the Farmers, etc., started to refuse to accept the meat, thereby breaking the idea of the distribution as a village-wide affair.

Second, the economic conditions under which goats were donated have changed. There is no longer as much grazing land available, and owners wish to conserve what they have for their own livestock. Further, there are more goats in the village than before. The Goatherd is now one of several men (Bhilalas, Weavers) with flocks; for the demand for meat has risen in the rapidly growing towns of Indore, Ujjain and Dewas where some immigrants are said to lose vegetarian habits. The headmen who, as Rajputs, are members of the main landholding caste, therefore prefer to purchase their goats from the goatherders, and make the latter pay them for grazing-rights. And, having bought the goats, they feel under no compulsion to divide the meat around the village; so they only give some to the village servants who have helped them in the night's work. This change in the headmen's attitudes is not only the result of economic causes; it also stems from the general lessening of the headman's authority in the village, with a correspondingly weaker obligation towards its population. This third feature of interest will become clear in this chapter.

Caste and Village Leadership

As with the Nine Nights, the Divali festival is made up partly of household rites and partly of a village celebration. It takes place on the last day of the dark half and the first day of the bright half of Kartik (October–November) month. This is just after the Nine Nights festival, and comes at the start of the cold weather, around the time of the first (sorghum) harvest.

The general part of the festival starts on the first night, with the singing of special songs called *hir*.[1] A *hir* party consists of two sections; one starts singing with three slowly rising notes, leading into a verse which ends with a long, drawn-out '*hir*', sung whilst the other section starts its verse. In former times, it is said, *hirs* used to be sung for many nights before Divali; but I heard only two parties which sang through the single night. One was of Rajputs and Weavers, the other of Farmers and Weavers, and neither numbered more than six or eight men. This is partly because the younger men think such singing is old-fashioned and prefer film-songs; partly it is because all non-vegetarian singers drink liquor (the reason given is to keep warm through the already chilly autumn night) and liquor is now very expensive under present Government policy.

Shortly before dawn, the *hir* singers approach the main headman's house. Awoken by them, he goes to the Tanner's ward, where the *caura* is prepared. This is the skin of a young calf, fastened with outstretched paws to a stout pole. As the Tanners do this work, they joke with the singers and the headman, throwing firecrackers at them and chasing each other with hot coals, which they try to drop down each other's backs. The upper caste villagers allow a certain amount of this frivolity, but withdraw to a safe distance when it seems to endanger their dignity. When the *caura* is ready the Tanners are given a token payment in cash by the headman on behalf of the village. The Weavers then take the *caura* and the small procession goes through the waking village, still singing, to each of the headman's houses. There, the women make a swastika of flour on the ground and put red powder (*kunku*) on the *caura*. Dawn breaks as this work finishes, and what started as a dozen men slowly swells until some fifty people accompany the *caura* to the yard of the headman, where it is left for a few hours, so that people can go home and decorate their cattle.

At about ten o'clock that morning, people reassemble round the *caura*, and a procession starts. At every open space two or three Weavers hold the *caura*, and a young calf is pinioned behind them.

---

[1] The Divali night is said to be the darkest of the year, and songs are sung to keep away harmful spirits.

The calf's mother, made very nervous by the deprivation of her calf and the smell of the calf-skin on the *caura*, charges the latter and is only prevented from rushing the Weavers by the pole they hold. As the crowd grows, so it presses in on the open space, and people frequently have to flee from cows which decide to run away and go charging up the streets away from it all. The year I saw this cow-baiting there were several very lively animals, and the procession took some time to reach the central village square, where almost the entire village population had gathered. Delays were also caused by disputes which broke out among the Weavers and other people (mostly Bhilalas and Rajputs) who had been drinking since early morning. The climax of the day was about to begin, with cow-baiting in the main square, when a sharper quarrel broke out. Thereupon the headman who had inaugurated the procession stepped in, took the *caura* away at once, and 'cooled' it by sinking it in a nearby pond. So the programme finished abruptly.

This end to the *caura* procession was by no means unexpected, for the occasion is always marked by disputes because of the liquor drunk and the degree of excitement promoted by the noise, dust and even physical danger of the cow-baiting. Indeed, the headman told me that because of fights the year before, he had determined to stay in his house at dawn; and without him the *caura* could not have been fetched from the Tanners. My presence changed his mind, he said, for he thought that I ought to see the cow-baiting. But I am not sure that my role was as significant as this. For in 1955 the *caura* was again taken round the village, after I had left; and I was told in letters that fights again occurred. There may, in fact, be a constant pull between the desire of the headman to prevent the risk of fights for which the Police would hold him responsible, and the weight of tradition, and the desire of the Weavers for drink and amusement and of the general village population for diversion. Nevertheless, although the headman may at present be powerless to stop it, he is able to cut short the procession at any time. And this he does when he feels that small disputes (which he himself could patch up later) are going to develop into a fight which might get out of control.

Later in the afternoon some of the villagers go to the shrine of Udeyrao Maharaj, about half a mile from the village. In 1954 two of the three village headmen went, with about forty other people, mostly younger men of whom Rajputs formed the largest caste group. Here the village priest reads the forecast (*pancang*) for the coming year; for Divali marks the new year of the Vikram era. This forecast is in a printed almanack, published in Ujjain, and contains two parts. One is largely political—in 1954 it analysed the international situation, for example, saying that India would become more friendly with China and Russia, and that the Western powers would continue to try to impose their policies. The other account is agricultural—it forecasts the prices of farm products, the number of rainy days in each month, etc. The discussion of the forecast afterwards centred entirely on this latter part, not a word being said about the political aspect.

When this is over, the Carpenter medium is possessed by Ram Deoji Maharaj. Again, there has always been a medium in action on this day, say Ramkheri people. But his activities differ from those in the Naumi procession. For now the medium is used for private consultation (as he is used during the Nine Nights). Many of the questions are confidential, and must be camouflaged in front of the crowd. Thus, a man asked about an object he had lost in the house. This in fact referred to his wife, and he was told that he would recover it 'after three periods'—this he took to mean three months, but friends maintained that the periods might be years or days. Other questions are asked openly; thus a man asked if his son, on whom he set much store, would grow to be an educated man. The reply was ambiguous: 'he will be first in his classes', said the medium, but did not say up to which class he would study. Again, a man asked for advice about his eye trouble, and was given sorghum grains to eat. In all, some dozen questions were asked, after which people returned to the village.

The programme at Divali does not contain acts so clearly meant for the village welfare as does that at Naumi. The *caura* is seen as an amusement; 'it pleases the cows', I was told, though it may once have had a deeper significance as a corporate village activity. Again, the forecast used formerly to be read by the village priests at each house in turn, and the public reading is more for his own convenience.[1] And the medium deals with individual, not village matters. Nevertheless, the programme is open to all villagers, is in the village's name and is supervised by the village headman.

THE HEADMAN—UNOFFICIAL DUTIES AT HOLI

The activities at the Holi festival resemble Naumi, in being concerned with general village welfare. Holi takes place on the last (full-moon) day of Phalgun month (February–March), and the first day of Chait month (March–April). This is at the end of the cold weather, when the wheat harvest is in progress, or has just finished.

Two days before the full-moon night, the Weaver village servants dig holes and plant the saplings which are to be used in the Holi fires.

[1] Cf. Dube 1955: 99, where a similar reading must be attended by 'all responsible village elders' and is held at the headman's house.

There are two of these; one is in the main square in front of what was the landlord's house, and is known as the 'government (*sarkari*) fire' because expenses were given by the landlord. The other is on the outskirts of the settlement, and is the 'village fire'. At present the small expenses for both are met by the headmen.

During the ensuing two days, the saplings are surrounded by a pile of cow-dung cakes as fuel. In former times these were collected by theft. Anyone could steal from any villager's house or byre; and if he put the cakes in a place with a flag over it, the owner could not take them back. All castes played at this theft, it is said, and the old men recall that Maharaja Krishnaji Rao II participated too, and was even chased and spanked by a house-owner who caught him one dark night. This privileged theft stopped about six to eight years ago, and people now give three or four cakes per house. People say that now there is no landlord to support the custom, some villagers have threatened to sue the thieves; and this reason is, I think, true. Many rites now suffer for lack of an influential patron who at the same time is outside the village system, and so can act as scapegoat if anything goes wrong. And since the wealthier people would suffer most from these thefts, they now feel free to protest against them, and to use their influence to stop them.

On the evening of the full-moon, the three headmen join the village priest at the 'government fire', perform a rite and light the fire. When it has died down, about thirty women come in procession, led by the drummer. They go to the shrine of the Sakti Mata and worship there—first the wives of the headmen, then the other Rajput women, who in fact make up most of the procession, and finally a few others (Oil-pressers, Farmers and Gosains). Then they cross to the fire and walk round it, some sprinkling water, and all dropping a mixture of rice, sugar and *ghi* on to the embers. When they have finished and gone to their homes a few Tanner women perform the same rite. This ends activities at the 'government fire'.

Next morning at dawn it is the turn of the 'village fire'. The headmen again light it, watched by a dozen or so men of nearby houses. Then they set off around the village, going to all the houses in which there has been a death in the past year. Here are gathered at least some, if not all, of the villagers who are agnates of the dead man, or of the husband of the dead woman. In two out of the eighteen cases close neighbours also sat with the bereaved ones; Muslims were visited as well as Hindus. The procedure is for the Barber to put some *kunku* on the lintel of the door, and on the foreheads of the men sitting outside, while the women keen in the house, particularly the widow who has been more or less secluded from the time of the death. As the procession leaves, the men who were sitting join it, and so it swells as more houses are visited. At Weaver houses, the Barber gives the *kunku* to each man, but does not actually put it on their foreheads; at the Tanners' ward he gives a large amount to one man for distribution among the rest. This illustrates the progressive exclusion down the caste scale of the Harijan castes (the Sweeper was not visited in 1955, so I do not know what happens there). On arrival back at the embers of the village fire, the mourners go round it sprinkling water, and then throw a coconut into the ashes. The morning's programme is over, and people sit and talk, some taking the ashes and mixing them with salt to give to their cattle.

In the afternoon, the wives of the headmen make a similar journey of condolence. Accompanied in the main by other Rajput women, with some from the allied castes and a few Farmer women whose houses lie near those of the headmen, they enter each house and sit with the keening women, comforting them, and sprinkling red water on the floor. The only difference from the men's procession is that the mourners do not join in the return to the Holi fire, where the women empty the rest of the water from their pots.

This ends the main ritual activities. For the rest of the day there is merriment. Groups of men singers (*geriya*), mostly of lower castes, go around the village singing and collecting money with which they buy liquor. Women, it is said, beg unrefined sugar from householders, on pain of dousing with red water.[1] The three or four traders set up small stalls of sweetmeats and cheap toys, and the less thrifty take their children there. At dusk the focus moves to the Swing (*gal*). This is a pole some fifteen feet high, with a cross-bar at the top forming a 'T' shape; a rope can be looped from one end of the bar, and a man can swing round and round, since the cross-bar is free-circling. Live coals have been spread between the shrine to the Lord of the Swing and a Bheru shrine some three or four steps away. About twenty women come to the place, led by the drummer. They have fasted during the day and purified themselves with turmeric paste. After making offerings to the Lord of the Swing they walk over the coals to the Bheru and worship there. This they do several times, watched by a large crowd (I estimated perhaps 40 per cent. of the village population). It is in fulfilment of various vows—in particular, women who are barren or who have lost many children, will make this act of faith in the deities.

When they have finished, the drummer escorts a man of the Basket-maker (Bargunda) caste to the swing. Previously he used to swing, but now he contents himself with a dance and a walk on the

---

[1] I was unable to see how much of this actually went on, for in 1955 I was the main object of attack.

embers. He has also purified himself with turmeric, and has drunk deeply. The swinging has been stopped for about the same length of time as the stealing of the cow-dung cakes. In the first place, nobody is willing to bear the expenses of the Basket-maker's liquor—in the old days, the landlord sponsored the affair; and in the second place, the headmen fear the results of an accident if the swing should break. For they think that they would be held to blame by the authorities. Previously, again, the landlord used to come and watch the swinging, thereby taking the responsibility for what went on; and even if he were not present, the headmen knew that he would support them if anything happened.

The fifth day of the month is called Colour Fifth (*Rangpancmi*). As on the Holi day, parties of men should tour the village, singing and dousing people with red dyed water and dust. I am not able to say whether the size of the parties was augmented by the fact that I presented an opportune target for dousing, but I was told that, like many other occasions, there is much less activity than before. People are touchy about getting their clothes stained, and one must now be careful whom one douses without specific permission. Again, this is partly because there is no leader who has power to maintain the old ways; for formerly much of the play went on in front of the landlord's house.

The final rite of the festival used to occur on the thirteenth day after Holi. I am deliberately leaving out a discussion of the mythology on which these festivals are based, but I should mention here that the fires lit on the first day are said to be in commemoration of the burning of the princess Holika, in punishment for her worship of false gods. Afterwards, I was told, her blind husband came to see the spot, and this was celebrated by Weavers in the Jamrai rite. A Weaver was blindfolded, led first to the Holi fire and then round the village, being given cooked food at all houses occupied by castes from which he could eat. The Weavers stopped doing this about ten years ago; they felt that it demeaned them, and hindered their attempts to raise their group's status.

The headman's leadership in the Holi festival, and his responsibility to the whole village in this, is clear. I expect other people could light the fires, but it is 'natural' for the headman to do so, as well as it is for him to visit the bereaved households. The headmen's wives have an essential task too. For their visit at the first Holi after a death marks the end of the widow's seclusion; and this is the occasion for quite a large feminine gathering, women returning to their parental houses for 'the first Holi' after a death there.

There is at present not the same burden on the headman to see that the programme runs smoothly as there is in the *caura* procession.

But this was not always the case, since in former times Holi was as productive of fights as Divali is now. At that time special songs (*kavali*) were sung by two teams in a competition consisting of each side's singing a verse to which the other had to find an appropriate answer, the victor being the side whose verse went uncapped. Recruitment of the teams was on a territorial basis and the boundary, which was marked by a special stone (*cira*), was also the line between the original settlement of Ramkheri and the newer Hamlet which was started by the seceding Rajput headman. The sides were called Turre and Kilangi; each had a flag and Turre, as representatives of the elder section of the village, were by tradition allowed to lead the procession. But the Kilangis would try to go to the front when they had won the singing competition; everyone having drunk freely, brawls would ensue. These had to be controlled by the headmen, though this was a difficult job since many of the participants were Rajputs. The State authorities stepped in after one particularly severe affray and forbade the contest, and the division is no longer formally recognized. Young men often know nothing about it and are genuinely interested to hear of the old custom. For others, 'Turre-Kilangi' is synonymous with 'quarrel' but the derivation is unknown. The older men are self-conscious of talking about such boisterous occasions to an outsider, and it is hard to assess just when the contest stopped—I imagine between twenty and thirty years ago.[1] With it stopped a context for the headman's authority, and a demonstration of the Rajput caste group's leadership—for Rajputs were foremost in the processions and the singing.

THE HEADMAN—UNOFFICIAL DUTIES AT OTHER RITES

The three festivals I have described are the major annual occasions for village gatherings. Almost the whole village assembles in one place; and the headman and other village officials act on behalf of the entire population. There are other times when an activity is open to all in the village,[2] though no more than a fraction of the population actually participates. Thus, on each Monday during the month of Sravan (July–August) the image of Bholanath is taken round the village by its Gosain custodian.[3] In theory, all could join the procession, and people of all households are free to pay homage to the deity as he passes in the street. But in practice only a dozen or so

[1] I understand that Turre-Kilangi matches still occur in some villages of Malwa but have been unable to get any further data. For similar data, see Mayer 1952*b*.

[2] When I talk of 'the whole village' one must always recall the limited degrees to which Harijan castes can take part.

[3] Monday is associated with Siva (Bholanath) all over India. Again, Sravan is his month.

men follow the palanquin, and the alms collected are so meager that the Gosain now finds excuses to miss several of the weekly processions each year.

Again, the Maka Sankrant festival occurs in the winter, when the sun starts to return from the south. In the morning the village cattle are brought to the open space in front of the village, are fed on sorghum stalks and given the rest of the day for leisure. The Naths beg from villagers; and the main common activity is the playing of *gulli-danda*. This is a game with a short stick and a piece of wood about six inches long which is carved into a diamond shape. The latter is placed on the ground, and when its end is hit, flies into the air. The hitter tries to send it as far as he can, and his opponent runs in from a distance and tries to touch him before he has succeeded in hitting the *gulli*. Most of the playing is done by younger men, as one can imagine. But at present a feeling of some apprehension attends it. If the *gulli* hits anyone, say people, there may be a fight. 'Before, we had people of power in the village, to whom such incidents would be reported and settled at once', said a villager. 'But now people would go to Dewas and start a lawsuit.' Hence there was in 1955 only a small gathering of players and watchers, the main group containing no more than thirty men, of whom eight were Rajputs, six Weavers, only five Farmers and a few others. Play stopped abruptly after half an hour, and I could not at first find out why; later I was told what I had missed seeing, that one youth had been hit on the ear, and the senior Rajput present had stopped the affair. (Here, again, the Rajputs take responsibility for the peace of the meeting, though they are not powerful enough to ensure a settlement of all disputes that may arise.)

There are some village rites which are only periodic. One such is the worship of the Smallpox Goddess, which is a thanksgiving made every twenty years or so by women with children who have had smallpox and recovered. I was fortunate enough to see the rite at Ramkheri. It consisted of a procession round the village, starting from houses next to the Goddess's shrine on the side of the main square, and gathering women as it went, until it returned to the shrine again. This was an innovation; for on previous occasions there had been separate processions from each of the headmen's houses, bringing people from that side of the village only. The headmen's wives went to the head of the 1955 procession but they did not initiate it. This may have been because the organizer was the chairman of the Village Committee, rather than a headman. And it adds to the picture of the headman's weakening authority.

Sometimes there are rites in emergencies. An instance is when there is an epidemic among the village cattle. On the first day the headmen do homage to the forty-four village shrines I have listed. The next day sees the *tana* rite. A procession forms; first, a man sprinkling wheat and sorghum grain on the ground; then a man bearing a pot filled with a mixture of liquor and water, with holes in its base so that there is a trickle on to the ground; and lastly a pig led by one man and prodded, so that it squeals, by another. When the pot needs filling the procession stops, a hen's egg is broken or a cock killed. Whilst a complete circuit is made of the village, the inhabitants and their livestock must stay inside. The route ends at the shrine of the Lord of the Village Gates. Here the pig is sacrificed and buried in the road. The cattle are led over the spot, and milk and cow urine sprinkled on them as they go. The main people concerned are Weavers, but other castes can also help (e.g. the Potter bears water to fill the pitcher). The headmen supervise, and make a levy on every landowner for expenses. In the same way, there is a similar ritual to the Cholera Goddess if that epidemic strikes the village. And if there is a drought, the headmen must call on Indra by performing the fire rite for seven days at the shrine of the Sakti Mata.

SUMMARY OF THE HEADMAN'S POSITION

Until the last decade, the headmen were the only people with statutory authority in the village. In former times this authority was very great, and operated in matters which have later been moved to the jurisdiction of the courts. But it still included tax collection and the responsibility for law and order. This power, backed as it was by the unanswerable sanctions of the Maharaja, could make village despots of the headman. It may sometimes have done so; but on other occasions (and I have no way of knowing how often) the headmen moved as much as possible with the approval of the leaders of other important caste groups. In this way the caste divisions in the village, which prevented the headmen from being the senior kinsmen as well as the State representatives, served to temper and 'democratize' the situation.

The headman also had the greatest unofficial power in the village. This followed as an overflow of influence from his official position. It was reflected in arbitration of other castes' affairs, and in the control he exercised over all-village rites. It is true that he needed some personal ability to maintain his unofficial position; but out of three (and formerly four) headmen one might expect that there would always have been at least one man thus qualified—a man of not too advanced an age (between forty and fifty-five years), with the desire to lead, and the intelligence, oratory and firmness of resolve to do so, quite apart from a sense of his own importance.

112

The sanctions he could wield were not statutory ones. But his power existed because people did not wish to get him against them in the spheres where he *did* have statutory authority (e.g. a man who flouted the headman's unofficial decisions, might find himself pressed into compulsory labour rather more frequently). I do not deny that there were sometimes other influential Rajputs, and that these might have as much unofficial power as some of the headmen. But these men appear to have worked through the headman most closely related to them (see p. 239) in all questions over which factions of Rajputs arose.

The influence of these Rajput leaders spread to the rest of the caste group. This was partly because the group was to some extent seen as undifferentiated by the rest of the village, and partly it was due to conscious efforts by all caste members to share in the prestige of their ruling caste mates. This tendency existed whether the caste members were wealthy and well regarded in the Rajput caste group or not. Hence, in Ramkheri even the poor relations of the headmen tended to lead other castes in informal situations. Important Rajputs would take the lead in any discussions which they attended, and here the lesser caste men would defer to them; but when no headman or other influential Rajput was present, the lesser lights of the caste would shine more brightly. Rajputs also attended village affairs more than other important castes (e.g. the Farmers), and this aided their general primacy in village matters. For the Rajputs, village leadership was a caste thing, for the other castes it seems to have been the role of one or two 'big' men of the caste.

As I have stressed throughout this account, the headman's position has changed in the last ten years. In the first place, he is no longer the only person with statutory backing and official outside contacts in Ramkheri. The members of the Village Committee also have the sanction of Government for their duties; and these tend constantly to encroach on the responsibilities of the headman, and to weaken his official position. Second, his power in unofficial contexts has diminished. Those others who have authority in the village are equally sought for arbitration of major issues. And though the headmen, in their roles at the major festivals, still supply the symbolic focus for village corporate action, these occasions are less important in the lives of the villagers, precisely because the headmen are now too weak to keep these festivals under close control (e.g. people are now more afraid of quarrels because these are not so easily settled right away by the headmen, and so they tend to keep away from the festivals).

It is time, then, to turn to the new positions of authority, and to the Village Committee which embodies them. From the description we shall be able to see to what extent the old pattern has changed—that is, to what extent the men in authority there have different powers to those of their predecessors, and whether the Rajputs as a caste group have lost the influence they previously possessed.

VILLAGE COMMITTEE AND COMPREHENSIVE COMMITTEE

There are four main contexts of village leadership in the new era which started with the foundation of the Village Committee in 1946. Two of these have been discussed—the statutory authority still held by the headmen, and the informal contexts in which the headmen retain some position as leaders. The two new ones are—the statutory authority now held by leaders of the Village Committee, and new informal contexts which come into the purview of the Comprehensive Committee. I say 'old' and 'new' now, to highlight my analysis. But as I have just stated, one of the problems is to see in how far these are new in form only, or whether they represent genuine differences in the principles and personnel of leadership from the traditional patterns.

The Village Committee (*Ganv Pancayat*) was inaugurated by the Maharaja's Government in 1946. At that time Ramkheri was given its own Committee of eight representatives who were elected by a show of hands in a village meeting. In 1951 there was another election; this time there were four seats for Ramkheri and two for the smaller neighbouring village of Krishnapura—this was because it was thought best to have a Committee for every 1200 people, and Ramkheri was too small to have a Committee of its own. In the third elections in 1956 a fifth seat was given and reserved for a woman. In addition, the village schoolmaster was appointed secretary on a salary of Rs. 5 per month.

The statutory powers given to the Village Committee have varied over the decade. At first they were considerable. The Committee was empowered to judge civil cases of up to Rs. 15 damages, and to give fines of up to Rs. 5 in petty, non-cognizable criminal actions. Some of these cases would formerly have been referred to the courts in Dewas, and others might well have been arbitrated by the landlord whilst he was in Ramkheri, or by the headman. During the years 1946–50, 110 cases were dealt with, and only 5 went on appeal to the courts. Of these cases, 73 were civil and 37 criminal; most were between people of different castes, though 13 and 15 cases respectively concerned those of the same caste. The Village Committee seems to have been effective in disposing of these cases quickly and cheaply. But in other villages the work of the Committees gave rise to more disputes than they settled,[1] and in 1950 the Madhya Bharat Government abolished this power in all villages.

Other functions of the Village Committee included the impounding of animals against a fine for their release, the allocation of house sites in the state-owned village confines (formerly the prerogative of the headman), and the collection of a tax on houses which, with a small percentage of the land tax, constituted its income. The Committee was encouraged to start making improvements to the village of the kind which are now sponsored through the Community Projects Administration and the National Extension Service.

Recently, there has been a move to give increased power to the Village Committee. It, instead of the headmen, is to collect the land tax; and it has already been given the power to demand five days' annual 'voluntary' labour (*sramdan*) from each adult male, on pain of fine, for work on development projects which the Committee itself inaugurates and controls. The present policy seems to be to give it all the powers formerly held by the headman. Even if the latter retains his responsibility for law and order, his post is to be made elective, rather than hereditary, and so members of the Village Committee may themselves be elected headmen. Government contacts with the village are increasing under the new plans of economic and social development, and most of these are with the Village Committee.

The Village Committee has been the preserve of the upper castes, of which the most prominent has been the Rajput. The first Committee had three Rajputs (of which two were headmen), and one Brahman, Trader (who later left the village), Farmer, Cotton-carder and Oil-presser. The latter was the chairman (*sarpanc*); having been the village schoolmaster, and so having taught many of the Committee members, it was thought respectful to allow him the chair. The second Committee consisted of two Rajputs (one a headman), a Brahman and a Balai Babaji to represent Harijans. The most recent Committee includes one Rajput, Brahman, Cotton-carder and Bhilala, and a Rajput woman. In both these most recent Committees the same Rajput has been the chairman and most powerful member,[2] but he is not a headman, and it is notable that no headman is on the

---

[1] This is said to have been particularly so in Gwalior villages. Here, the landlord and his agents had had great powers, and their departure left no established authorities in the village like the Dewas headmen, who could run such courts. The Dewas villages thereby suffered, for they were integrated with the much larger Gwalior territory in a State where legislation had to be uniformly applied.

[2] The Brahman spends his time in Dewas. He has great prestige in Ramkheri, which he uses to reinforce the authority of the Rajput; but he does not play so great a part in the details of the Committee, preferring to set the broad lines of its policy and supervise from afar.

most recent Committee—again, a sign of the headman's decreasing influence, since it was not for want of trying that the headman was not re-elected. Neither has there been any Farmer on recent Committees—partly because there is no outstanding leader in the caste group, partly because Farmers do not take such an interest in public affairs and are anyhow regarded as comparative newcomers, and partly because the caste group is too divided internally to be able to support a single candidate solidly enough to have him elected. The composition of the Committee, then, shows the continuing dominance of the Rajputs in the public life of Ramkheri, though there is some strain between the chairman of the Committee and the headmen who are jealous of his power.

About six months after the first election to the Village Committee, a body called the Comprehensive Committee (*Sarvjanik Samiti*) was formed by the villagers. It had the following members: President, Vice-President, Treasurer, Deputy Treasurer, Secretary, Auditor, Organizer, and *ex-officio* the head of the Labour Council (a body set up to regulate the rates of wages payable to farm labourers, which expired after a few months). In addition, there was a committee of twenty-two men. Further, the village sent representatives from each of fourteen wards, and this added ten men to the Committee who were not already serving in other capacities. The total number thus on the Comprehensive Committee was forty-three—and this out of a total male population of 250 adults made it indeed comprehensive! The election was said to have been by vote, but I suspect that it was largely a selection by the three or four men who had started the Committee and filled its main posts. There have been no further elections to this Committee. Records of meetings and resolutions have been kept, though they are not subject to inspection by officials, as are those of the Village Committee.

One reason for the formation of the Comprehensive Committee was the rivalry between the Village Committee's Oil-presser chairman and the powerful Rajputs who were his committee-members. The latter disliked playing second fiddle to a man of lower caste and so formed their own association (and we must recall that there had previously been some feeling between Oil-pressers and Rajputs over the former's demand to eat in the same line as the allied castes). In part, the Comprehensive Committee did the work entrusted by Government to the Village Committee. Under its auspices, for example, the construction of a village meeting-house was started, though this was a kind of improvement the Village Committee might have been expected to make. The Village Committee chairman, however, was unable to act without the support of the Rajputs who, though they remained in his Village Committee, lent their support to the new association. But the Village Committee continued to operate in those fields where the Comprehensive Committee could not be its substitute, e.g. in the petty civil and criminal cases. The Comprehensive Committee, moreover, was not simply formed to spite the Oil-presser chairman. For it was hoped through it to co-ordinate all aspects of village life which were to be improved, and thus to deal with matters outside the compass of the Village Committee.

Chief among these were disputes of a kind which could not have gone to the Village Committee. These were raised through a formal mechanism which reflected the influence of the now emerging democratic patterns. Four Caste Associations (*Jati Sangh*) were set up; one for Rajputs and all other castes in divisions 1-4 save Farmers; one for Farmers; one for Muslims; and one for Harijans. These bodies were supposed to hear disputes among members (which might thus be intra- or inter-caste) and report them to the Compre-hensive Committee when they proved intractable. I do not know if this machinery ever worked; there are no minutes for any Caste Association, and it is very likely that this was only an ideal pattern.[1] Cases of the kind envisaged did, however, reach the Comprehensive Committee.

Such, for example, was the quarrel between brothers as to how their jointly held property should be divided, and what should be set aside for the maintenance of their widowed mother. The Compre-hensive Committee set down terms in a document signed by the contenders, and this has been effective. Again, a series of quarrels among Farmers ended with arbitration and the signing of a docu-ment which read: 'We are united now, and will not tolerate any divisions of caste. Anyone who causes a quarrel or breaks this unity can be fined by the Comprehensive Committee, which is given this authority by the undersigned, who realize that as sons of India, they must have unity.' Documents like this could be drawn up in the hey-day of independence, when there was great enthusiasm for improving the life of the village, and when the Comprehensive Committee was newly established and its authority untarnished. At present, however, there are again disputes between Farmers. People said that in theory these could be brought to the Comprehensive Committee, and the guilty fined as provided for in the document. But nobody was pre-pared to do this any more. 'Look,' they said, 'the last arbitration did not stop disputes, why should any further attempts succeed?'

Besides this arbitration, the Comprehensive Committee took upon itself the welfare and morals of the people. It disposed of such

[1] It is not without interest as such. For it shows the isolated position of the Farmers from other upper castes.

matters as defecating too close to a well (fine of Rs. 1¼), ploughing on the dark-night day of the month, which is a rest-day for bullocks (fine of Rs. 1½) and so forth. In all these affairs, the Comprehensive Committee partly followed the pattern set by the headmen and other 'big men' in former days; but partly it broke new ground, when it acted over matters which had been nobody's concern in former times, but which were judged now to matter to the entire village (the fine for defecation is an example). In these cases the Comprehensive Committee took upon itself a village-wide authority and responsibility which found its climax in the boycott of a refractory individual by the entire village, of which more below.

The Oil-presser chairman of the Village Committee died during his first term of office, and at the next election, as we have seen, a Rajput became the new chairman, with a Rajput headman as fellow-member. At that time there was no ill-feeling from the latter for not having been made chairman; for the headmen did not yet feel the loss of their power, and regarded at least one seat on the Village Committee as 'theirs'.[1] In short, the Village Committee comprised a united membership, and there were no serious opponents outside it, with the exception of an Oil-presser about whom I have more to say later.

Under these conditions, the Village and Comprehensive Committees ran side by side, being scarcely distinguishable one from another. The same number of people came to meetings, whether they were officially styled Village or Comprehensive Committee gatherings. And the only occasions on which I saw the four Village Committee members meet alone was when they were drawing up projects for the Second Five-Year Plan, which they later presented for discussion in the larger assembly. The only difference that I could see between the two bodies was that meetings of the Comprehensive Committee were announced by the village Barber, who went calling the news down the streets, and that just before the meeting was due to start, a conch shell was blown to call the people. Neither of these things was done for the meetings of the Village Committee, which can thereby be seen as less of an all-village affair. But the villagers appeared unaware of such distinctions; the two words 'Village' and 'Comprehensive' were used apparently interchangeably about meetings (only those which were obviously Village Committee gatherings were always talked of as such—e.g. when an election was held, or an official came to check the books). At the beginning of

[1] In 1954 the headman refused to entertain the possibility that he might not retain his seat at the next election. His disillusion was all the greater when I saw him after the 1956 election, when he had been forced out to make way for a Muslim Cotton-carder.

fieldwork, I had difficulty in finding out the composition of early committees. For when I asked about the Village Committee, I was sometimes given a list of its members, sometimes of the Comprehensive Committee's members, and yet other informants gave me a mixture of the two. Nevertheless, there were certain features which belonged to the Village Committee, and certain to the Comprehensive Committee; the merging of the two can be seen as an attempt to amalgamate the desirable features of each, under a single leadership. What are these features?

The size of membership is important. As I have said, the formal membership of the Comprehensive Committee included one-sixth of Ramkheri's men. This meant, in effect, that all interested people attended any meeting and were full parties to any decision, though this may have been formulated and pushed through by the four or five men who were the effective leaders. It is unlikely that there would be any important people left outside, for all those men likely to have views were precisely those who had been selected for the Committee; and with no election for the last nine years, the idea of 'ordinary member' of the Committee has in any case become progressively vaguer, and more inclusive of any interested person.

People would like the Village Committee to be run on the same lines. The chairman told an official, 'Yes, we have only the four members of the Committee from Ramkheri, but any others can help in the work, and they are just as much members as I am, and so are all the people of the village.' This is why, in practice, meetings of the Village Committee are open, and anybody can speak to any issue. But since formally there is a membership of only four men, those who have ambitions to be leaders get bitter if they are unsuccessful in the elections. The restricted numbers turn the Village Committee into a factor of dissension; and the amalgamation with the Comprehensive Committee is a way of alleviating this. But the Government's object of having a small, well-organized and so quickly-acting group of executives is thereby defeated.

It is also weakened through a second feature, the desire to take action on a subject only when everyone is agreed about it. This is a very widespread characteristic of meetings in Ramkheri; we shall see that in the subcaste councils there is also a desire for unanimity before a decision is made; and it is reflected in the preponderance of uncontested elections for Village Committees.[1] What it means in these Committees is illustrated in the words of a villager. 'There are

---

[1] In recent Village Committee elections, six out of eight were uncontested. The issues are decided in pre-election canvassing, and unless the decision is too close for candidates to know their prospective fate, those who reckon they would lose will stand down in the name of unanimity.

three kinds of man in a village. The first speaks out loud at any meeting; the second is silent there, but will give his opinion in public later; and the third speaks only in private, largely to intrigue. All three must have their say before a decision can be taken, or else the village will be divided. That is why we cannot move on any matter for several days.'

This man was being optimistic when he gave the delay before taking a decision as being in days. For if there is any sort of controversy, it may be weeks or even months before things sort themselves out, and the feeling of the village is recognized by everyone. Now this approach can be followed on a Comprehensive Committee. If an issue proves intractable, postpone it; later, the difference may become quite unimportant to the contestants, when a decision can be reached. This is the case, for example, with the work begun on a village meeting-house. After a year or two the contributions dried up, and there was a general lack of interest over the half-finished building. The Comprehensive Committee leaders tried to raise more money, but finding that this would only exacerbate feelings about the project, they dropped the idea. After four or five years, a different opinion started to grow; people became self-conscious about the incomplete building, and felt that it reflected on their village. Under this turn of events (never openly acknowledged) the recalcitrants were less strongly opposed, and now the Committee leaders have started building again.

It is less possible to sustain this approach in the Village Committee; for this is an officially-sponsored body with specific functions, and the Government expects regular progress. Minutes are kept of meetings, and these are inspected by officials. When the Village Committee used to try cases, there was provision for adjournment, whilst members collected evidence in their own—often devious —ways. But the affair, once entered in the minutes, could not be indefinitely postponed. And so a judgment was made, which often antagonized the losers and resulted in their obstruction of the other work of the Committee. Because not enough time was left to get a consensus, there were even minority opinions delivered in some cases. It is true that few appeals were made from these decisions, but this was rather because of the expense involved than because the feelings of all concerned were that they had been rightly dealt with. The same thing happens now, in the development projects which are the responsibility of the Village Committee. If there is resistance towards contributing money or labour for, say, a road or drinking well, the matter can be delayed for some time. It was alleged, in fact, that minutes had been entered of imaginary meetings about one deadlocked issue, to satisfy inspecting officials. But sooner or later these will ask about what is happening, and then action must be taken. Work on an approach road had been stalled for the year I was in Ramkheri. Finally, official pressure on the Committee chairman grew so strong that he had to threaten everyone with fines. At this some work was done, though many people did little save curse the chairman.[1]

The wish to have unanimous action not only impedes the work of the Village Committee, but makes its members want to have their actions supported by people in a Comprehensive Committee. It is because of this that the largest meeting of the Comprehensive Committee which I witnessed was precisely about this matter of the road —formally a matter for the Village Committee's decision, and nothing to do with the Comprehensive Committee. The chairman felt, in fact, that he had to get all influential villagers committed to the road project before he could get work started; and he had to do the latter because of official insistence.

We see, then, that the two Committees work very closely, and are distinguishable only in a formal and rather unreal membership, and in the duties enjoined on the Village Committee. I am not prepared to say that the Comprehensive Committee must have been created, even if it had not been for the rivalry between Rajputs and Oil-pressers which was its immediate cause. But I would maintain that something like this body is felt to be necessary—a gathering which is open to all, which has no time-table, and which can deal with any issues it thinks fit.[2]

If we remember the situation before 1946 we see that there were, in fact, contexts for leadership which paralleled these two Committees. First, in former times the orders from the Maharaja or his officials represented the occasions when the line of authority passed through a limited number of people armed with sanctions (the headmen) and where action had to be taken within a limited time. At the present day this situation exists at least in theory in the Village Committee. That the time limits are lax is not because there are no effective sanctions (for the Village Committee chairman can fine people for not obeying his order to pay their house tax, etc.); it is rather because the Government's policy is to have action come from the villagers themselves, for objectives which they themselves want to attain,

---

[1] I must, in justice, add that when the road was almost complete, these men were among those who acknowledged that it was a useful addition to the village. They just did not apparently want to work on the road themselves.

[2] In some areas the importance of the wider body is officially recognized. Thus in Amaravati District, the *Vikas Mandal* is a statutory village body with no fixed membership and no concrete constitution. Any villager can belong if he wishes, and sub-committees are set up to supervise particular development projects (Anon. 1955: 264–70).

rather than to push on with something that the official thinks should be done forthwith.[1] Second, in former times the headman's council provided a forum for all interested and influential people to discuss matters and to arbitrate disputes. And this kind of leadership is now expressed through the Comprehensive Committee.

I can be more general about these two kinds of body, and say that the one typifies the 'committee procedure' and the other the 'council procedure'. A council is defined as 'an assembly or meeting for consultation or advice'. In our context the executive aspect would be a little more important, as in the now obsolete definition of 'an assembly called together for any purpose'. But two important elements are present in the former—the fluid membership, and the lack of compulsion to decide issues. The committee, on the other hand, is defined as 'a body of persons appointed or elected for some specific business or function'.[2] Here is the delegation of authority by a larger group, here is the restricted membership, and here is the need to make (and enforce) decisions, which I have shown exist in the Village Committee. This difference is mirrored in the Hindi, too; the dictionary translates council and committee by the term *sabha* and by different words—*parisad* and *pancayat*;[3] in the village there is also a distinction, for though both kinds of body can be called *pancayat*, the word *samiti* is only used for the committee.

The council, then, is the traditional and the committee the new type of assembly. The procedure by which the headman acted together with influential villagers and through which, as we shall see, affairs are carried on within the caste, is of the council type. The new Village Committee is of the committee type—but the tendency is to turn it into a council. Again, the Comprehensive Committee is in form a committee, as befits its modern origin, and I have called it such; but it is in fact the council which supplements the Village Committee.

We must note that the pressure towards acting through councils is nowadays very great, because of the new kinds of subjects with which the village associations deal. Decisions were in the old days confined to subjects which had been raised many times before, and about whose validity people were agreed. Thus, a headman's council to decide on what date a village festival should be held, or how compulsory labour for the Maharaja or the landlord should be allocated, was a repetition of many other such meetings, and did not need a

[1] See Mayer 1957 for further discussion on the problem of compulsion in Village Committees working in development projects.

[2] The definitions are from the *Shorter Oxford English Dictionary* 1955: 350 and 404.

[3] Bhargava's *Dictionary of the English Language* 1951: 158 and 186.

wide body of men to decide it or to discuss the issues. But the matters now in the hands of the Village Committee are new. To decide how to build a road, and where to lay it, needs agreement on the fundamental facts that a road is necessary and that it must run over somebody's land to get to the village. This is an unfamiliar situation, and hence the leaders wish to have everyone discuss it. This is, in fact, why Village Committees are really councils. Perhaps, after a decade or two, the work of the Village Committee will be routine, its members will feel able to run it alone, and the villagers in turn will allow them to do so as they formerly allowed the headmen to run most village affairs.

CASTE AND THE CHANGING AUTHORITY STRUCTURE

The situation after 1946 brought changes in the relations of the different castes towards village leadership. I have said that the Rajputs dominate the Village Committee as well as continuing as headmen. But they are no longer as united a caste group as they were, and are no longer as powerful in the village, for other men are trying to become pre-eminent, too. The focal point of rivalry is the boycott of an Oil-presser, which arose over his defiance of a decision made by the Comprehensive Committee. This occurred at the time when the Village Committee and the Comprehensive Committee were still separate and rival bodies headed by different people. The former, it will be recalled, had an Oil-presser as chairman, and the latter was composed mainly of Rajputs. The leaders of the Comprehensive Committee decided to stage a play at a Holi festival, and arranged for a performance called *mac*, in which there is considerable bawdiness. The head of the Village Committee maintained that it was the Village Committee's duty to put on such plays, since the whole population would see them, and that in any case a religious play of greater moral value should be staged instead of the *mac*. But he found himself with only one supporter, a caste mate, and was forced to change his mind after the Comprehensive Committee had ordered him to be boycotted. His supporter refused to give way, and has remained boycotted to this day.

This supporter had differences of longer-standing with the powerful men in the village, and an economic stake in defying them. Several years ago, he had started to cultivate a patch of grazing land (of perhaps half an acre) which formed the boundary between Ramkheri and a village to the east. This blocked the most direct access of livestock to some other grazing land, and also of course lessened the area available to the animals. Villagers had protested in vain, for the trespasser had his own contacts in the relevant

Government offices, and had managed to defer the case. From this incident had grown a general dislike for this man on the part of village leaders; and this was now to be expressed in a boycott over a quite different issue.

At first this boycott is said to have been complete. Nobody smoked with the man, nor gave him invitations, and no craftsman or labourer worked for him. The last was especially serious; it meant that he had to engage labourers from other villages at higher rates, and had to contract with outside craftsmen too, with inconvenience when his farm equipment needed mending, etc. After five years, the boycott has softened slightly, though maintained in its essentials. No village craftsmen yet work for the man, but he is now able to engage labourers for his farm work, mostly old, single men who do not have anything to lose by this, and whose acquiescence is not viewed so seriously by the leaders of the boycott. Almost all his agnates now attend rites at his house and eat his food, though they do not invite him in return. This, again, is excused by the man's main opponents, for the obligations of near kin in the ritual duties of the agnatic lines are acknowledged to be paramount. But more than this, other people are now slowly starting to make social contacts with the boycotted man. These can be roughly classed as—ritual kin; people who have had specific disputes with men who lead the boycott; and people who have ambitions of leadership in the village, who resent the present dominant group because of this, and so show their independence by accepting the invitations of the boycotted household. In all, these people are about a dozen strong.

Villagers say that the entire settlement has never before boycotted a person in this way. For nobody has ever defied the village thus. On the only other occasion when the Comprehensive Committee declared a boycott, its object was quickly brought to heel (see p. 263). Rather, a man has been turned out by the people of his subcaste group, and other inhabitants have boycotted him in sympathy, because they hold common ideas about the morality of the acts over which he has been judged. The most common boycott of this sort is when a man kills a cow or bullock (involuntarily, of course). He is boycotted by his own subcaste group in the village; and because cow-killing is believed to be highly polluting, everyone else will shun him until he has made penance.

Whilst agreeing that this may be the first boycott imposed directly by the whole village, I do not think this means that nobody ever disagreed with the recognized leaders before. The difference, I would suggest, is that a man can now disagree and stay in the village. Before, the headmen had such power that they could force a man to leave if he tried to defy them. But now, a man like the Oil-presser, who derives some of his income from outside and can arrange for alternative services from craftsmen, etc., can afford to weather the boycott. And in doing so he becomes a focus for village opposition to the established leaders. For all the villagers must make up their minds over whose side they are on. The apology of a boycotted man must be made to the whole village, not just to his subcaste group, and so everyone is involved, and the issue becomes linked to wider alignments. In this case, for instance, some of the man's close friends who were starting to disregard the ban were village accountants, being only incidentally farmers. There have always been such men in the village; but with the increased interest in education, such clerical workers are more looked up to, and also have influence through their official contacts. Their opponents rather represent the group of traditional leaders, being of higher caste and having the headmen in their ranks. Their concern is to maintain established patterns in the village, whereas the man who is boycotted and his close associates hold that the Rajputs and other upper castes should not have sole power in Ramkheri.

The village-wide boycott is a two-edged weapon. In so far as it is effective, it is clearly a potent weapon for strengthening the power of the leaders. But there is an obvious tendency for such a wide boycott to be eroded by ties of self-interest, as well as of ritual kinship, propinquity or friendships which existed before the boycott was imposed. When this happens, the boycott turns into a factor of division in the village, as is happening in Ramkheri. The fact that one man is successfully defying the village leaders, and may be even recruiting supporters (though covertly) weakens the authority of the leaders in other fields; for their authority flows from one situation to another. Thus, because the boycotted one does not pay any subscription towards the meeting-house fund, other people refuse to do so, not because they are his supporters, but because they see in this a way to avoid spending money. If the Village Committee leaders ask them to give, they will tell them to collect from everyone in the village before coming to them; and even if they finally pay up, it is only after a delay which weakens the leaders' position. Thus, the atmosphere in a village can change bit by bit, until there is little agreement over matters requiring village-wide co-operation. As people say 'the village work has gone bad' (*kam kharab hogaya*) and the leaders have lost their effectiveness.

Looking at the broad position, we see that hitherto Rajputs have had both statutory and unofficial authority in their hands; they have been the headmen of the village, and the services of any members of their caste group might be called for the arbitration of disputes of other castes. It must be noted, though, that the Rajputs do not

125

appear to have had as much power as is reported of dominant castes in other Indian villages. Srinivas, for example, writes that people in a Mysore village consider it wrong to take cases to the courts, and disadvantageous to have them settled by a caste council, rather than by the village elders who are of the dominant caste.[1] In Ramkheri, on the other hand, most cases seem to have been decided by the courts or by subcaste councils.[2] And when arbitration was made within the village, the Rajputs were not necessarily the only men to be called in. True, Rajputs of prestige were called most often but there was an influential Cotton-carder whose advice was taken, and there are instances of Oil-pressers and Farmers acting as judges in disputes too. The fact that the Rajputs' power was not more overwhelming may partly be because its numerical dominance was not so great as in the village described by Srinivas (whose dominant caste comprised half the village population), and partly because there were newly-arrived castes in the village which tended to settle their own affairs, and were not used to the village tradition of Rajput authority (e.g. Farmers and Oil-pressers).

Even with these qualifications, it is true to say that the Rajputs have been dominant in leadership, just as they were economically and ritually important. In the last ten years, however, Rajput control of the village has been shaken. This is because the headman's authority has lessened, other positions having been created to rival it. If the headmen had controlled the Village and Comprehensive Committee (which they do in some other villages) there might have been no change in the position. But this control has mainly been in the hands of a Rajput who is not a headman. The Rajput caste group is divided thereby, and its authority is lessened, even though it has managed to maintain a dominant position which it would have lost had some other caste member become chairman of the Village Committee.

If the solidarity of the village rests on the solidarity of the dominant caste,[3] then when this caste is divided internally, there is less solidarity. For it is possible for individuals to defy the boycott which one section of the dominant caste may order, but which the other section may tacitly oppose. In this way the Oil-presser, representing a group of men largely economically independent of the village, was able to challenge the 'village decision' of the Comprehensive Committee. Not only did he enlist friends among Farmers and others jealous of

---

[1] Srinivas 1955*a*: 18–19.

[2] Even were these the only cases about which I was told (those decided by the headmen being considered of less interest because they were more informal) it still means that a number of cases were not considered by the Rajput elders.

[3] Cf. Dumont and Pocock 1957: 30.

Rajput primacy, but he may even have had allies among the Rajputs. It is significant that the Rajput head of the Village Committee accused the Rajput headman whom he had ousted from the Committee of siding with the Oil-presser. The headman denied this, but the Committee chairman himself saw breaches in the unity of the Rajput caste group as being connected with the failure of the village boycott.

Ramkheri is going through the transition between a hereditary system of clear-cut village leadership, and an elective pattern of authority in which the hitherto dominant Rajputs will have to compete as individuals with people of other castes, often hierarchically inferior to them. The advance guard of the new leaders is made up of men of the Oil-presser and Farmer castes. We have seen the former to be a caste group which is trying most strongly to change its commensal status, and which is also one of the wealthiest caste groups, supplementing a fairly high standard of landholding with clerical work. Most of the Farmers take little part in village affairs, but a few are of the same type as these Oil-pressers.

If Farmers or any numerically large combination of other castes were to challenge for leadership, the Rajputs would have to enlist new allies. This will continue in the future because Rajputs do not have at present as high a live birth rate as Farmers, with at the same time a higher child mortality rate.[1] The number of votes which they themselves can provide for caste mates is thus a decreasing proportion of the total village voting strength. One way to get allies would be to concede to castes like the Goatherd that they are 'former Rajputs', and at the same time loosen commensal restrictions towards them.[2]

There has even been a covert wooing of the Harijans. The spokesman of these castes has hitherto been a Cotton-carder; but the Rajput leaders now tend to try to supplant him (Harijans do not have enough votes to make up their own party). It is too soon to predict changes in inter-caste relations because of the new democratic basis for leadership. But one may note that the main opposers of the established leaders are village accountants, who by Government order cannot hold office on the Village Committee. Cases of this kind make the observer wonder whether it might not be worthwhile rescinding this order, and so perhaps reducing the criticism of such men and harness their undoubted abilities by allowing them to be on the Village Committee.

[1] Mayer 1955: 1147.
[2] Srinivas (1957: 545) gives an example of this trend towards liberalization for the sake of votes.

Caste and Village Leadership

The village has hitherto been treated as a separate administrative unit. The revenue records applied to each settlement only, and the headman's power did not extend outside the village's boundary. The majority of landlords (sixteen out of the twenty-four in Dewas Senior) had grants of single villages only. Unofficially, too, leadership was confined to the village. The major festivals like Divali and Naumi brought together the village's inhabitants only, and arbitration was usually between men of the same village (an exception being the arbitration of compensation for remarriage). Matters arising between people of different villages tended to be considered by councils within their subcaste if they had the same affiliations, and by the courts if they did not.

The main outside contacts with other authorities, then, were with officials in Dewas, rather than with men of other villages. Usually the headman had the most intimate acquaintance with officials, since these dealt with him more than anyone else. But I have mentioned others who might also have contacts. One man, for instance, was a contract labourer for a landlord; and he came to know many important officials in the town from being sent on errands to them by his master. Because he was 'recognized' by such people, the man gained influence in Ramkheri. For he used these contacts to get favours for friends, and to aid people in trouble.

The start of a system of local government in 1946 heralded major changes in these outside contacts of village leaders. First, the pattern of the ties with Dewas officials changed. The contacts with revenue, judicial and police departments remained important; but a new side of Government now emerged—that concerned with rural development, with setting up Village Committees, with running co-operative banks, with operating agricultural extension schemes. Officials of these departments paid more frequent visits to the village, and they arrived ready and willing to distribute money. Small wonder, then, that contacts with these officials quickly became an important part of any leader's role. Here the chairman of the Village Committee was especially prominent, since the development schemes worked through that body.

The leader's functions *vis-à-vis* the villagers were not very different from those of former leaders. Whether it was through contacts with Palace and the court, or with the development officers, the resulting role of the leader in his village was much the same—it maintained a clientele whose support was forthcoming when he took decisions, for as long as he could smooth their ways in the town.

But the new leader has to be a more versatile person and probably

128

better educated. The old headman had limited jobs; the chairman of the Village Committee needs to learn about improved agricultural methods, about new types of well and latrine, about the workings of co-operative societies, and he should probably have an idea of book-keeping, to name a few necessary accomplishments. On the whole, the older men in Ramkheri are not so highly educated, the Rajputs included; and this may help explain the jealousy among accountants and other younger men who feel themselves superior in this new context.

The leaders' relations with officials have generally become a great deal more impersonal, since officials are now members of the civil service of a large Government, liable to transfer hundreds of miles away, rather than members of a small State service in which they retained contacts with the same public through a lifetime of work in and near Dewas. In the second place, development officials now try to cast themselves in the role of adviser and helper, rather than superior and commander.[1]

A more radical change in the village's external contacts is the institution of committees composed of representatives from several villages. The smallest of these is, in fact, the Village Committee. This is almost always an inter-village body, since the required 1200 population per Committee is rarely filled by a single settlement. I have already said that there were two representatives from Krishna-pura on the Ramkheri Committee. But I have been able to treat the Committee as if it consisted of Ramkheri people only, because the Krishnapura men have played no part in Committee affairs. I only saw them attend one meeting, and they have not started any projects in their village. I did not know Krishnapura well enough to be able to account for this indifference; but it may be that since Ramkheri is so much larger, its members feel that the Committee is 'their' body. This is by no means the case in some other Village Committees, where there may be inter-village relations ranging from close co-operation to open hostility and rivalry for the Committee's funds.

Each Village Committee sends one member to the Justice Committee (*Nyaya Pancayat*), started in 1952 to replace the Village Committee as a body with minor judicial powers. Ramkheri is joined to four other Village Committees at present. Finally, there is a representative on the Central Committee (*Kendra Pancayat*) which supervises the work of the Village Committees, allocates funds for development projects, etc. Until 1956, Ramkheri formed part of a thirteen-Village Committee body, but now the Central Committee comprises no fewer than fifty-two Village Committees, and the power of its chairman (and the money at his disposal) is great.

[1] See Mayer 1956b: 38–9 for further discussion of this change.

Representatives to these two larger Committees meet men from a wide area with whom they might otherwise not have had contacts. For, as I shall show later, ties between villages have hitherto largely run on lines of kinship, and there have been few occasions to meet men of other castes in places where no kin exist. Only the Weavers are represented in all villages and of the more powerful Ramkheri castes Rajputs and Farmers lived in only eight and nine of twenty-four nearby villages respectively, Brahmans in seventeen, and Oil-pressers in four. The large Central Committee enables leaders in this administrative region to meet.

These contacts are intensified by the elections for Central Committee offices, particularly the chairmanship. This, as I have said, is a powerful position, and there are prospects of elevation to the District Committee (*Mandal Pancayat*), comprising men from several Central Committees and senior officials, the board of the Co-operative Bank, and other advisory committees in Dewas. Men who like town life and are not tied to daily chores in the village are most anxious to occupy this post. In 1956 there were two candidates, a Rajput and a Brahman, and for at least two months beforehand they and their supporters were trying to arrange the election of favourably disposed Central Committee members from each village. As the time of the elections drew near, the two candidates thought of little else, and spent most of their time canvassing voters. To some extent their arguments were based on their superior abilities for the post; but a great deal of support was recruited by appeals to common caste links and/or kin ties which the voter had with the candidate or the supporter who was sent to persuade him. Candidates condemned this as a regression to 'casteism' but both practised it.

These elections add an element to inter-village contacts. Even where a man has supported a candidate because he is a kinsman, something new has been added to the content of that kin tie. And in some cases neighbouring villages have been brought into closer contact through their common participation in the Committee. This can mean an increase in co-operation—e.g. two neighbouring villages found they supported the same candidate, and their leaders were soon talking of sharing the expense of bringing a roller to work on their roads. On the other hand, villages may be estranged. One day, for instance, I was talking with close supporters of one candidate when the chairman of the neighbouring Village Committee went past. He gave us a brief greeting but did not stop when I invited him to. I was told that he had been canvassed and found to support the other candidate, and consequently did not want to risk getting into an argument by sitting with us; so he sat fifty yards away, waiting for his bus. The Central and Justice Committees have been running for too short a time for me to give a detailed analysis of the inter-village contacts which result; but it is clear that village leaders now operate in another dimension. And their prestige in their own villages may depend on the power they wield in these larger Committees, or at least the terms on which they stand with the chairmen of these bodies.

The Central Committee is significant for our theme—the relation of caste to village leadership. For the last election of its chairman was apparently fought on the lines of Rajputs and allied castes against the rest; this I say from my acquaintance with the politics of only some half a dozen of the fifty Village Committees, it is true. But as far as I could see, the Brahman candidate was supported by fellow-caste mates, and by Farmers and others. The Rajput had his own caste behind him with few exceptions, and tended also to be supported by powerful allied caste leaders (Gujars, Dakkars). Even if a full analysis would qualify this, the filling of posts indicates that caste was at least an important factor. The Rajput candidate was made chairman; and Rajputs were then appointed to the two other powerful posts—the vice-chairmanship, and the membership of the District Committee.

The election shows that, even though they do not dominate in every village, Rajputs are the most influential caste in the area around Dewas; they are themselves numerically largest in the region, and can call on the support of other allied castes, some of which are powerful too.[1] This dominance was not made politically manifest[2] until these elections forced an open trial of strength. Because villages were so separate, Rajput primacy was rather reflected in the general prestige held by the Rajputs, of which I have talked in Chapters IV and V.

[1] It is notable that the 'higher' allied castes (e.g. not the Potter or Barber) are headmen of most villages in which they reside. Thus, Rajputs were headmen in 7 of 8 villages, Gujars in 2 of 4, Dakkars in 2 of 4 and Ahirs in 3 of 4. By contrast, Farmers were headmen in only 4 of 9 and Brahmans in 2 of 17.

[2] I am only talking of the rural pattern. In the town the Marathas had political dominance, of course. (For a detailed analysis of the concept of the dominant caste in Dewas Senior, see Mayer 1958.)

VII

THE VILLAGE AS A UNIT

T HE description I have given of inter-caste relations has emphasized the separateness of caste groups in Ramkheri. In the
commensal hierarchy only the allied castes break this down
to a great extent; the economic system is less caste-oriented with its
neutral ground of agriculture, but here again the traditional link with
an occupation is still effective in distinguishing many caste groups;
and positions of village leadership are only now beginning to be
filled by other castes than that of the headmen to any extent.

Nevertheless, it would be a mistake to think of the village as a mere
collection of separate caste groups. For many of the people's interests
centre inside the village and provide village-wide participation in
some events (e.g. the major festivals of the year). And differences of
custom and caste composition in other villages add to a feeling of
separateness which quickly turns into village patriotism. Besides these
general ways in which caste divisions are over-ridden, there are two
specific features making for a wider unity. One is the closeness based
on daily contacts in work and/or residence. The second is the link of
ritual kinship, which cuts across caste lines and also spatial separation, to bind people otherwise unrelated. This chapter, then, discusses
first the territorial division of the village into wards, etc., and the
degree to which common ward membership binds people, and then
ritual kin ties.

WARD, SITTING-PLACE AND THRESHING-FLOOR

Ramkheri is a large place, and not every inhabitant is in close touch
with his fellow-villagers. There are several roads leading from the
village to the outside, and men living in one part may rarely see others
who reside at the opposite end of the settlement, and have their fields
in that direction. This is the negative side of settlement patterns; the
positive side is that people in the same division, or ward, of the village
may have informal, everyday contacts which overlay otherwise existing differences of caste, or kinship.

In my account of the history of Ramkheri I mentioned the initial
settlement on the high ground, the splitting of the senior Rajput
headman's family and the founding of a separate hamlet on the

132

northern edge of the higher land. Later, I indicated, the village expanded around this nucleus and the houses of the lower and less powerful people, which were grouped on all sides. Previously, there were half a dozen wards, but now their number varies from the ten or twelve names which everyone gives when asked to name wards (*bakal*), to the fourteen wards recognized in the division of the village for representation to the self-appointed Comprehensive Committee. This latter figure gives an average of eighteen men per ward.

How is a ward defined? It is a division of the village, in part distinguished by differences of terrain (natural features like trees or high ground), in part by village activities which take place there, and in part by differences of caste. This can be seen in the ward names (I give the number of men in each in brackets). Chamarpura (18) and Balaipura—sometimes divided into Malwipura (12) and Gujaratipura (10), according to the Malwi and Gujarati subcastes which live in each—contain but one caste of Tanners and Weavers respectively. Again, Khatipura (21) is a one-caste ward of Farmers, formed of houses opening on the single street in what was formerly the fort area, before its settlement after the famine. These are the only completely caste-based wards—and largely concern the Harijans, as would be expected from their exclusive hierarchical positions. A few other wards are called by caste names, but have people of other castes living there too. Bhilpura (23) contains Naths as well as Bhilalas, Malipura (12) has Rajputs and Farmers as well as Gardeners; even the Patelserai, or Headman Street (25) which contains the 'big house' of the senior Rajputs, also has Farmer, Gosain and Brahman houses therein. These wards are thus called after the main caste there, past or present, but have a sufficiently mixed population to support my characterization of wards as multi-caste divisions.

Other wards are named after shrines. Hanumanpura (10) has the shrine of the Lord of the Village, Galpura (29) is the place of the swing used at the Holi festival, Pirdarga (24) has a Muslim saint's tomb (this ward can also be called Musulmanpura, though it contains Hindus too). Finally there are wards called after physical features. Bazaar (28) centres around a broad street where, it is said, there was once a market; Chauk (22) is another broad street and crossroads; Ghantipura (11) is a ward situated on the high ground forming the centre of the Khera hamlet; and Amlibar (12) commemorates the several large tamarind (*imli*) trees in the ward.

I have marked these wards on a map of the village. They are formally recognized in the Comprehensive Committee, and in the use to which their names are put in conversation; thus, if one asks, 'Where is A?' the answer may be 'I saw him at Galpura.' There are no activities restricted to the members of a ward. But wards are significant

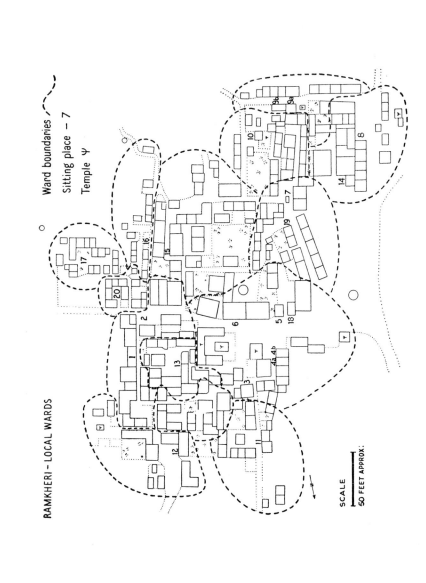

RAMKHERI – LOCAL WARDS

Ward boundaries
Sitting place – 7
Temple Ψ

SCALE
50 FEET APPROX.

in two ways; as nuclei of casual congregation, and as centres of informal co-operation between households at several rites.

There are various spots in Ramkheri where men tend to gather
when they are not working in the fields, or of an evening. These are
called sitting-places (*baithak*). There is nothing institutional about
them—no expected regularity of attendance, no particular activities
there (unless it be to smoke one another's tobacco), and no formal
correspondence of the sitting-place with the populace of the ward in
which it is situated. It is possible that there was a steadier and more
sustained attendance in the days when the hubble-bubble (*hukka*) was
smoked; for this required some time to light and get working, and
represented more of a communal effort. But with the present fashion
of country cigarettes, or the little clay pipe carried in the pocket, a
man can smoke casually with a friend; and he can smoke with him
when and where he finds him, too, rather than at a place where there
is a hubble-bubble.

The sitting-place is the spot where one thinks of looking for a particular person, and the membership, though loose, is predictable
enough to permit this. I have marked twenty sitting-places on the
map of the village wards. This is to some extent an arbitrary number.
For the word *baithak* can be used for the veranda in front of any
house, and covers both less and more frequented places. Nevertheless, I think these spots represent places of fairly permanent neighbourly visiting.

There are three kinds of sitting-place. One centres on the place
where there is a craftsman; his clients will gather there, and passers-by
will stop, too. Thus, there are always men at the blacksmithy and the
carpenters' workshops; they may be waiting for repairs to their tools,
or simply watching and sometimes helping the craftsman (blowing
the bellows or holding pieces of wood). Again, the tailors and the two
storekeepers almost always have company at any part of the day, and
so do the barbers when they work on the verandas of their houses.
These account for the sitting-places 1, 3, 4a, 4b, 5, 7, 8, 9a, 9b.[1] The
other craftsmen either have work of a less steady kind (e.g. the potter)
or are too low to support a sitting-place (e.g. the tanner).

Other sitting-places are set in the middle of wards. Here there are
few people found during the day, but after work people gather there
because the sitting-place is nearest to their houses. Some of
these places are uni-caste (e.g. the Harijan wards and the Farmer
ward); others have several castes in the surrounding houses. These

[1] 4a and 4b are sitting-places of two tailors, and 9a and 9b of two carpenters
who do not speak to each other after household disputes and divisions. Clients
tend to sit in one place only, for it would be embarrassing to cross from one to
the other.

sitting-places are numbered 17, 16, 20, 19, 12, 14, 13, 10 and 15. Last, places are popular because they are 'public' places, having unrivalled opportunities for seeing the comings and goings of the village. Such sitting-places are 18, 6, 11 and 2; they include the Village Committee house, the school house, and places at the main entrances to the village.

The map shows that there is a sitting-place in all wards but one. Any individual has the choice between going to a sitting-place where he will mostly meet people of his ward, or to a place where a more representative group is gathered. The choice depends on many variables—present relations with other people, pressure of work, time of day, etc. Wards, though recognized as centres for casual intercourse, do not form any kind of boundaries in the village. But even where most of the casual contact takes place within the ward, this seldom means a restriction within a caste; for most wards have several castes in them.

Women have less chance to meet people from other parts of the village than have men. True, the village well provides a meeting-place for all women of non-Harijan castes, and the opportunity for gossip there is well taken. But there is a limit to the time that busy women can stand and talk while they draw their water, and afterwards they must return home, where the occasions for talking to people outside their own household are limited to meetings with other women of the street, and so to fellow-ward members. Nevertheless, though feminine contacts are more ward-centred than masculine ones, one cannot say that this makes the wards much more solitary. In many cases there is a feeling of common neighbourhood, as contrasted with 'those people over there'. But precisely because the contacts are so much closer, there is more chance of petty quarrels, over straying animals or fighting children; and so there may be sharper antagonisms within the ward than between women of different wards.

In the absence of particular hostility, common ward membership may run beyond just talking together and being friendly into positive co-operation. This is mainly in ritual matters. I have already mentioned how in a few cases near neighbours came and sat with bereaved families at Holi. Again, one man had his head shaved in the purificatory rites after the death of a neighbour; this is an act reserved for agnates but I was told by the man that he felt like a neighbour-brother, and people of the descent group did not dissent. People from the same ward, though of different caste, may more easily attend small rites than fellow-caste mates at some distance in the village. A case is the installation and daily procession of a bride or bridegroom before the wedding. Here, women are needed to sing songs in the background of ritual and procession. At the installation of a

Rajput bride living in Amlibar, for example, there were present Rajput women living close by but of a different clan, and Brahman women of Ghantipura, but very few women from the bride's own clan who were living in Patelserai, some distance away.

This co-operation between ward mates extends less to economic affairs mainly because wards are, roughly, distinguishable between those of the 'haves' and those of the 'have nots'. Landowners and their labourers tend to live in different wards; e.g. only three of the twenty contract labourers in 1954–5 lived in the same wards as their masters, a further five living in adjacent wards. Again, while small loans may more easily be made between ward mates, any considerable borrowing does not necessarily take place between neighbours. But an important link through economic activity comes not by being neighbours in the village, but through sharing the same threshing-place (*khala*).

As I have said, there are two harvests in Ramkheri, that of sorghum at the beginning of the cold weather, and that of wheat at the start of the ensuing hot season. Both crops are cut by hand, and the ears are dried and then threshed by cattle on floors made of beaten earth covered with a binding mixture of earth and cowdung. The winnowing, too, is done at the threshing-floor, which is thus the scene of considerable activity for several weeks during the first harvest and a lesser time during the wheat harvest since the crop is smaller. Both men and women take part in the work. It is the women's job to smear dung on the earth which the men have packed by driving bullocks over it. The men thresh the grain, whilst the women guard the crop from marauding cattle or goats and rake clear the threshed ears. Winnowing is done by both sexes. The time at the threshing-floor is pleasant for the entire family—it is a sort of camp—for the women, of course, bring their children with them.

In the days when the village was under the jurisdiction of a single landlord, all farmers used the same place to make their threshing-floors. This was ordered, it is said, so that the landlord's agents could keep watch on the harvest and the headmen could take grain on the spot for any arrears of rent. When the village was put directly under Government control some farmers moved into other parts. But thefts of grain, and the depredations of wild pigs, at that time very numerous, drove them back to two main places, one on each side of the village. These continue to hold many floors; they are easy to reach from the village, and have the advantages which come from co-operative efforts—mutual aid in guarding the drying crops, sometimes loans of livestock to help the threshing, and companionship. In the last seven or eight years, however, increasing numbers of farmers have again been setting up their floors in or near their own fields. The recent fostering by the Government of crops which need irrigation during the time the harvest is on the threshing-floor means that men are more tied to their wells, and find it easier to thresh there. Again, the danger from pigs no longer exists, now that these animals are not protected for sport. The position is now that there are twenty floors at the traditional places, and seventy-one elsewhere.

There is an average of $3\frac{1}{2}$ floors in each of the twenty-six places. Six places contain a single floor; three have several floors belonging to members of a single caste (usually of the same extended family) and seventeen are multi-caste places. Of these, four contain two castes, eleven have three castes, and there are two places having four and five castes. All but two Rajput landowners still make their floors in the two traditional places near the village. The land belongs to the Rajput headmen who are more willing to have their caste mates than to give the use of their land to others. This is part of that generally lessened feeling of public responsibility felt by the headmen as their powers are reduced, and adds a reason for the dispersal of floors.

The co-operation in a shared threshing-place is not vital for the harvest; its importance lies rather in the informal ties which grow up there. Farmers more or less live at their floors whilst the grain is on them. Although they would not have started to share the one place had they already not been friendly, this nevertheless deepens the attachment, and it is on precisely such bases that their children become ritual kin. A common threshing-place, then, provides another possibility for a tie bridging caste differences. This is not so much based on being neighbours in the village—though this can also lead to sharing a threshing-place—as on having fields in the same vicinity, if not contiguous.

Having adjacent landholdings can, of course, produce just the opposite effect. Disputes over boundaries, rights of way, etc., occur, and sometimes have far-reaching repercussions. There are many petty frictions which never get to the courts, and others result in litigation. Again, some remain issues between the disputants only, and others bring in the respective kin-groups and may even divide other villagers.[1] Especially productive of such quarrels is the periodic re-survey of all holdings to reassess the land tax due on each. For there are opportunities of engineering alterations in the boundaries on the village accountant's map. The last settlement in Ramkheri was in 1942, but disputes stemming from that event still smoulder in the

[1] E.g. an aspect of the coolness between the Village Committee chairman and the major headman (see p. 127) was a dispute over a right of way between the headman and a neighbouring landowner of different caste whose case the Village Committee chairman supported.

village; sometimes they provide underlying causes for people's alignments over quite different issues.

RITUAL KINSHIP

There are several ways in which people of different castes can be linked as kin through ritual acts. The most important occurs on the full-moon day of Asarh (June–July) month, when groups of young people 'hear Ram's name' together from a teacher (*guru*), and are then considered to be ritual brothers and sisters (*gurubhai* and *gurubahin*). The rite is in two parts. On the night before, the candidates come to the teacher who is a Bairagi;[1] each makes the *tilak* mark on the teacher's forehead, and he does the same in return, and blows three times in the candidate's ear. The next morning there is again a procession to the teacher. This time he whispers the verse in the person's left ear,[2] and is then given a coconut which the candidate has been holding, and a small cash present. The rite ends with the teacher pouring water into the cupped hands of the candidate, which is then emptied on to the ground.[3]

A person can only hear Ram's name once; and his ritual kin are thus confined to the group with whom he was instructed. This averages around five or six people (in theory it should contain an odd number, but in practice if there is an even number the teacher himself is included to make it odd). The duties of these ritual brothers and sisters should, if anything, be taken even more seriously than the corresponding real kin ties. For, it is said, 'That is the sister of sin (*pap*), this is the sister of religious duty (*dharam*).' The main manifestations of the link are those exchanges of presents which are also prescribed for real kin. Thus, the brother should bring gifts of clothes for his sister and her new-born baby; and he should take gifts at the marriage of his sister's children. In return, the sister should make presents (though of less value) at the major ceremonies of the brother's children. Again, at the festival of Gangaur in the month of Bhadon (August–September), women who have taken a vow to do so are

---

[1] The Bairagi is a Vaishnavite. The rites were twice performed during my stay—once at the shrine of Narsingh (an incarnation of Vishnu) and once in front of the Sakti Mata shrine. The latter is a Sivaite place, managed by Gosains, but I was told that this did not prevent a Vaishnava rite from being held there.

[2] The words are said to be '*Om namo Bhagavate Vasudevaya*'. This is a common invocation of God, and can be said or printed without restriction. When, however, it is whispered by the teacher, or is uttered in any context where its latent power is to be used, it becomes a verse which must be used in secrecy.

[3] On another occasion this water rite was omitted; and instead each brother and sister exchanged *tilak* marks. Such variations in rites with different teachers may be common. But the verse is said always to be the same.

ducked in a stream by their real or ritual brothers. Since this takes place in their village of marriage, where they have their ritual kin, these are more prominent than real kin. After the ceremony the ritual brother and his ritual sister's husband give each other turbans, a common sign of friendship between affines.

In practice, few follow completely the ideal pattern of exchange; but all ritual brothers give presents to at least the eldest of their ritual sister's children, though they may not have the resources or the inclination to do so for the others. The connection is in any case kept alive by the tying of a thread of protection by the sister on the wrist of the brother at the festival of Raksha Bandhan each year. I must stress that the ritual kin tie is quite distinct from the real kin tie for the membership of a descent group; thus, ritual kin are not allowed to worship the agnatic descent group's tutelary deity, nor do they shave their heads when a ritual brother dies, as they would were he a real sibling.

Almost all people in Ramkheri had ritual kin. Only the village priest and the Gosains had not 'heard Ram's name'. The first said that Brahmans would demean themselves by being instructed by a Bairagi, and the Gosains said that, as attendants of Siva shrines, they should not have a Vaishnavite as their spiritual master. The rite has been called an initiation without which 'no man can go to God'.[1] While this belief may be held by some in Ramkheri, it was not expressed to me and the presence of people who have not heard Ram's name indicates a variation from Fuchs' material (which deals with Weavers' beliefs only).

A major significance of this ritual tie is the way in which it gives support to a woman in her conjugal village. For women hardly ever hear Ram's name with men of their parental village,[2] which they leave in virilocal marriage; and ritual ties between people of more than one village are exceptional. By this tie the woman makes allegiances after her marriage in a village where she is at first alone, and thus feels she has supporters and friends there.[3] It is perhaps for this reason that the main emphasis of the rite is on the brother-sister relationship, rather than the equally valid relation between the two ritual brothers. Further, informants always explained the rite by say-

[1] Fuchs 1950: 320. I am told that there is no classical basis for this.

[2] In the only two cases I recorded, one girl had been abandoned by her husband and had returned home with the intention of staying there. Her action was nevertheless badly regarded, and the feeling was that she should have stayed without ritual kin rather than contracting these ties in her parental village. The other case concerned a girl who was a transvestite. Since her role was that of a boy, public opinion allowed her this variation in the location of the ritual kin.

[3] She will, of course, have affines there, but these are not regarded in the same way as people who are as siblings to her.

140

ing that a woman coming to her conjugal village (*sasural*) would wish to make brothers; they never saw it as a means for the man to make a ritual sister in place of the real sister who had left the village after marriage.

This explanation would also account for the fact that the main organizers of the rite are women. For it is they who agree to have their sons or their sons' wives hear Ram's name together, and the entire congregation at a rite I saw in 1956 was feminine. Men agree that everyone should hear Ram's name, and should meet at least the minimal obligations that flow from this, but they admit the selection and organization to be women's work. A headman, for example, held that Ram's name should only be heard by boys old enough to know what it all meant; but he allowed his three-year-old son to go through the rite because his wife wanted it, and because he did not wish to upset friends whose children she had already suggested might become the boy's ritual kin.

The choice of partners goes on for several weeks before the ceremony. Women know who are the brides newly arrived in the village, and the young boys who have not already heard Ram's name. Suggestions are made—at the well, when travelling together to market, when on the road to nearby fields, or when sitting at doorsteps in the same street. All are insistent that friendship and the possession of a 'good name' are the only criteria for selection. And, indeed, the data give many instances where no financial or political gain could have been expected from the tie.[1] (One might speculate that, were they expected, the men would take more interest in the selection of partners.)

In how far does residence of the same ward, and common caste, determine the selection of ritual kin? One must, of course, first separate the Harijan castes, for each hears Ram's name from its own teacher and has no ritual ties with other castes. Next, the Cotton-carder Muslims have a separate, though similar, ceremony, which results in ritual kin called *pirbhai* and *pirbahin*. My data for the rest includes 20 cases concerning 127 people, whose residence at the time of the rite is known. Of these, 77 had ritual kin in their own ward as well as outside it, and 50 had all their ritual kin in other wards. To calculate statistically the influence which neighbourhood has on ritual kinship would require other data—one would need to know the eligible population of each ward at the time of every choice. But I can say that each person has at present an average of one ritual kin in his or her ward, and a further 4·7 ritual kin in other wards. This may seem a low proportion of ritual kin in the same ward. But if we

[1] The secondary nature of mutual aid and economic benefit is reported from other areas, too (Okada 1957: 214).

recall that the average ward contains only about one-tenth of the available people, we can very tentatively draw a positive correlation between ward membership and ritual kin ties. This, however, does not contradict the fact that most ritual links stretch outside the ward and are significant in bringing villagers, rather than ward members, into closer contact.

The degree to which ritual kin ties are made with caste mates varies with the size of the village caste group; there is no great feeling that ties should be made inside or outside the caste. Farmers, as the largest caste group, appear to be more self-contained than others. Thus, of the 148 people hearing Ram's name together where Farmers figured, 67 were Farmers and 81 came from 17 other caste groups. Of the 156 people where Rajputs were included, only 50 were Rajputs and 106 were from 21 other castes. The linkages of smaller caste groups, such as the Gosain or the Potter, would be almost entirely with people of other castes.

To some extent, also, the inclinations of the caste group direct the pattern of selection outside the caste. The table below shows the different emphasis of the Barber and Oil-presser caste groups in their ritual relations with the two main caste groups of Rajputs and Farmers.

TABLE 1

Caste	Ritual Kin for:	
	Oil-presser	Barber
Farmer	18	15
Rajput	9	14
Oil-presser	10	*
Barber	*	14
Others	28	42
	—	—
Total	65	85
	—	—

* This caste is included in the category 'others'.

We see that Oil-pressers have more Farmers than Rajputs as ritual kin; the Barber, on the other hand, has an equal number from each of these castes, though the Farmer caste group is nearly twice as big. Remembering that the Oil-pressers have had friction with the ruling Rajput group, and that the Barbers are part of the allied caste nexus, this is not surprising. So ritual kin ties to some extent correspond to the broad relations of castes within the village—as is natural, since they are founded on friendship.

There are other occasions when ritual ties are contracted. The festival of Raksha Bandhan is primarily centred around the tie between real brother and sister. It falls on the full-moon day of Sravan month, during the rainy season, and is the time for women to return to their parental villages. As I have said, these tie a thread of divine protection round the wrists of their brothers, and are given presents in return. It is not necessary to be a real kinswoman, nor even to have heard Ram's name together to tie the thread (*rakhi*), and anyone else who ties it is also regarded as a ritual sister. But this form of ritual tie is weak, and is usually only recognized at Raksha Bandhan; there are no other obligations of gift exchange such as bind the ritual kin who have heard Ram's name together. Only for the Harijan castes does this tie assume added importance. For Harijans cannot hear Ram's name with upper castes, and the tying of the *rakhi* is the only means they have of making a ritual connection with a non-Harijan. Several Weavers had done this, and called their ritual siblings *gurubhai*, though they were actually only *rakhi bhai*. They treated the relation like a Ram's name relation, in fact, and I saw a Weaver make a present, through an upper caste intermediary, of clothes to his upper caste *rakhi* sister at her marriage. I knew of no such ties between Tanner and Sweepers and upper castes, but I do not see why these are not possible.

Another ritual tie is the relation between a woman and her ritual father (*dharam ka bap*). This is contracted on the last day of the wedding. The groom's party (*barat*) gather, sometimes in the bride's house and sometimes in a place set aside for them. An elder member of the groom's party sits cross-legged on a carpet, and the bride sits between his legs; one or more men of the groom's party then offer a coconut, a piece of money, and small pieces of sugar to the bride. The man in whose lap she has sat is her ritual father. His main subsequent duty is the presentation of clothes at the weddings of his ritual daughter's children, and he complies as far as his means permit. He is, in addition, to some extent the protector of his ritual daughter. In general, as I have said, women marry into villages where they have no close relatives; and people say it is a good thing to have some man who will keep an eye on the way her affines treat her. In cases of domestic discord, the ritual father may even attempt to arbitrate and smooth things down, it is said. I must admit that I found no case where the ritual father had played a major part in household affairs, but this is at least thought to be a basis for the ritual tie. Nowadays, it is said, the force of the relation is less strong, since women are more powerful in the home, and do not need such protection. Some men treat it as a joking matter (though I do not know to what extent this also is a recent development). Thus, a man called out to his wife's ritual father's wife 'Hallo, mother-in-law'.

And when she went by silently, though smiling, his companion shouted after her, 'She won't talk, for if she did she would have to give him a coconut and a rupee.' (These are gifts normally made to a son-in-law when he visits his affines.) The real mother-in-law would never be joked at thus; in fact, the speaker said he had never been to his conjugal village because he felt shy in front of his wife's relatives. But this ritual tie provoked no such inhibition in him.

As with other ritual kin, the ritual father can come from inside or outside the caste (save for the self-contained Harijan castes). My data indicate a fair spread of inter-caste contacts by this means, though the castes of division 4 tend more than the upper castes to have ritual fathers from inside the caste. This is in part a function of their wealth. For a groom of the upper castes may take a large wedding party which includes men of many castes, one of whom will be persuaded to act as ritual father; but people of lower castes tend to take smaller parties, and confine these to their own kinsfolk.

Ritual kin ties provide a means by which differences of caste or ward membership can be bridged. In theory, ritual kin ties should be as binding as real ties. In fact, the wide extension of ritual links and the lack of corporate activities on the part of ritual kin seems to belie this expectation. Most ritual kin behave towards each other as good friends and nothing more. One can, it is true, sometimes connect support or hostility in disputes, or creditor-debtor relations, or organization of match-making with the ritual connection between the parties. (It may be more than a coincidence that the Oil-presser who was boycotted by the Rajput-dominated Comprehensive Committee headed a household with no Rajputs among its ritual kin.) But ritual kinship seems to provide a justification for action, rather than a compelling reason for activity. A man may support his ritual kin in their disputes; but at the same time he will often be going against someone with whom he can also trace a ritual tie. For each of the members of his household has four or five ritual links, and this makes him tied to very many other households in the village. He supports one man rather than the other because of an economic or other reason, but talks of it in ritual terms. The wide ramifications of ritual kinship make alignments on it as sole basis almost impossible.

VILLAGE KINSHIP

Kin terms of address are used by fellow-villagers unrelated by either real or ritual ties. This is in part an extension which enters into all social intercourse. A man meeting a total stranger in another village or a town will, if he is a contemporary, call him brother (*bhai*) or elder brother (*dada*), and if he is of the succeeding generation, call him father's elder brother (*ba*). It would be considered a slight to call him by his name, even if he knew it. A story is told, for instance, of a shopkeeper who built up his trade from small beginnings. His son took over on his death; but he was haughty, and instead of calling people by their kin terms, used their proper names. Within a few years his customers had left him, and he was penniless.

This wide use of kin terms is little more than a form of courtesy. It is different from the attitude of fellow-villagers towards each other, for these call each other 'village kinsmen' (*ganv ka rista*) whether or not there is any mutual obligation between them. This village kinship is not uniformly felt, of course. At the one extreme, the Harijans (especially the Tanners) have little contact with the rest of the village, and the use of kin terms towards them is hardly stronger than their application to people of other villages. On the other hand, close relatives of one's ritual kin are called by the appropriate term (e.g. the cousin of a ritual father would be called father's brother), and are felt to be part of a local kin-group.

Strangers occasionally settle in the village without already having kin there. At first, such a newcomer will call everybody of the same age and older *bhai* and *ba* respectively, without distinguishing the relationships between them. But later he will become friendly with someone (often of his own ward), and will suggest that he and his friend's wife become ritual brother and sister (through tying the *rakhi* only, since they will both have heard Ram's name already). Henceforth he will have a whole range of village kin (sister's children, sister's husband's kin, etc.), and will thereby enter the village kinship universe. It is significant that there is no move to make such men brothers. As I have indicated, the emphasis is all on the brother-sister tie. It is as if the brother tie, as a main feature of patrilineal kinship, were considered to be too exclusive to be thus contracted, in contrast to the brother-sister tie which is primarily one of affectionate co-operation rather than duty.

Another type of integration into village kinship is provided by the man who comes to live in his wife's village. He will be known as 'A's sister's husband (*jiyaji*)'; he, in turn, will call all older men father-in-law (*baji*) and men of his own age wife's brother (*salaji*). His children will be known as 'sister's sons of the village' (*ganv bhanej*). They will call older people mother's brother (*mama*), though allowing also for ritual kinship relations. The *ganv bhanej* considers men of his own age as cousins, and calls them *bhai* and *dada*. Hence, his own children will call men of ascending generations *ba*, and of their own generation *bhai* and *dada*, exactly as do the people who have lived in the village for generations. Thus, in two generations after the immigrant arrives, there are no traces to show the outside origin of his descendants, and they are absorbed into the system of village kin terms given to those of long-standing residence.[1]

The account shows a feeling that village membership should be expressed in kin terms. I do not, however, think that this means that it is more than the application of a much wider principle—that *all* people should be addressed by kin terms, if complimentary names for the appropriate caste are not used.[2] Whilst the feeling of being members of a specific village is strong, there is only preferred rather than prescribed village exogamy as a rule of behaviour on which an idea of 'village kinship' could be based.

One can divide kin ties into three kinds. The first and strongest consists of real ties and those ritual ties derived from the *guru* and the ritual fatherhood at a wedding. Here, there are definite obligations with a minimal amount to be fulfilled on pain of general public disapproval. Next come minor ritual kin ties (*rakhi*) and strong friendships which have become expressed in a kinship idiom; the latter are not ritual ties, but are a stronger form of village kin tie. For the people concerned are in definite kin roles (e.g. they may give money at weddings, as brothers do, rather than give clothes, which is the duty of the mother's brother). Last, there are the village kin ties, brought about by mere co-residence, and involving obligations incumbent on every village member equally (e.g. all women, Muslims as well as Hindus, should come and weep at the house of a newly widowed woman between the day of her husband's death and the subsequent purificatory rites). Ward membership plays no definite part in all this. Friendships, and later ritual ties, may be formed through being in the same ward; but they may equally be made by people with nearby fields, or by those who patronize the same shop or other sitting-place.

THE VILLAGE AS A UNIT

This account has shown how it is that a village containing twenty-seven different caste groups, each with its barrier of endogamy and often occupational and commensal restrictions, can nevertheless exist to some extent as a social unit. Common residence and a ritual kinship which overlays most caste barriers join with the administrative,

[1] This is only absorption into the village kinship system, not into any descent group, of course. The newcomer cannot become assimilated to any clan group in the village.

[2] Thus, it is equally in order to call a Rajput 'Thakur (lord)', a Farmer 'Chaudhuri (leader)', a Sweeper 'Jamadar (captain)', etc., as to call them by a kin term.

economic and commensal separation of the village from other settlements as the main factors.

The village is on the one hand a unit like any nuclear settlement
which is by definition spatially separate from other units, and on the
other an official unit based on a Government policy which makes use
of this spatial separation for the enforcement of law and order, tax
collection, etc. Co-residence, of course, breeds a kind of local
patriotism and a feeling of identity with neighbours, and this is aided
by ritual kinship. It produces a reluctance to move from the known
to the relatively unknown, and makes for a fairly stable and 'solid'
village population. This reluctance is obviously supported by any
economic stake in the village, e.g. land holding. In time, the accretion
of the reputations of many village leaders, and of a multitude of
incidents within the village, gives it a collective reputation. Thus, one
village is known in the region as hard-working, another as hot-
tempered, and so forth. People accept the fact that their own village
is seen in this way. And purely structural features are thereby
augmented in defining the village as a social unit.

PART III

The Constitution of the Caste

VIII

INTERNAL STRUCTURE OF THE CASTE

THIS book has so far focussed on the relations between people of different castes. In particular, they have been relations within a single village, and this is because most of the contacts people have with other villages are with members of their own caste or, more particularly, their own subcaste.

It is now time to turn to these contacts; in general terms, to analyse the internal nature of the caste. The account shifts from the caste to the other levels mentioned in Chapter I—the subcaste and the kindred, as well as to the clan, lineage and household. In this chapter, I am concerned with these divisions of the caste, the way they are defined, and their inter-relations. Later, I examine the rights and obligations held by their members, and the mechanisms by which these are enforced.

The enquiry has two main problems as its themes. One is to see in how far the effective groups within the caste cover a wider area than the single village, and just how this area is defined. This concerns the second half of the distinction made in Chapter I—between largely village-centred inter-caste relations, and mainly regional intra-caste relations.

The second problem is to find out in how far the effective local group within a caste is a kin-group, and what categories of kin are most important in its operation. This information is needed before we can understand the nature of the subcaste.

These problems fit into my wider argument that there are two levels of definition for both the caste and subcaste. The first is in terms of their 'total' population, and concerns the formal definition considered in most of the literature on caste. The second, on the other hand, is the level of the effective caste group and subcaste group; and here we step down to purely local relationships. I have already suggested that the effective caste group is the caste population of a single village, and I will now try to show that the effective subcaste group comprises the people of a region composed of several score settlements. These people are at the same time kin, and there is thus an important way in which the local subcaste group can be defined as a kin-group.

151

THE SUBCASTE

The largest division within the caste is the subcaste. It is called this because, whilst it is clearly only part of a larger unit, it has enough properties common to the caste to be a caste-like unit. Its place subordinate to the caste is shown in the way its name qualifies the caste name. Thus the Weaver (Balai) caste is divided into subcastes called Malwi Balai, Gujarati Balai, etc. All are Weavers, but all are also distinct within the caste. The similarity of the nature of caste and subcaste, on the other hand, is shown by the substitution of terms to denote them. *Jat*, the general word for species, is the most commonly used term for 'caste'. But the word *biradari* can also be used, and both can equally easily refer to the subcaste. On one occasion I asked a Gujarati Weaver, 'Are Gujaratis living in X- village?' He answered, 'No, it is Rattan's *jat* [naming a Malwi Weaver, and so using *jat* to refer to the subcaste]; my *biradari* lives only in Y-village [this time using *biradari* for subcaste].' Again, if you ask a man 'what is your *biradari*' or 'what is your *jat*' he will answer according to the context. If he has never met you, he will give the caste name; but if he thinks you already know his caste, he will tell the subcaste. In everyday conversation, *jat* tends to denote a larger population than *biradari*. If one says, for example, 'The Farmers are a hard-working caste' one would use the word *jat*, though to say *biradari* would also make the meaning clear. Conversely, to talk of the *biradari* gives an indication of a more local group. This is doubtless why the Weaver used *biradari* for his own subcaste group, which he saw in its local context, but when talking of his friend Rattan's subcaste in a more general way used the word *jat*. Again, a man was describing a breach of commensal rules. 'The *biradari* was greatly offended in the old days,' he said, meaning the local group which had the power to punish such wrongdoing. There is not a complete distinction between the use of *jat* for the entire subcaste and that of *biradari* for the locally effective group, such as is made by Blunt;[1] for the headman of the local group is called a *jat patel*, rather than a *biradari patel*, and the local subcaste council in which he acts is the *jat*, rather than the *biradari pancayat*. I suggest, however, that the use of the words *jat* and *biradari*, more than indicating differences in scale, shows the caste-like nature of the subcaste and thus renders them interchangeable.

The subcastes in Ramkheri, with their populations, are given in a table which shows that in only two cases is there more than one

---

[1] Blunt 1946: 51. His use of the word *bhaibandh* as a synonym for *biradari* is contrary to Malwi usage, as will appear later.

subcaste of the same caste in the village, a fact whose significance will be discussed later.

TABLE 1

Caste	Subcaste	Population
Goatherd	*Malwi*	10
Barber	*Gujarati*	14
Mina	*Ujle*	8
Gardener	*Gujarati*	13
Potter	*Malwi*	9
Weaver	*Malwi*	57
	Gujarati	28
Drummer	*Nababansi*	8
Sweeper	*Saticuri*	8
Carpenter	*Malwi*	25
Tanner	*Purviya*	69
Oil-presser	*Malwi (Rathor)*	29
Dairyman	*Goalbans*	26
Brahman	*Kanauji*	11
	Sanodiya	13
	Srigaur	4
Blacksmith	*Gujarati*	8
Tailor	*Gujarati*	9
Tobacco-curer	*Maru (Marwari)*	14
Nath	*Rajguri*	14
Balai Babaji	*Ramanandi*	9
Rajput	'Khas'	118
Farmer	'Khas'	181
Bhilala	'Khas'	64
Gosain	'Sansari'	45
Bairagi	'Sansari'	5
		Total 799

Most subcastes are one of many similar divisions in the caste, whether with fission, or a different regional or ethnic origin as their base. It would be impossible to make a survey of all the subcastes existing in most of the Ramkheri castes. Some castes, like the Brahman,[1] Tanner and Barber range over the whole of India (though under different names), and only a few like the Farmer have any sort of local concentration within a hundred-mile radius. In most castes, then, there are many subcastes. Even within Malwa, the scene of constant migration, where there are people from all parts of north

[1] There is good reason for regarding the Brahman as a section (*varn*) composed of several castes (Hutton 1946: 58). I do not have detailed data on Brahman organization in Malwa, and thus follow the customary terminology.

India, Gujarat and Maharashtra, it is possible that many subcastes exist which are not to be met within the neighbourhood of Ramkheri. Again, there may be variations of behaviour between the same sub-castes in different parts of the province. Just as I have noted that in Ramkheri Rajputs and Farmers do not eat together, but that in other villages they may do so, so relations between subcastes may differ. My data on the subcaste, then, are confined to my own observations in Ramkheri, and the information provided by the people there about other subcastes in the area.

The average informant in Ramkheri knew of between three or four other subcastes in his caste and supposed that there were more elsewhere. A few exceptions exist, one being the sectarian castes, of course. Here there are only two divisions—the celibates, and the *sansaris* who have taken up a family life. The former is hardly a subcaste since it depends for recruitment on outsiders; the latter is exactly the same in structure and operation as other subcastes. Again, the Bhilalas stem from alliances of Rajputs with Bhil (tribal) women. Since these unions were informal, the issue were not recognized as Rajputs. Neither were they accepted as Bhils, however, and the Bhilalas nowadays disclaim any connection with them, though others may call them a subcaste of the Bhil tribe. I think it best to take the Bhilalas as a unitary caste, rather than as a Bhil subcaste; for they have no tribal distinctions, and act exactly as other castes.

Besides these, the Rajputs and Farmers are castes with a very limited number of subcastes.[1] The former are mainly divided between people who call themselves 'real' (*khas*) Rajputs, and those whom they call 'eastern' Rajputs. The latter are presumably immigrants from Bundelkhand and other areas to the northeast, and are in a minority in the country around Dewas. They do not eat or marry with the local Rajputs, though this distinction is now starting to break down. The local men regard the easterner as being somewhat lower. Partly this is because the latter are fewer, and as immigrants are less well connected (however remotely) with powerful landlords (*thakur*); and partly it is because of the Rajput tradition that the better Rajputs live in the west, a fact which is significant in the later analysis of marriage patterns.

In addition, a group of Rajputs live in some twelve villages of the region. These are called Pancholi Rajputs, are endogamous and commensally quite separate from all others. They are said to have been put out of the caste, but the date on which this was done, and the crime over which such drastic action was taken, are both in-definite. The caste genealogist is said to know the details, but such

[1] Their subcaste structure appears similar to what Blunt calls 'tribal' as opposed to 'functional' (Blunt 1931: 5).

154

information is jealously guarded. It could only be divulged at a general caste council, called to decide whether to readmit the Pancholis. Such a possibility was in the air at the time of my stay, and this division may, in fact, be a more temporary one than those marking other subcaste separations.

The Farmers are practically a unitary caste, and have no regional subcastes comparable to the eastern Rajputs. The only group which approaches being a subcaste is the Rajgeria Farmer population, inhabiting several villages to the northeast of Ramkheri. These people are said to stem from the children of Rajputs and their Farmer servant girls, and for this reason are separate, ideally having no intermarriage with other Farmers.[1] Unofficially, however, there appear to be some matches between poor Farmers who cannot find mates among the main body of the caste, and the Rajgerias. Indeed, one would suspect some sort of contact of this sort; for these 'out-caste subcastes' are so small that it is hard for them to find marriage partners within the group. Pancholi Rajputs, for example, were said to allow cross-cousin marriage in their efforts to contract marriages though this is generally regarded as a forbidden match. But there must be pressure to marry in normal ways into the majority subcaste, whose poor families will no doubt do so if they are given presents by the minority group.

Subcastes have the same properties whether many or few exist in the caste. I have said that these properties are castelike—so one would expect endogamy and restricted commensality between sub-castes. The Table 2 shows to what extent this is the case in most of the Ramkheri subcastes.

It shows that fifteen out of the nineteen subcastes are quite endogamous, and either have no commensal relations with other subcastes, or are able to eat with some of them.[2] The term 'limited' refers not necessarily to the commensal relations themselves, but to the number of subcastes with which they were allowed. In no case did anyone say that they could eat with *all* other subcastes.

Four subcastes, besides having commensal relations with other

[1] For a similar kind of subcaste, see Dumont 1957a: 149. The connection of the Bhilala and Rajgeria subcastes with the mother's rather than the progenitor's subcaste goes against the data I obtained from contemporary unions (see p. 25). One cannot explain this without knowing more about the origins of these sub-castes. The women may have had only temporary unions, perhaps before marriage, their children forming a category of 'second class member' which could crystallize into a separate subcaste.

[2] In some cases subcastes not eating together would also not smoke together, in other instances the latter was allowed. I was rarely able to test these statements by observation, since people of different subcastes seldom had occasion to eat together. My data about the remaining subcastes listed in Table 1 conflicts, and I do not think it safe to tabulate it.

TABLE 2

Subcaste	Endogamy of Ramkheri Subcaste	Commensality with other Subcastes
Malwi Goatherd	Complete	Limited
Gujarati Barber	,,	,,
Ujle Mina	,,	,,
Malwi Potter	,,	,,
Malwi Weaver	,,	,,
Gujarati Weaver	,,	,,
Purviya Tanner	,,	,,
Gujarati Gardener	,,	None
Nababansi Drummer	,,	,,
Satichuri Sweeper	,,	,,
Farmer	,,	,,
Rajguri Nath	,,	,,
Goalbans Dairyman	,,	,,
Gujarati Blacksmith	,,	,,
Rajput	,,	,,
Malwi Carpenter	Limited	Limited
Malwi Oil-presser	,,	,,
Gujarati Tailor	,,	,,
Sanodya Brahman	,,	,,

subcastes, also had limited marriage relations with them. Some were hypergamous (e.g. the Gujarati Tailor said that he could take wives from the Mewara Tailors, but not give girls) but in some cases there was reciprocal marriage—e.g. between Malwi and Mewara Carpenters, and Malwi and Mewara Oil-pressers. This, of course, did not preclude the existence of other subcastes with which there was no such intermarriage.

In only one case was I told of subcastes classified on the basis of occupation. This involved the village Tanners, who tan the hides as well as manufacture slippers, etc., and the town Tanners, who only work the finished leather and are known as Mochis. Subcaste differentiation by occupation is, of course, well known,[1] but does not seem to be common around Ramkheri, though I understand a distinction exists in another part of Malwa between oil-pressing Oil-pressers and those who merely deal in the finished product.[2]

Distinctions in eating, in occupation and endogamy—these certainly indicate that the subcastes are like smaller castes. There is also an attempt by some people to rank the subcastes of their castes, using these criteria. This is less successful, at least from the objective

[1] E.g. Hutton 1946: 45.
[2] Written communication from Sri K. S. Mathur.

viewpoint, than caste ranking; for there is much less possibility of checking any conflicting statements by reference to the actions of outsiders. If castes A and B did not eat from each other's hands, it will be recalled, it was often possible to deduce that A was higher, since caste C ate from A but not from B. This can be done only occasionally between subcastes. Thus, the Malwi and Ujle Goatherds do not eat from each other; but Rajputs eat with the Ujle, but not with the Malwi Goatherd, and the latter is forced to admit that he is inferior. Usually, however, people of other castes take no notice of subcaste divisions; they will eat (or not eat) with all subcastes, and this makes ranking of subcastes difficult. It does not, of course, stop people from saying that their own subcaste is superior —and this is the significant point at present, since it shows that people think of their subcaste as being in a hierarchy similar to that of the castes.

The only exception to this characterization of subcastes as smaller editions of castes would seem to lie in the cases of those subcastes whose members both eat and marry reciprocally.[1] What keeps such subcastes separate, it may be asked? In the cases I know of, it is largely the fact that they are differently named, and not much else. Take the Malwi and Mewara Oil-pressers. The first intermarriage and interdining between these subcastes took place forty years ago, it is said; and at about the same time the Malwi Oil-pressers started calling themselves Rathor Oil-pressers. Now, one member maintained, the Mewara Oil-pressers were also starting to call themselves Rathor, and he agreed that the two subcastes might easily amalgamate into a single Rathor subcaste. He held that the Mewara subcaste was slightly lower—more of its members ate meat than did the Malwi Oil-pressers, he said—but this is a difference that can be quickly remedied. I would maintain that subcastes are primarily endogamous bodies, and would see this example as portraying a changing situation in which two subcastes are merging and at the moment are neither separate nor fully united.

A provincial study would be needed to say more about this merger —whether it is taking place because there are few Mewara Oil-pressers in Malwa, whether there is a similar move in Mewar, etc. But it does not appear to be a common process; that is, the subcaste coming from the outside province does not usually merge with the Malwi subcaste. The Gujarati Weavers have been in Malwa for many centuries, according to local opinion, and have not yet merged with the Malwi Weavers. Indeed, there is just as likely to be fission within the immigrant subcaste; there has, for instance,

---

[1] This fact of weak endogamous rules is the one stressed by Blunt to show the difference between a caste and a subcaste (see p. 7).

been a division of the Mewara Carpenters into Old and New endogamous bodies, on the basis of the time of immigration.

The reason why marriage is a more important criterion of sub-caste distinction than commensal restrictions or a separate name is that people are thereby actual or potential kin.This means that they attend each other's ceremonies, and participate in the councils of subcaste control, which take place there, as did Mewara and Malwi Oil-presser kin. And the council is the major instrument for keeping the local subcaste group a separate social entity, as well as being the main regional focus for most subcastes.

The local subcaste is the group within which sanctions are exerted to maintain the rules of both internal and external behaviour. When subcaste members act over the external behaviour of a fellow, it can either be over actions towards people of another subcaste, or those of another caste. For there is no caste body to enforce inter-caste behaviour. This is seen from the outside to mean that when a council composed of men of a single subcaste deals with inter-caste matters it is acting on behalf of the entire caste. For outsiders do not usually differentiate between different subcastes; they see that a Weaver has been disciplined, for instance, for eating with a Tanner, and they say that the Weaver council has taken this step. They do not see it primarily as the sanction of a council of Gujarati Weavers on a member of the subcaste. And they are generally not mistaken; for the Gujarati Weavers are acting in the interests of the entire Weaver caste in such a matter, since all Weavers refuse to eat with Tanners and would also penalize members of their own subcastes who do so. Men of the other subcastes might, in fact, also boycott the Gujarati Weaver for having contravened an inter-caste law.

Exceptions exist when subcastes have different inter-caste be-haviour. Thus, a Malwi Goatherd council which penalized a member for eating with a Barber would not be supported by the Ujle Goat-herds, who are allowed to eat with Barbers and other allied castes. Such cases appear to be rare. Thus, the Rajputs and allied castes eat with the meat-eating subcaste of Gardeners, but not with the vegetarian Gujarati Gardeners. Again, I have already suggested that differences in origin make for differential behaviour of subcastes towards other castes. The Minas have a Deshvali subcaste, said to be descended from the unions of Rajputs with Mina women,[1] and an Ujle (high) subcaste. Members of the latter say they eat with Rajputs in the east, though not in Malwa; but the Deshvali are classed as lower and do not do so. (This may also be the case with the two Goatherd subcastes, since the term '*ujle*' also occurs here.)

There may also be differential behaviour towards members of a

[1] Venkatachar 1933: 276.

newly arrived subcaste. Thus the main subcaste of Dairymen around Ramkheri is Jadavbans, and these form part of the allied caste group. Recently, some Goalbans Dairymen have come from Bundelkhand and the northeast, settling mainly in Indore. A family which came to Ramkheri is not yet included in the allied caste group; but if it is later admitted, there would again be no difference in the Rajputs' and other castes' treatment of all Dairymen. Again, the representatives of the Kanauji and Sanodya Brahmans are from the north. And though most Ramkheri people do not know their subcaste names, some are unwilling to eat from them at present; this is also said to be partly because these Brahmans are farmers, rather than practising priests. The distinction is as much between 'native' and 'foreign' and between occupations, as between subcastes.

For the most part, behaviour is uniform towards all subcastes of a caste. And even when this is not so, differential rules are seldom applied because there is rarely more than one subcaste in a village. We have seen that only the Brahmans and the Weavers, out of the twenty-five castes in Ramkheri, are represented by more than one subcaste. This appears usual for the area. Data for thirty-eight villages inhabited by Weavers show that there are only three multi-subcaste settlements. Again, only two out of twenty-eight villages of Barbers contain more than one subcaste; and only one of eighteen villages has two Potter subcastes. There is, in fact, seldom the occasion for other castes to make distinctions between subcastes. Their dealings within the village are uncomplicated and if they go to a village where different subcastes exist, they follow the example of their hosts, as I have already shown. Thus, a Rajput of Ramkheri eats with his Barber who is of the Gujarati subcaste. If this Rajput goes to another village on the invitation of a Rajput, and the Barber there happens to be a Malwi, he will eat with the latter if his host does so, or abstain if that is the custom of the village —that is, he is guided in his relations to other Barber subcastes by the actions of his own caste mates, not by those of the Gujarati Barber of his own village, who may or may not eat with Malwi Barbers. It is only on the few occasions where two subcastes living in the village are treated in different ways that this procedure would be inapplicable.

Though subcastes are generally equal in the eyes of outsiders, these know that there are different subcastes in each caste, of course. But there is usually a need to identify these subcastes only in matters affecting the caste internally. Hence, in this book, I refer to the 'caste' when I am dealing with inter-caste relations of an entire caste group or one of its subcaste groups, and to the 'subcaste' when I am interested in the subcaste group's relations to other subcaste groups, and in its internal structure. This distinction does not cover certain contingencies, as I have indicated, but it is sufficient for my data. More important, it emphasizes what I think is a main aspect of the situation—that the subcaste group in the village also represents the entire caste, e.g. the Barbers in Ramkheri are regarded as Barbers, not Gujarati Barbers, by all non-Barbers.

There may be complications in making this a general usage for India. For the differences between subcastes in some areas may be so marked as to make them readily distinguishable by other castes. In Malabar, for example, the various subcastes of Nayars include washermen and barbers as well as warriors and aristocrats. Since, moreover, several of these subcastes live in the same settlement, it is clear that here subcaste membership colours a man's relations with other castes in the same village. Mostly, however, subcastes having radically different status tend to become separate castes (e.g. the Mochi is no longer considered to be a 'real Tanner' by Ramkheri people, since he only cobbles and does not tan the leather). Hence, in the majority of instances, I believe my distinction might hold good, and put it forward as the basis for comparative analysis.

As I have indicated, some writers have held that the subcaste is 'the real caste' since the main group activities—social control, endogamy, etc.—occur at subcaste rather than caste level. I would take a rather different view. Whilst acknowledging the importance of the subcaste, I would point out that both caste and subcaste membership are possessed by every individual, and that there are appropriate roles for each. Thus, one cannot say that the subcaste alone is the effective social unit. When a man acts in an inter-caste matter, he represents his *caste* (with rare exceptions), because all his fellow-caste members have the same inter-caste rules. The same man can later be involved in an issue with other subcastes of his caste, or with people of his own subcaste, and he is then acting as a *subcaste* member. I would conclude that both roles are important, and that it is necessary to distinguish them. For there can be regional variations in the content of these roles. Thus, in Malwa I believe that both endogamy and councils for social control are matters for the subcaste, and point to the merging of the Malwi and Mewara Oil-pressers in a Rathor subcaste to illustrate this. But in Mysore, for example, a village's population is made up of subcastes[1] which it is presumed are endogamous, but the councils are on a caste basis.[2]

My analysis has shown that the caste roles are primarily concerned with inter-caste relations *within* the village, and the following chapters will suggest that subcaste roles are mainly between fellow-subcaste mates of *nearby* villages (though where the subcaste group

[1] Srinivas 1955*b*: 24.   [2] Ibid: 29.

in a village is large, there may be considerable activity within it). But the subcaste itself is not a formal local unit, save where there is endogamy within a handful of villages (see p. 4). The roles are instead made manifest in what I term the 'kindred of recognition' and 'kindred of co-operation'. The small area in which these kindreds exist is the area within which both inter-caste and intra-subcaste relations take place—and this area I call the 'region'. It is the area of effective relations, rather than of formal membership of bodies like the subcaste. Indeed, subcaste mates coming from outside this region are not given the privileges of membership until their *bona fides* are established. In this way the total habitat of the subcaste can be seen as made up of many overlapping regions.

THE CLAN

All subcastes are divided into exogamous sections which can be called clans. The word *gotra* was most often used by villagers for these sections, though they have nothing to do with the traditional Brahminical *gotra*. The clan has a dispersed membership, as far as is known coterminous with the subcaste. It is based on agnatic ties, putatively assumed from the patrilineal succession to a common clan name, and a common Clan Goddess, as well as from the records of the clan's genealogist. A man or woman is born into the clan of the *pater* in the same way as into his caste. Nothing alters this allegiance for men; for a man does not lose his natal clan membership if he is adopted into a different clan. Thus, a man who was adopted by his father's sister's husband did not become a full member of the latter's clan though he should have done, according to traditional usage. He performed some minor rites reserved for the agnatic line of his adoptor, but his main tutelary deity continued to be that of his natal clan. For women the position is more changeable, for after marriage they have allegiances of varying strength to their conjugal clan; but some sort of tie to their natal clan always remains.

Clans are said to have an origin contemporaneous with the mythical founding of the caste. Take the clans of the Farmer caste, for example, which I was told dated from the time that Parasurama waged war against the Kshatriyas in the myth I have already recounted. Part of the myth, said a genealogist of the Farmers, was that King Sahasrarjun fought Parasurama mainly through his 10,000 sons (begotten from 10,000 wives). Parasurama killed many of these sons, and made the different castes from some of the survivors. But 105 sons were left, and these went to Raja Janaka (the King of Mithila) and asked for his protection. He assented, and put them to work in the fields, telling Parasurama that they were Khatis and not

Kshatri(ya)s. From these brothers the Farmer caste, in the form of 105 clans, issued. Since then twenty-one clans have become extinct, and the remainder are listed in the books of the genealogist. This story varies with the different genealogists;[1] but the villager in any case seldom recalls the details of these histories, and though most of the castes in divisions 2 to 4 also said their clans started from the time of Parasurama, they were not always clear in what manner. In general, Ramkheri people do not know their clan origins, nor how many there are in each subcaste. Some said, vaguely, that there were 'hundreds', others gave precise figures—101, 1001, 1446—but I would hesitate to place too much reliance on these.

There is little information about any fission of clans or foundation of new clans. Though the genealogists I met were prepared to give instances of clans dying out for want of members, none could recall a case of a new clan being started after the initial 'creation'. A possible process is suggested by the number of clans whose names coincide with village names. Thus, the settlements of Baroli, Dhamanda, Ajnod, etc., are linked by name to the Barolia, Dhamandia, Ajnodia clans. This may have come about through a man's having settled a new village, his descendants then becoming separated genealogically as well as spatially, taking the name he gave to the village. But this is pure speculation, and the opposite may equally well have occurred—the making of a new settlement by people of, say, the Barolia clan, who then called the village Baroli.

Clans presumably divide when a new subcaste is formed. For example, the Kawaria clan is said to exist amongst both Malwi and Marwara subcastes of Potters.[2] One can speculate that the Kawaria clan was originally a single exogamous unit, but when the Potters broke into provincial subcastes, the clan also divided. Such fission might also occur when new subcastes emerge on occupational lines.

A possible source for the emergence of new clans is suggested by the number of clan names of one caste, and especially Rajput branch[3] names, which are used by subcastes of other castes as clan names. The branch name 'Chauhan' for example occurs as a clan name in the Gujarati Barber, Ujle Mina, Purviya Tanner, Bhilala, Rajguri Nath and Gujarati Blacksmith subcastes of Ramkheri. Altogether, thirteen out of the twenty-seven subcastes for which clan

---

[1] Another account gives the number of sons as 1000, and the number of survivors as 108, with twenty-four clans becoming extinct (personal communication from Sri K. S. Mathur).

[2] I say 'said to exist' because my data were verbal, rather than written records, and what I may have heard as the same clan name might, in fact, be a different one (e.g. Kamaria in one case, Kawaria in another).

[3] I discuss my use of this term below (p. 164).

names were collected had Rajput branch names for at least one of their clans. And there is nothing to suggest that several more would not have been found to have them, had more clan names been collected.[1] Local opinion explains the incidence of the same clan names in several subcastes by the outcasting of a man for living with a woman of lower subcaste. The children would become members of the lower subcaste, but would keep their father's clan name. This may explain some of the spread; but it does not account for the fact that most of the clan names which occur in this way are indubitably Rajput branch names—such as Chauhan, Solanki, etc. Only four out of twenty-seven subcastes possessed a common non-Rajput clan name—there is a Bhensaudia clan among both Farmers and Malwi Carpenters, both Malwi Weavers and Mewara Carpenters have a Barolia clan, and the Tajpuria clan occurs in Farmer and Malwi Carpenter subcastes. Nobody maintained, however, that it was practically only Rajputs who lived with women of other castes (though Rajput landlords were often said to have relations with the maidservants who attended their wives). One may suggest that there is here a desire to copy the Rajput overlords, and to claim traditional connections with the Rajputs through the correspondence of clan names, thereby gaining an improvement in caste status.

The conjectures into which one is forced if one wishes to discuss such structural features of the clan emphasize the essentially local and genealogically shallow interest of the villagers about their clans. These mainly provide affiliations which are invoked in the rules of exogamy and in ritual acts performed by the small local clan group only. The entire clan does not meet as a group (it is far too dispersed for that) and there are few clans whose members are distinguished in any way. Some Rajputs told of branch and clan rankings, but could provide no clear and consistent hierarchy. Again, certain Farmer clans were said to be eminent, e.g. the Sunanya clan is the largest and is said to be a 'good' clan with which to ally oneself, and the men of the Kajuria clan are called 'arbitrator' (*mandloi*). But I could find no actions on which these distinctions were based. No system of hypergamy emerged from the data on marriages, the Kajuria men were or were not arbitrators according to personal capability. The 'big man' (*mukhati*) of the Farmer caste group can belong to any clan, in the same way as Rajput lords and eminent Oil-pressers (*modi*). The clan as a whole is a body with minor influence on actions,

---

[1] I listed 259 clan names, but this is only part of the total number in the subcastes of Ramkheri. In only one case am I sure that there are no Rajput clan names, for I have a list of all Farmer clans, and they do not occur there. No plausible reason was suggested to me why this should be, but it shows another small but significant difference between the two major castes of Ramkheri.

about which people have little information above the bare fact of their membership, though this membership is clearly recognized by every individual.

This can also be seen when we consider the rather more complex clan system of certain castes. Most important of these is the Rajput structure. This is in three tiers.

Traditionally, the Rajputs were divided into lines (*vans*). Villagers maintain that these lines existed before the time of Parasurama, and so before any clans existed, and that they were then the exogamous units. In some quarters, three lines are arranged in a hypergamous progression, again traditional, the Sun line taking women from the Moon line, and the Moon from the Fire.[1] But this is not done by the peasant Rajputs in Ramkheri and its region. Indeed, few people knew more than that the lines existed; those that did, knew only that Rama was a member of the Sun and Krishna of the Moon line (nobody had heard of the Fire line, it seemed). For the most part, people did not know to which line their branch belonged. One or two men gave affiliations which differed from the traditional writings (saying, for example, that the Chauhan branch belonged to the Moon instead of to the Fire line), or even gave different answers when subsequently questioned. It is safe to conclude that the line is not a significant factor in the organization of Ramkheri Rajputs, and nowhere enters overtly into their activities.

There are a number of sections within each line. These have been called 'race' by some,[2] and 'clan' by others.[3] I prefer to use the term current in Ramkheri, 'branch' (*sakha*). This avoids historical complications implicit in 'race' and also the association of complete exogamy with the word 'clan', a connection which I shall show is not justified in Ramkheri, though perhaps valid elsewhere.[4]

Each line has several branches, and people know at least something of the mythical emergence of the latter. An important group of Rajputs in Ramkheri are of the Chauhan branch; this is part of the Fire line, of which there are four branches. A comparison of the story told me by the genealogist and that recalled by a Chauhan villager will give an indication of the degree to which traditional data exist in Ramkheri about such matters. According to the genealogist, the four Fire branches were created one day when a host of Brahmans gathered to eat. An evil spirit came down and stole their food. So Brahma took some earth and made four images of man, passing

[1] Karve 1953: 141.
[2] Tod 1829: 68.   [3] Karve 1953: 140.
[4] Cf. ibid.: 140. The names given to the various divisions of Rajputs vary from writer to writer, and sometimes even in a single account. Thus, Tod sometimes calls the 'race' the 'tribe' (1829: 96).

164

them through the fire which had been lit (hence the connection of the line with fire). As he made the first one, he stretched out his four arms, which bore the sacred symbols (the conch, the wheel, the lotus and the club); the first was therefore called Chauhan (*chau* or *char* = four). The second clutched Brahma's clothes (*sal*) and was called Brahmachal or Solanki; the third fell down some steps and was called Parihar (*parna* = to fall) and the fourth was told to beat the evil spirit and was called Parmar (*marna* = to beat) or Ponwar.

The villager's story is less detailed. He stated that the Rajputs came from a model of a man made from Brahma's arm. After making the model, Brahma washed it and left it in a well; from this there emerged in order—Chauhan, Parihar, Parmar or Ponwar. He knew the names of other branches but could not give their order of appearance. His story has two essentials which correspond to the genealogist's. The Rajputs come in both from models made by Brahma, and they come in a certain order, led by the Chauhan. The reference by the villager to the Rajputs being made from Brahma's arm may refer to the waving of Brahma's arms as the Chauhan was created—the informant was himself a Chauhan, who would best remember this part of the genealogist's story. Further, the villagers thought that this myth referred to the creation of all Rajput branches, whereas the genealogist gave it as applying to the Fire line alone. Again, then, the line is left out of the calculations of the villagers. But the separate creation of the branches is to some extent remembered. There is also a general idea that some branches are higher than others—but no specific order can be cited, and no system of hypergamy rests on it.

Within each branch there are clans (*gotra*). The Solanki has sixteen clans, the Chauhan has twenty-four, etc. Marriages can take place between people of the same branch if their clans differ. Thus, a Balecha Chauhan in Ramkheri married a Sanchora Chauhan woman; again, a Devra Chauhan has married a Balecha Chauhan. This, however, is exceptional: for of forty-nine marriages in which Chauhans took part, only four were within the branch. Indeed, some people say that the branches are themselves exogamous. This would accord with much of the writings on Rajput structure, and with the use of the term 'clan' for what I am calling a branch. Cole, for instance, writes that the branches are exogamous.[1] More comparative data is needed, and I can only record the situation in Ramkheri.

Another feature Cole notes is that the clan may become so well known that it is regarded as being as important as its branch, and finally becomes to all practical purposes a separate branch. The best example is perhaps the Sisodia clan of the Gahlot branch. This even

[1] Cole 1932: 134.

has its own subdivisions (e.g. Ranawat Sisodia) and in such cases one should talk strictly of sub-clans, though people like those in Ramkheri see the Sisodia as the branch and the Ranawat as one of its clans.

In contrast to those who forget the branch, others knew their branch name but not the name of the clan in it. This knowledge they left to the genealogist or the more knowledgeable men of the caste group, since it was in any case only necessary at the time of marriage negotiations. It may be such ignorance that made 20 per cent. of the people who said that they were members of the Kachwaha branch unable to give their clan name in the 1931 Census of Rajasthan, though they were shown a list of the twenty-four clans in the branch.[1] The latitude of knowledge allowed to people about their branch and clan suggests that, in the Rajput as in other castes, these affiliations are mainly for ritual and exogamous purposes. This means that they are only of occasional application, and also that they are of *local* application, and hence allow variation. It does not matter, for example, if a local agnatic group calls itself Khichhi and considers that Khichhi is a branch, or calls itself Khichhi Chauhan, recognizing that Khichhi is only a clan of the Chauhan branch. The main thing is that its members recognize a common name, which means a rule of exogamy if they consider it to be proper. Thus, provided the genealogist is not called in, the situation is one where the clan or the branch is equally an exogamous unit, depending on the knowledge of the members.

The Gosains and Bairagis have a two-tiered system of the same sort as the Rajput. The Gosain, for example, comprise ten branches, within which there are clans. Marriage can take place within or between branches. There are no other castes in Ramkheri with similar complex structures of more than purely formal import. Thus, some subcastes may have a superstructure of clans. The eighty-four Mewara Carpenter 'village clans' (*ganv gotra*) are formed into twenty-seven 'sage's clans' (*rsi gotra*), according to their genealogist.[2] But not one inhabitant of Ramkheri could tell me about these in any subcaste; and even the genealogist admitted that the sage's clans played no part in rituals or in marriage negotiations. I do not think they are of any importance in the village now.

---

[1] Cole 1932: 136. Some people may have been assuming Rajput membership and thus have been unable or unwilling to tell more of their affiliations. On the other hand, in the cases known to me where people have assumed a Rajput branch name that was not rightfully theirs, they have taken care to take a clan membership at the same time, and to know about this in some detail.

[2] The *rsi gotra* may here refer to a *pravara* system adopted by the Carpenter genealogist to enhance the status of his clients (for the connection of *rsi gotra* and *pravara*, see Brough 1953: 7).

Internal Structure of the Caste

Within the clan, there are various words used to describe the unilineal descent group with a depth of more than three or four generations, in which descent is calculable. But all of them can also refer to other kinds of kin-group. This is in contrast to the word *gotra*, which is used for the clan alone. *Kutumb*, for example, is a word used to denote the family, and is as flexible as its English translation. Thus, one can call the elementary or extended family a *kutumb*, or can talk of the agnatic line as a *kutumb*, in the English sense of 'a noble family'. Generally, however, the former use is meant. *Kul* refers to the agnatic line, but in rather a special sense. The tutelary goddess of the clan is called *Kul Mata*; and though one could legitimately call either members of the lineage or clan by this word in any context, it is usually reserved for this ritual activity only.

Two words remain, *bhaibandh* and *khandan*. Each can be used to mean both lineage and clan. Thus, if a man is asked 'to what *bhaibandh* (or *khandan*) do you belong?' he will give his clan name, in the same way as if the questioner had used the word *gotra*. Partly this is because the lineage does not have a name—either of the founding ancestor or the place of origin, etc. But were he to be asked 'whereabout is your *bhaibandh* (or *khandan*) living?' he would not answer with the area covered by his clan, but would rather tell of the local region in which his lineage lives. The size and depth of this lineage will vary, being primarily defined by the extent of his own interaction with agnatic kin in other villages. Again, this group of people does not have a name (one would simply call it 'the nearby (*as pas*) *bhaibandh*'). Only if one asked about clan mates in the same village would the name of the senior man be used to designate the group (e.g. 'Lakshman's *khandan*') but such a group will often be of less than four generations' depth.

A unilineal descent group without a name, whose precise extent and composition may differ according to each individual's view of it —is this no more than an abstraction made by the outside observer? I think not, because at least some villagers see clearly the difference between the small scale, local unilineal descent groups, and the clan population as a whole. And there is actual co-operation, or a history of such co-operation, which marks the lineage and distinguishes it from the clan.

The people who make this distinction tend to be those whose clan population in the area around Ramkheri is large. Thus, one man said, 'My *bhaibandh* are in villages X- and Y-. I am not sure how many generations' gap there is between us, but we still invite them; there are one or two houses in each place. My father's father's father was from Z- village. There are seventy houses there, but I do not invite them any more.' The man's brother, referring to the Z-population, added, 'They are in our *bhaibandh*, I suppose, though we do not invite them. If Z- were a village next to Ramkheri, it would not matter how many generations' gap there were between us, we should still invite. But if they are at a distance [Z- is thirty miles from Ramkheri], we drop the relation after five or six generations have died.' A bystander then concluded, 'Then, the lineage passes into the clan (*bhaibandh gotra men jata hai*), and the people become clan mates (*gotra bhai*) only.'

Another opinion on this last point was: 'The *bhaibandh* goes back for many generations, even up to ten generations, and to twenty miles away when members have settled elsewhere. No, it is not the same as the *gotra*. For if a man came from Delhi and said he was of my *gotra*, and worshipped the same Clan Goddess, he would be a clan mate, but not of my *bhaibandh*.'

Both speakers emphasized that the *bhaibandh* is limited in genealogical depth, but that it is also influenced by its spatial spread. As one man put this, 'if you are living in the same village, you can have a thousand generations' gap between you [from the common ancestor], and you will still invite each other, and talk of a single *bhaibandh*'.

The significant thing is that these speakers are members of clans with fairly large local populations. Villagers with few clansmen in the neighbourhood were more likely to make statements like, 'the people in villages X- and Y- are our *bhaibandh*. However many generations' gap there may be, and whether we invite them or not, they will continue to be our *bhaibandh*, so long as they worship the same Clan Goddess.' Here there is no distinction between the local lineage and the clan group. I suggest that this is because the people with the greater density of clan population have very practical reasons for distinguishing lineage from clan. If it can be said that only the lineage people must be invited, then for economic reasons one will try to curtail the lineage at the earliest proper moment. It is perhaps no coincidence that, in the first statement, the speaker did not say that the agnatic links between him and the people of village Z- were any more remote than with villages X- and Y-. But he did say that the latter had few houses, whereas the former had a large clan population. Generally, there are few occasions where people can afford to invite very large numbers; only at the largest funerary feasts (*nukta*) are guests numbered in the thousands—and here the invitation is usually issued for the entire subcaste population of a village (*pancayati nyauta*) rather than merely for the lineage or clan mates in the settlement.

168

There appear to be two kinds of lineage, therefore. One is recognized to contain agnates who come to one's social functions (and since these functions are the main occasions for local subcaste action, this is more important than it may appear). This lineage tends to be at the most of five or six generations' depth from its founder, unless members live in the same or perhaps neighbouring villages, when it will last indefinitely. People may not know the names of all the ascendants through whom they are linked, but they know at least the approximate depth of these ties. One can call this the lineage of co-operation; I use co-operation rather than a stronger word such as obligation because, as I shall describe, even these close agnates have freedom to decide whether they will co-operate or not in activities which concern them both.

The other kind of lineage is that which is based simply on recognition of a previous agnatic link; this link may not be known in any detail to members, but it can be traced through the records of the genealogist. We can call this a lineage of recognition. It extends to about ten generations from the founder; and the degree of mobility in Malwa has been such that there are few cases where nearby agnates would have a greater generation gap. Neither of these lineages exists where men have no fellow-clansmen within the region of the village. Thus, the Vagela Solanki Rajputs in Ramkheri knew that they had clansmen seventy miles off; but they said that these were 'not really our *bhaibandh*'.

My distinction between the two kinds of lineage is based on the presence or absence of certain activities, rather than on 'genealogical depth'. And the data provide little opportunity to use such terms as 'major' and 'minor' lineage. The Hindi terms I have mentioned to some extent fit the two kinds of lineage. In the same way as *biradari* meant the entire subcaste but was used largely to denote the local subcaste group, so *bhaibandh* can mean the whole clan, but is used more often to refer to lineages of recognition. Again, *khandan* can be used for wider unilineal descent groups, but more often refers to the agnates of four or five generations' depth (this is connected with its special use as a term in the selection of marriage partners, of which more below).

EXTENDED FAMILY AND KINDRED

Smaller in scale than either of the lineages I have described is the unilineal descent group of up to three generations ascending from the men of about thirty years now in Ramkheri. This group differs from the others in that the names and relationships of all component kin are remembered. For nearly all men can recall the name of their father's father, though they seldom remember details beyond this.[1] I have indicated that the word given most often to this group is *kutumb* (*parivar* has a similar meaning but a less frequent use). This term has ambiguities, however, and I must note these and, in doing so, outline the limits of bilateral kin-groups. For at this shallow depth we are really dealing with an extended family whose members recognize agnatic ties in some circumstances and uterine links in others.

Kutumb, I have said, means family in an indefinite way. On the one hand, it can be used in the same sort of contexts as the word *bhaibandh*; on the other hand, it more commonly refers to kin tracing relations through both males and females of one or two ascending generations. The patrilineal axis of the society makes agnatic links more important (in inheritance, settlement pattern, ritual duties, etc.). But at the same time uterine ties are important enough to be remembered. For a man has obligations towards his uterine kin and his affines as well as towards agnates; he thinks of these people as being in his kin-group, and uses the word *kutumb* for them.

Some people therefore distinguish between what they call the 'main family' (*khas kutumb*) and what they designate as 'the family' (*kutumb*), i.e. between the smallest agnatically defined group and what I call the co-operating kindred for reasons I give below. The difference between the two is illustrated by the following diagrams, which show the views of one Rajput informant.[2] For the main family he designated these kin:

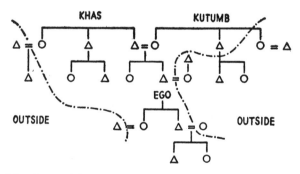

The *khas kutumb* here set out is a patrilineal group, composed of one or several households, save for the inclusion of the mother's

[1] The greatest generation recall I found was amongst the headmen, where some men (though not all) could give the names of four generations of deceased ascendants.

[2] I regret that I do not have sufficient data from lower caste informants to say whether their views of kin-groups are markedly different.

brother.[1] This person has a special place in the affairs of the family, and is no doubt included because of this; but the contravention of unilineality does not go as far as his children. The *kutumb*, on the other hand, has extremely debatable limits, and there appears to be no constant criterion of membership. This is brought out in the diagram below, which shows some of the relationships on which the Rajput gave judgment.

The remoteness of relationship seems to have little to do with membership. A, for example, is separated from Ego by only one

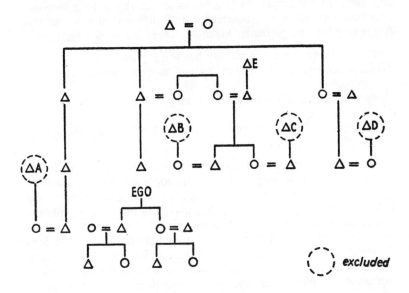

marriage, yet is excluded, whereas E is related through two marriages and is included. The *kutumb*, like the lineage of co-operation, seems to be defined by social contacts. If a man is not invited by his cognates or affines for one reason or another (e.g. personal dislike which may overcome a not very strong obligation, or economic inability to invite), he may be recognized as a relation (*ristedar* or *natedar*) but may not be included when the *kutumb* is talked of. The *kutumb* in such contexts is a group of varying size, and I think it best to call it the co-operating kindred, meaning those cognates and affines who regard themselves as related and have some sort of interaction. This is distinct from what one might call the kindred of recognition, which includes all those with whom a kin tie is calculated by a

[1] The mother is also included, though the informant placed other women in their natal *kutumbs*.

particular person.[1] This latter is, naturally enough, a somewhat shadowy group. There are some people who would call it a *kutumb* also, but on the whole feeling appears to be that the kindred of recognition is an intermediate stage between the kindred of co-operation and the local subcaste population in much the same way as, on the unilineal level, the lineage of recognition is said to 'pass into the clan'.

People in Ramkheri make a clear distinction between kin ties which exist only in theory and those which are maintained by coactivity. Many people say that the latter are the real kin ties, the foundation of which is a combination of sufficient money and the desire to invite the particular kinsman. There is a verse which goes:

Without money, a mother will say her son is wicked,
Without money, the mother-in-law will say, this son-in-law is not mine,
Without money a brother will say, let us give the brother trouble and wound him,
Without money the wife will say, my husband is lazy [though he works, he makes no money].

This verse may seem a cynical equation of kinship with the economic benefits it brings, and not all people are as materialistic as this. Some, certainly, measure the minimum obligations they need fulfil, and try to get more than they give; but for many people the relevance of money is that of maintaining kin ties which are seen as meritorious. All kin relationships are connected with obligations to invite and to make gifts, and money is basic to this. Without enough money, the tie will lapse just as surely as it does if one party withholds his proper contribution when he does, in fact, possess the money.

KIN COMPOSITION OF VILLAGE SUBCASTE POPULATIONS

Some of the kin-groups I have been discussing are of a size which might be found in a single settlement. What, then, is the kinship composition of the subcastes in Ramkheri, and in what types of households do they live?

The simplest kind of subcaste is that composed of a single elementary family (parents and children)—e.g. the Bairagi, Srigaur Brahman and Kanauji Brahman subcastes.

Second, the Ujle Mina, Rajguri Nath, Gujarati Gardener, Gujarati Blacksmith, Malwi Potter, Gujarati Tailor, Nababansi Drummer and

---

[1] It is in this sense that the term kindred is usually used, but I think it appropriate to qualify it in this way.

172

Satichuri Sweeper subcaste groups comprise a single extended family going back one or two generations to the founding ancestor—e.g. a man with his married sons and grandchildren, or two brothers and their children.

Next are those subcastes composed of an elementary or extended family with one or more elementary families of uterine kin or affines linked to them. An example is the Malwi Goatherd subcaste which consists of an elementary family and the daughter's husband and his elementary family who have recently come to the village. Again, the Gujarati Barbers comprise an extended family with an elementary family of affines. In this category also fall the Goalbans Dairyman, Malwi Carpenter, Purviya Tanner. These subcastes consist of a *kutumb* rather than a *khas kutumb*, in the terms used above.

The organization of Bhilalas presents the temporal progression from this, when the linked elementary family becomes itself an extended family. Thus, Bhilalas are in two large extended families of different clans, linked by a marriage some eighty years ago which brought the founder of the newer family to Ramkheri as an affine. In addition there are one or two elementary families affinally attached to these larger groups.

Another variation is presented when there are two kin-groups unrelated to each other through kin ties between village residents. Thus, the Marwari Tobacco-curer subcaste consists of an elementary family of one clan, and the same of another clan with an affinally linked family. Again, the Cotton-carders have two unrelated kin-groups of exactly the same composition—two extended families of cognates, and an affinally linked elementary family. The Gosains and Balai Babajis have similar subcaste configurations.

The large Farmer population is organized with somewhat greater complexity. Overall, it forms a single kin-group, as the accompanying diagram shows. But within there are three main clan groups (marked A, B and C). Two form large extended families, and one is a smaller extended family based on a man, his son and grandson. These three are prior because they stem from the first Farmers to come to Ramkheri at the end of the nineteenth century. The remainder are affines and uterine kin, some the descendants of those who followed the founders to the village.

The last three subcastes differ from the others because they contain lineages. In each case—those of the Solanki and Chauhan Rajputs, and of the Malwi Weavers and Gujarati Weavers—the exact descent pattern and number of generations to the founder of the lineage is not known by the inhabitants, though they say it can be ascertained from the genealogists. These provide examples of the situation where a lineage which might otherwise be one of recognition—or if the ties

173

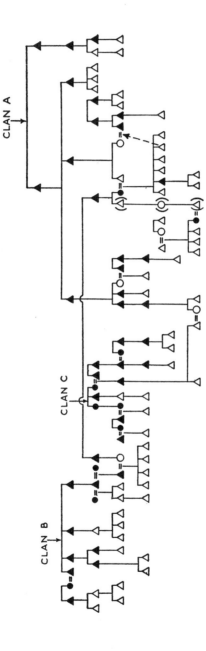

RAMKHERI FARMERS : KINSHIP CHART.

▲ or ● = dead person

(△) or (○) = absent from village

--→ = adoption

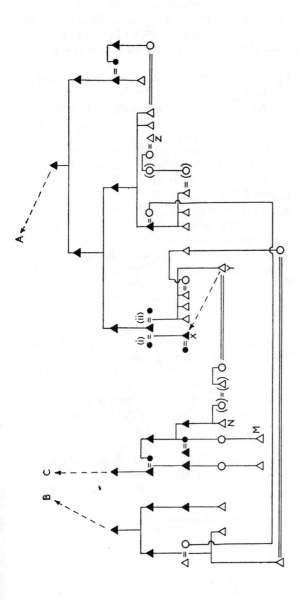

BALECHA CHAUHAN RAJPUT LINEAGE

▲ or ● = dead person

(△) or (○) = absent from village

(i) and (ii) = first and second marriage

◄ — — — = adoption

are of greater depth be no longer recognized at all—is maintained as a lineage of co-operation because of common residence. All the lineages have other elementary and/or extended families linked to them, and the subcaste population is completed with a few households of unrelated people.

As an example, I give a diagram of the Balecha Chauhan Rajput lineage, showing adult males only. This has two branches, A and B; a third, C, originally came with these from the village of immigration to Ramkheri; but no descendants remain, though the settling of a wife's brother at one stage means that there are more distant kin (M and N) still here. Family A is the senior branch of the lineage, and the senior house of the entire kin-group was occupied by X, the son of his father's first marriage, and is now held by Y who was adopted by X's widow to fill the headmanship the latter held. There is an affinally linked elementary family (Z). The other branch comprises an extended family with no affinally linked kin. These branches of the lineage are not separate units. If a branch's heirs were to die out, the land could be claimed by the other branch's men as collateral kin. The fact that all worship the Clan Goddess together, and have a single Bheru in the fields outside the village also shows the unity of the group. Only the division of the headmanship, whereby there is a headman of branch A as well as of B, shows a division of the lineage.

These Rajputs are also connected by affinal ties through other villages (e.g. Y to N), but most of these are held to be secondary to ties existing in each village before the matches. This is important because many people in all subcastes are related in both ways. For it is only the rules of exogamy and lack of partners which prevents repeated marriages into the same extended family in another village. And it is seldom that people related within Ramkheri cannot trace kinship through mutual relatives outside the village. These secondary ties can influence the behaviour of villagers towards each other; but they are usually at least formally subordinate, as the following example shows:

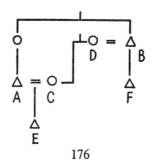

B is A's maternal uncle (*mama*), and the two men have married full sisters. They are thus related by their previous uterine tie and by the more recent link of their marriages into a different village. Which tie takes precedence for the various people involved? The two wives call each other sister (*bahin*) rather than sister-in-law; and A calls B maternal uncle rather than wife's sister's husband (*saru bhai*), and in return is called sister's son (*bhanej*) by B. In short, the ties existing before the marriage are prior. Again, F calls A cousin (classificatory elder brother), but he calls C mother's sister (*masi*), rather than brother's (cousin's) wife (*bhabhi*). B calls C wife's sister (*sali*) rather than sister's son's wife. When E was small he used to call B mother's sister's husband (*masa*). But B himself stopped this, and asked him to call him *ba*, a general term accorded to men of ascending generations, including the father's maternal uncle. The only exception to the pattern is that A calls D mother's brother's wife (*mami*), instead of recognizing the link between the two sisters as prior, and so calling D wife's sister. The reason lies in the special position of the mother's brother (see p. 222), which is one of affection and economic importance. A thus feels it would be inappropriate to call B's wife by a term applicable to one with whom informality, rather than respect, is possible. The distinction drawn in the terms of address is reflected in activities. Thus, at E's wedding in 1955, B played the part of mother's brother, rather than mother's sister's husband. Most outsiders, be it noted, do not take into account the ties that A's and B's wives had before their marriages. They see them simply as 'wives of the village', thereby rather putting their own village's relationships first.

THE HOUSEHOLD

A 'household' refers to those people who share a cooking hearth, pool their incomes and have their living expenses in common. There is no specific Hindi word for this group in Ramkheri. *Ghar* means a dwelling, and *gharwale* refers to the people in it. But *ghar* can also be used in the sense of the household, which may not comprise all people in the dwelling. The question 'how many *ghar* are there in the village' would therefore receive an answer in terms of either dwellings or households, depending on the context of conversation. Thus, if one asked 'how many *ghar* of Carpenters are there?' the answer would be in terms of households; if one asked 'how many *ghar* are there in Khatipura ward of the village?' one would probably get an answer in terms of dwellings.

The physical and social meanings of the word *ghar* conflict when several men forming the household group separate their domestic arrangements into separate households but remain in the same dwelling instead of moving into different houses. This is not hard to do, if not too many people are involved. An interior wall is built to divide the house, and an extra entrance can easily be made.[1] When this is the case, a stranger will be directed to 'A—'s *ghar*' giving the name of the senior man, but told to use the left- or right-hand door (*darwaja*). 'To make one's own door' is a way of describing this kind of household partition. The term *darwaja* is only used in this qualifying way (one does not, for example, ask 'where is A—'s *darwaja*' upon entering a village).

Other terms for residence do not have this alternative reference to the inhabitants. *Makan*, for example, always means the dwelling house. *Mukam* means a person's present place of residence; it may therefore indicate his house, but could also be used by a traveller to describe the hotel at which he was staying. He could then distinguish this from the chief residence (*khas mukam*) which would refer to the place of his domicile. A man living for several years in a village would not speak of this as his *khas mukam*, for example, but would use that term for his parental village if he had any ideas of returning there.

Ghar is the word in commonest use for household, and the implied pattern is for each household to be in a separate dwelling. As I have said, houses in Ramkheri are relatively simple in construction and plan. As the number of people in a household grows, it is easy to erect half walls or large storage bins, so that some sort of privacy can be maintained by the various couples living jointly. All belongings are held in common save for the ornaments of the wives,[2] and these and the couple's clothes are kept in metal trunks. Sometimes these are piled in one place, but if they are kept separately, they tend to become the 'headquarters' of that couple in the house. There is usually little room for expansion of the house. Most dwellings are on streets, contiguous to their neighbours, and it is thus impossible to build on at each end; even if there is room at the back, the building of a new roof is expensive. It is commoner to build a separate cattle byre in any space at the back, and use the old byre in the house as an extra room. Sometimes a new byre must be built or purchased elsewhere. But the household usually divides before the pressure of population is thus great; the strain of living in cramped conditions

[1] There appear to be no such changes in the exterior gates of larger houses with courtyards. In one village, the headman's household was divided. Each brother claimed the door of the courtyard as his, and for this they fought protracted battles in the courts, rather than make another gate. Again, an important household had divided in Ramkheri, but both brothers continued to use the same gate, though they had made separate doors in the house.

[2] The kitchen utensils, bed, etc., given as a wife's dowry are also separate, but are pooled for household use.

may, in fact, contribute to the division in the form of petty quarrels, though this is not seen as a cause by the people themselves, who do not reckon privacy as an essential feature of a household. In a division, it is usual for the seceding party to build a separate house, either in the courtyard if there is space, or in a vacant plot which is often quite far off. The internal partition of the house is rarer.

The key to household membership is that marriage is primarily virilocal. In Ramkheri 184 couples were living in the husband's parental [1] village (or a village of his own choosing in the few cases of emigration), 6 were living in the wife's parental village, and 2 in the husband's mother's parental village. Lastly, 2 marriages were made within the village. Again, there were no fewer than 61 widows who continued to live in their conjugal village, as contrasted with 6 in their parental village, and 6 in a third village.

This pattern fits a patrilineal system of inheritance in which the daughter has no share in the parental property if there are sons alive. The latter will therefore stay at the place of their patrimony, whereas the daughter will only return if there are no other heirs, or if exceptional conditions (such as shortage of labour) make her husband welcome in his conjugal village. Again, a woman usually stays at her conjugal village in widowhood—for her sons maintain her, and even if these do not exist, this is the village in which she has spent her adult life, and in which there are usually a few of her husband's kin to help her.

The table on p. 180 lists the ten most important types of household composition, which together comprise some two-thirds of the village's people and over half its households.

Many of these households differ only in detail. Parents may live with sons, all or only some of whom are married. One or all the brothers in the same households may be married. But together they clearly show the emphasis on virilocal settlement, and agnatic ties. Married daughters with their parents comprise a class of only 12 people in 3 households, and there are no sisters and their husbands living with brothers.

Widowed mothers make up the largest category of what can be called accretions to the core of the household; of 73 widows in the village, only 9 are living alone. Besides these, we find relatives such as unmarried, divorced or widowed siblings (where the parents are dead), widows of brother or father's brother, sister's son, wife's mother, and widowed father. The majority of households having a

[1] I use the word 'parental' rather than 'natal' to cover cases of adoption (always of males) where the adoptor's would be the parental, but not the natal, house or village; also included are cases where parents have moved to another village after the birth of the person concerned.

TABLE 3

Household	Population	Number
1. Parents and their children*	329	74
2. Parents and their child(ren) and husband's widowed mother	91	18
3. Parents and their child(ren) and married son(s) with wive(s) and child(ren)	44	6
4. Parents and their child(ren) and married son(s) with wive(s)	30	4
5. Brothers, their wives and children	30	4
6. Brothers, one married with children, other(s) unmarried or without wives with them	29	5
7. Brothers, their wives and children and widowed mother	24	3
8. Parents with married son(s) with wive(s) and child(ren)	23	3
9. Widower and his child(ren)	18	7
10. Husband and wife with husband's widowed mother	18	6
Total	636	130

* 'Children' includes those who are married, but whose marriage has not been consummated (a fact that does not make the marriage incomplete) and who have not gone to live permanently with their husbands, or had their wives come to them.

pair of spouses do not include such people; 102 households with 488 people do not have them, against the 60 households and 339 people containing them. This, of course, is because one-third of the populace live in households composed of the elementary family. And lest it be thought that these households are formed through death or emigration of other members, I must stress that the heads of 47 of the 74 households (containing 207 of the 329 people) have brothers in the village with whom they were at one time jointly organized. It is only a minority of 17 households (77 members) who are without any agnates at all, since a further 10 household heads (45 members) have the father's brother's son also in the village, with whom there might have been a joint family household had there not been a division in the previous generation. This underlines the importance of the simple elementary family household, as well as that of family divisions.

The household organization of men above eighteen years is, in fact, one of two types.[1] First, the simple household, where only one

[1] Women play a part in household activities and policy, but households are distinguished externally by the males therein, and these have at least outwardly the controlling say in the household. In the proportion between different kinds

man resides; second, the joint household, where there is more than one man and where incomes and expenses are pooled. The figures for the two categories are:

TABLE 4

Category		Number	
		Household	Adult Men
Simple Household		139	139
Joint Household		46	113
	Total	185	252

One cannot correlate joint household organization with possession of land, which is best if worked together by kinsmen. True, Farmers tend to remain in joint households, and even if these divide may continue to farm the land jointly. But Rajputs divide both the property and the household when they split, and appear to do so more often than Farmers, though possessing more land per head. It is the attitude towards the land, rather than its mere possession, which is significant here. For Farmers are true husbandmen, whereas Rajputs look on land more as a source of wealth only. Again, the largely landless Bhilalas divide households a great deal, whereas the Tanners, with the least land per capita in the village, have a fair amount of joint organization, perhaps because a common craft keeps them together. I hope to analyse this position in greater detail elsewhere.

Few joint households have a complex structure. In only one case were there more than two generations of adult males together:

TABLE 5

Household Type		Number	
		Household	Adult Men
Father and son(s)		26	64
Brothers		19	43
Father, son(s) and grandson(s)		1	6
	Total	46	113

of households, then, only males have been taken. There are 11 households, containing 21 people, which do not contain any adult male; and these have been omitted for simplicity's sake. They number 3 per cent. of the village's population.

181

The position in the most complex of the households is this:

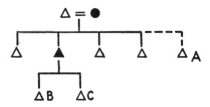

And since the time of research, I learn that B and C have formed their own joint household, and so the structure has again been simplified. The relation of brother A to the household is that he lives in a separate house but continues to have a share in the property which is held jointly by all the men shown. Here one must distinguish the joint household from the joint family. The latter is a corporate property group of patrikin, not necessarily a discrete living unit. There are 14 cases where brothers share the land and farm it together, yet reside separately and divide the crops. Again, 5 households containing 5 adult men of Ramkheri have coparceners of the joint family who live outside the village, yet retain their share in the joint property, which is run on their behalf by relatives in Ramkheri. The corporate kin-group may not always coincide with the corporate residential group. But one does not find very large joint families whose members have split into many separate households, for usually the division of the household is the occasion for a division of property too.

This review of the internal structure of the caste has indicated that there are well-defined groups at the 'top' and 'bottom' of the scale, but that the middle reaches are less clearcut. Everyone knows to what subcaste and clan he belongs, and everyone is definite about his affiliations to the property group, the household, and the patrikin within his village. Membership of the clan implies certain rules of behaviour (e.g. in marriage regulations); and people know their rights and obligations as collaterals in the small kin-groups. But the extent and operations of the lineage are ill-defined. The terms used are imprecise; recognition is governed by such changing factors as patterns of settlement; and the obligations towards lineage mates, as I have hinted, can be varied in specific circumstances (see p. 250). Again, the kindred is a group which, by definition, changes from person to person, and thereby allows opportunities for manipulation by the individual.

This lack of a structure of descent groups of 'middle range' is one factor in the relative isolation in their separate villages of the subcaste populations. Inter-village subcaste gatherings are held mostly on the basis of the individual's kin ties; and we shall see that there are few cases where the subcaste in settlements of the surrounding countryside has a well-defined organization. This contrasts with accounts given for the local organization of groups with well-defined lineages.[1] Within the village, the subcaste populations are for the most part of very simple kin structure, and the households and property holding groups also show a tendency towards containing no more than the elementary family. There are few complex and far-reaching kin-groups, then. And this means more chance for individual decisions about one's obligations to all but the nearest kin, and a greater dependence on impersonal factors such as money to fulfil them.

[1] E.g. both the local organization of the Pramalai Kallar and their descent system are much more clearcut than this picture from Malwa; and this cannot entirely be attributed to the fact that they inhabit *all* the villages of the surrounding area, but must also be connected with their system of clearly defined, named lineages (Dumont 1957*a*: 167 seq.).

IX

THE PLACE OF THE UNILINEAL DESCENT GROUP

I HAVE described clan affiliations as being known to everyone and as quite exclusive, in contrast to the more indefinite membership of the shallower descent group, the lineage. On the other hand, no activities take place at clan gatherings, whereas the lineage, being of local extension, tends to have co-operation amongst members and even to be itself defined through this co-operation. The differences between these two levels of unilineal descent is clearly shown in the religious sphere, in the pattern of worship of the Clan Goddess (*Kul Mata*) and the Bheru, deities of the clan and lineage respectively.

CLAN GODDESS WORSHIP

Worship of the Clan Goddess is a test of common clan membership even more than the clan name. A stranger can easily say he is a member of X- clan; but it was said to be a much more serious matter for him to claim that he worships the same Clan Goddess, and actually to do so.[1] In practice he will not be allowed to worship with clan mates in the village to which he has come until they are satisfied that his credentials are in order, through the existence of mutual kin or the guarantee of someone they trust.

The Clan Goddess is worshipped on one of the nine days before the festival of Dasahra, in September–October.[2] The image of the Clan Goddess, if this exists, is placed on a wood stand (*patli*) and all who are qualified then worship her with food and fire. Afterwards, sweet offerings (*parsad*) are eaten in honour of the occasion. The significance of the rite in Ramkheri consists for us in the people who participate, and in the degree to which it is exclusive to them.

To start with, all male agnates (married or widowed or bachelors) are expected to worship their Clan Goddess. A man adopted from

---

[1] This is duplicated elsewhere. Karve, for example, tells of the Maratha *Devkar* (an artefact or a living symbol) whose worship, more than the common clan name, precludes intermarriage (1953: 157).

[2] I have described the public rites of the Ninth Day (p. 99 seq.). There is no correlation between the status of the caste of the clan and the day on which it worships the Clan Goddess. Both high and low participate on the same days, notably the seventh, eighth and ninth.

184

any but a collateral branch will not usually worship. A villager told me that he did not worship his mother's brother's Clan Goddess, though he had been adopted into that clan. He let his mother worship, and when she died would bury the image so that it would require no ritual. In another instance, a man said he lit a fire in his house and performed a short rite to his father's sister's husband's Clan Goddess; for he had been adopted by this relative, who had lived in Ramkheri. But then he went to the house of his natal clan group and did the 'proper' worship there. Occasionally, it was said, a man might worship his adoptive Clan Goddess when all the collateral agnates were dead. But whilst they were alive he would only make an act of private supplication if he were in trouble, saying 'Oh *Mata*, I have come to your line (*kul*), please help me now.' This he would not mention to the clansmen, lest they beat him for such an intrusion into clan affairs.

There are two attitudes towards worship of men who have married women of the clan. Some clans (e.g. Detlya clan of the Farmers) maintain that since these men are not members of the wife's natal clan, they should not be allowed to worship, or even to see the worship. Others point to the fact that the man worships the Mother Goddess (*Mai Mata*) in the house of his wife at the time of marriage. People in general are not clear as to the precise difference between the Clan Goddess and the Mother Goddess, saying that both are 'goddesses of the house'. And some clans therefore maintain that the son-in-law can worship the former, since he has worshipped the latter. The issue crops up rarely. For the man will seldom be at his wife's parental village at the time of the festival. Men who have settled permanently in their conjugal village continue to worship their own Clan Goddess.

The main occasion of a woman's connection with her conjugal clan's Goddess is the worship by a wife in her husband's village at the first festival after their marriage. I was told by a Rajput that the couple go before the image or drawing of the Goddess together, the girl bows down before it with her face veiled, and touches the ground with her forehead. Only after this will the men of the clan group worship. This obeisance does not make the marriage complete (this has already occurred in the wedding ceremonies), but it does give the woman her proper status in the conjugal house. After that time, women may or may not worship the Clan Goddess each year. If the girl has been married before puberty, she will not come again to her conjugal house specifically to worship the Clan Goddess. But after she starts to live permanently in the household, she will usually be present each year; sometimes the men only will worship, sometimes the women join in.

The Place of the Unilineal Descent Group

The connection of a woman to her natal Clan Goddess varies. Some clans (e.g. Bhensaudia clan of Malwi Carpenters) allow girls to worship her; others say that, because the girl will eventually worship the Clan Goddess of her husband, she should not be allowed to worship any other, though she may witness the rite (e.g. Narbal clan of Rathor Oil-presser). Yet others (e.g. Detlya clan of Farmers) do not allow girls of the clan even to witness the worship. Again, there is a variation in the status of women who have made a re-marriage. Some (e.g. Rajputs and some Farmer clans) will not allow such a woman to worship the Clan Goddess of her second husband until she has borne him a son; others (e.g. Bhilalas and other Farmer clans) will allow her to worship from the time of her remarriage. Again, Rajputs do not allow a woman whose ancestry is 'unequal' [1] to worship her conjugal Clan Goddess.

Analysis shows a luxuriant variation of procedure between castes, subcastes and even different clans of a subcaste. And there is no certainty that clan members in different areas would conform to the rules I have noted. There are nevertheless a few general features. The personnel eligible to worship the Clan Goddess is clearly defined either agnatically, or by being closely related to agnates. In all cases the woman at marriage transfers her main worship to her husband's Goddess. And, indeed, she never formally renounces her right to worship. If she deserts her husband or is cast out by him, her right only lapses without any ceremony to end it.

This limitation of personnel is reinforced by other features. The rite is secret, for example, not only from members of other castes but also from non-qualified people of the same subcaste.[2] Any offering which is left over, and any ashes from the fire of worship, are buried lest they fall into the hands of outsiders. Again, differences in the Clan Goddess worshipped, and the wood of the platform on which she is placed,[3] also distinguish both subcastes and the clans within them.

The name of their Goddess is known to many clansmen. For instance, the Balecha Chauhan Rajputs worship Annpurna Mata, the Vagela Solanki Rajputs have Kimach (? Kamaksha) Mata, and the Ranawat Sisodia Rajputs Annpurna Mata as their deities. Many people, on the other hand, have forgotten the name of their Goddess

[1] I discuss this term later. It refers to a physical or moral defect in the girl or her proximate ancestors.

[2] Again, there is an exception; for the Gurarya clan of Farmers performs the rite on the doorstep, where anyone can see it.

[3] A few Farmer clans say they put the Clan Goddess on a turban, and a Tailor clan worships her on a red cloth. I am not able to say whether this is because they have always done this, or whether, at one time, the type of wood to be used was forgotten or disregarded.

and call her by the number of the day on which she is worshipped; thus Satam Mata or Atam Mata are worshipped on the seventh and eighth days of the festival respectively. Such people could if they wished learn the name of the Goddess from their genealogist, for he has this inscribed at the beginning of the clan's history.

The wood from which the platform is made is sacred for each clan, and must never be burnt by its members.[1] This is in addition to the wood of the *pipul* and *nim* trees, which no one should burn. The Vagela Solanki Rajput, for example, has his platform of *kankra* wood; the Balecha Chauhan and Ranawat Sisodia Rajputs have the same Clan Goddess, but the platform is different, being mango and *sevan* wood respectively. Sometimes the same wood is used by different clans, and sometimes the Goddess is the same; but it is believed that the combination of Goddess and platform wood is not duplicated.[2]

The commonest reason people gave for not knowing the name of their Clan Goddess or the wood of her platform was that there was no image of the Goddess in the village.[3] There is then no need for a platform, for the worship takes a different form. An auspicious pattern (*cauk*) is drawn with flour on a newly cleaned floor, and worship is made there in the name of the Goddess. Some men said they mentioned their clan and village as they worshipped, but others said that this was not necessary. There is no bar to purchasing an image of the appropriate Goddess, but nobody had done this to my knowledge.

Lack of an image, besides curtailing the rites, also militates against their corporate nature. For besides identifying the clan, the Goddess should be the focus of joint worship by the clan membership. Ideally, all clan members should worship together in the house of the senior man. Thus, the Rajputs in Ramkheri belong in the main to two clans, and each of the clan groups comes together at the house of the first man of the senior branch (see p. 176), which is known as the 'big house'. But this is the pattern of a minority only. Forty-eight men gathered from different households for joint worship, whereas seventy-two clansmen who could have done so worshipped separately in their own houses.[4] There are several cases (e.g. the Narbal clan

[1] People who do not know of which wood the platform is made cannot, of course, observe this prohibition, and are apparently undeterred from burning any wood by their ignorance.

[2] The forms of worship are probably different among clans (see Fuchs 1950: 237–53 for details of variations in different Balahi clans).

[3] Images were described as either three-dimensional figures, or as outlines on a plaque. They were usually said to be of silver rather than gold. Because of the secrecy surrounding the Goddess, I was not able to see an image.

[4] I do not include joint worship by men in a joint household, for this represents no departure from their daily routine.

of the Rathor Oil-pressers) where the change from corporate to individual rites has taken place in the last decade. In three cases an almost identical tale was told of the theft of the image; and this suggests a formal rationalization of the trend, since the absence of the image need not in theory stop corporate worship. Another reason given is that the people of the big house are unwilling to have the expense of feeding agnates from other households after the ritual. In those clans where corporate worship continues, there is clear knowledge about which is the big house, since the image is handed down by one incumbent of the big house to another. But in others, the big house has often been equated to me with the house of the eldest or most influential man of the present clan group. When there is no corporate activity depending on the primacy of this senior line, such a confusion may easily exist. It means that people of a village's clan population tend to see their relationships less in genealogical terms, and more in terms of present age or importance.

The pattern of worship of the Clan Goddess is of the kind to be expected in a widely dispersed clan. The Goddess represents a clan population whose corporate worship is physically impossible, and there is instead worship attended by no more people than are bound most closely with ties of descent and common residence. I have no record of any corporate worship by the clansmen of several nearby villages, that is, Clan Goddess worship is not made by the lineage of co-operation. Nor did I hear of any place central to the clan (e.g. a place of origin or first settlement in the province) where a wider worship might be held. At present, even the corporate worship by the small clan populations of each village is less and less carried out. But this does not affect the significance of the Clan Goddess, in providing a validation of clan membership of each member individually which is not necessarily linked to a larger, local group of clansmen. This contrasts with the pattern of the Bheru cult, to which I now turn.

BHERU WORSHIP

Bheru [1] is a ferocious aspect of the god Siva. Ramkheri people say that he is the son of Siva, born from Parvati his wife. The true son is 'fair' (*gora*) Bheru. But one day, it is said, Parvati called for Bheru and not finding him rubbed her skin; with the dust that came off it another son was created, known as 'dark' (*kala*) Bheru.[2] Each person

---

[1] This spelling of Bhairav is the transliteration of that used by Ramkheri people.

[2] Carstairs (1957: 93) says that in a Rajasthani village *kala* Bheru required blood sacrifice whereas *gora* Bheru abhorred this; I do not know if such a distinction exists in Ramkheri. Worship of Bheru is widespread in northern

owes allegiance to either fair or dark Bheru, but not to both. Dark Bheru is thought to be the more powerful, but people can otherwise tell of no difference between the two; many, in fact, say they do not know why there are two kinds of Bheru. 'Bheru is one.' they say, 'fair and dark aspects do not make any change in him.' Some go so far as to assert that the aspect of Bheru depends on the desires of the worshipper; if he asks for family prosperity and wealth, he will address fair Bheru; but if he wishes profit from theft or wants to gain power over others, he will be heeded by dark Bheru. This, however, seems to be no more than an attempted explanation for the differen: Bherus, and conflicts with the exclusive allegiance of every man to one or other aspect, as expressed in his genealogy.

Bheru's most important function is to protect and make prosper those who acknowledge his power. (His duty as guardian of wells is an aspect of this general contribution to the prosperity of farmers.) This acknowledgement is made most importantly at an annual ceremony on the full-moon day of Asarh month. It can also be made on any of the dark-night days which happen to fall on a Monday (*somvati amavasya*), Monday being Siva's day. In fact, such days are only made the occasion for rites when there is a special reason —e.g. the Ramkheri people held a village-wide worship on one such Monday in 1956, in gratitude at their deliverance from a cattle epidemic the previous year.

The physical manifestation of Bheru is a stone, or stones, painted with lead oxide. These often resemble the phallic representation of Siva, but there is no base to them, nor are they artificially shaped. Men are supposed to worship at the shrine established by members of the unilineal descent group. On one occasion a Gujarati Barber worshipped in this way. He went about two furlongs from the village, to the field in which his Bheru was, sat down and cleaned the twelve small stones with water and then freshly repainted them. Having stuck incense sticks at each side, he sprinkled the stones with puffed wheat and dried peas. Two small balls of unleavened bread were placed in front of the Bheru, and a coconut was broken on the largest of the stones. Pieces of coconut flesh were placed on eight of the stones, and the rite was over. The performer did not speak during his worship. He took home the rest of the coconut meat and gave it as *prasad* to his household. There are variations in content from this, but in general the rite is short, inexpensive and requires no priest. The only occasion when more complicated arrangements are needed is when a vow to Bheru is fulfilled. Some fathers promise

India. In some places he has an anthropomorphic form; in other places he is known as Khetṛpal (guardian of the fields), but this was not mentioned to me in Ramkheri (see Rose 1919: 317–18).

the god that they will not shave their son's hair until after his fifth year, when they will worship Bheru in return for his protection of the boy. Such a rite includes the sacrifice of a goat, for carnivorous castes, and a greater expense of other materials too.

I have said that the kind of Bheru a man has is written in his genealogy. In addition, he has a territorial link with Bheru, for his main Bheru image (*khas Bheru*) exists in a village whose name is also noted in the records and which is, in theory at least, the place of origin of his clan. We see, then, that Bheru is a deity almost entirely undifferentiated by clan (for there is only a single division of fair or dark) but instead distinct in terms of location. This contrasts with the pattern for the Clan Goddess, which is highly differentiated for each clan, but which has no territorial links. The Bheru rite is only correctly performed in front of the main Bheru, or one of the 'copy' (*namuna*) Bherus. But if there is no image, a truncated rite is made; no coconut is broken, and there is only a fire rite.

The spread and migration of clans makes it inevitable that very few people worship Bheru at the place named by the genealogist. If a family moves very far away, it will either have to content itself with a substitute rite each year, or will have to set up another shrine. Only in rare cases is the main Bheru ever said to have been moved with the family; as one man said, 'It hurts Bheru to be moved.' In one genealogist's book the phrase occurs 'X family came from Mewara, bearing the Bheru in a cart'. But this is said to refer to an emigration of the whole subcaste from one region to another, in 1100 Vikram era (A.D. 1044). If only one group of households emigrates, the people remaining will continue to minister to the shrine, and no physical transfer will be necessary.

The time taken before a substitute Bheru is set up by emigrants in the village where they have settled varies greatly. One clan group moved only four miles to Ramkheri, and set up a separate Bheru during the second generation (no special ceremony is required to do this). But another descent group had been living in the village for 'a great many generations' (more than four) and had not started its own shrine, though the former one was at the same distance. On the whole, the new Bheru appears to be started after three to four generations have died, and it is rare to find Bherus of more recent immigrants. This is a significant period, for it occurs shortly after the time when the memory of the oldest man who can recall the move is extinct. Further, it roughly coincides with the unilineal depth at which social relations between the agnates in these two villages are frequently ended—that is, it tends to occur at the time when the lineage of co-operation expands into the lineage of recognition. Thirteen descent groups at present living in Ramkheri have a Bheru within the village boundaries. Some are in the village itself, others in nearby fields. Of these, ten were included in the headman's round of annual obeisance to village shrines as the village's representative (see p. 102), the remainder having been forgotten (I do not think there is any other significance in this omission).

The responsibility for worshipping a 'copy' Bheru falls on the descendants of the persons who set it up. That is, it is a lineage responsibility. In theory, perhaps, any clansman would have this duty, since the shrine is ultimately a copy of the clan Bheru, but in practice this does not happen. Thus, Bheru worship is differentiated by its local definition at the lineage level, whereas Clan Goddess worship is a matter for the individual, since it has no local shrines.

But Bheru is the same for all clans and castes; he is a god who can be invoked to guard the descent group, but he does not himself define the descent group, as is the case with the Clan Goddess and her exclusive attributes. Hence, there is not such stress placed on the worship of Bheru exclusively by all agnates. Men worship the Bheru of their adopted father (if this differs from their natal Bheru) whereas they seldom worship their adoptive Clan Goddess. Again, whereas every male of the household or clan group worships the Clan Goddess (including babes in arms), a single male may perform the Bheru ritual on behalf of all his agnates, whether they are living in the same household or are scattered around the village. Neither do I know of any case in Ramkheri of a lineage group worshipping Bheru together. Further, people may also worship other gods on the same occasion; the Barber mentioned above went to the shrines of Hanuman and Adyapal Maharaj after he had worshipped his Bheru. He regarded the day as one of homage to all deities of protection (others worshipped Sakti Mata and the Muslim saint's tomb in the village). Occasionally, a particular Bheru may be acknowledged as particularly efficacious, and people of other castes may worship there, though this is not their responsibility as descendants of previous worshippers of course. A Rajput told me how he had been sitting up through the night of Divali, singing *hir* songs, when over the meadow he had seen a light dancing on the Bheru of the village barber. He knew then that it was an especially strong Bheru, and could have worshipped there had he wished. This would be absolutely prohibited, of course, with the Clan Goddess, whose worship cannot even be witnessed by other clan members, though these are of the same subcaste.

Few people ever return to the place where the former copy of Bheru exists. Though all people can tell one the name of this village —it usually lies between twenty and thirty miles from Ramkheri— hardly anyone can say that he has ever been there for the rite, though some talk of the 'old days' when people gathered from several villages at the focal Bheru shrine.[1] People now assume that a collateral lineage still lives there and continues to minister to the shrine, but this may not always be the case. An example is provided by the Brahmans who were the headmen in Ramkheri before the Rajputs. These people had their Bheru in the village. But nobody had come to worship for at least 60 years, and there were no agnates in the village either. When some Brahmans did return to worship in expiation of a vow, it was in ignorance of the location of the shrine, and only through the memory of the Ramkheri elders did they learn where it was. In such circumstances, old Bheru shrines can drop out of circulation at the same time as new ones are created. Again, I was told by people of other villages possessing similarly abandoned shrines that when people returned to worship it was not on the Asarh Punam day, as members of the lineage, but rather in fulfilment of vows about their children, and so in connection with individual not lineage purposes.

Though joint worship of the Clan Goddess and of Bheru is ideally different—one being by any clansmen who are neighbours, and the other by all the people of a lineage in a given locality—in practice the worship of both deities usually now concerns the individual villager only. In fact, the Clan Goddess attracts more of what joint worship there is, through her demand to be worshipped by every member, whereas the Bheru shrine has lost its efficacy as a centre for agnates of the locality (if it ever possessed it) and has not gained any compensating position as a centre of corporate worship in individual villages. Nevertheless, there still remains the difference that though both deities are concerned with unilineal descent groups, the Clan Goddess stands for the clan and the Bheru for the lineage—e.g. any member of the Balecha Chauhan clan could in theory worship at the Chauhans' Goddess in Ramkheri; but he would not worship at the Ramkheri Chauhans' Bheru shrine, for his Bheru would be in some other village, and he would either owe allegiance to that shrine or would set up a copy shrine of his own in Ramkheri.[2] As I have said, a man coming to Malwa from Delhi would be accepted as a member of a particular clan, with duties towards the Clan Goddess;

[1] I cannot say how far these gatherings actually occurred in the nineteenth century; it was notable that only the oldest men said they had ever been to another village to worship Bheru.

[2] The Clan Goddess and Bheru cults can be compared with rites in other areas. Thus, the Persa Pen of the Raj Gonds is worshipped in specific places, like the Bheru, but at the same time is thought of as a clan deity, like the Clan Goddess (Fürer-Haimendorf 1948: 240 seq.). More comparative data is needed before we can assess in how far Bheru is primarily a god connected with locality (e.g. the worship at Bheru shrines by headmen on behalf of the village, and the role of Bheru as Guardian of Wells) as distinct from the role I have stressed, as a tutelary of lineages which are themselves localized.

192

but he would belong to no lineage in Malwa, and so would not share any of the Bheru shrines there.

Similar to the worship of Bheru is that of Sati Mata. When a woman immolates herself (*sati*) on the funeral pyre of her husband, a memorial is set up in the village, and worship is made to her as a goddess by members of her husband's clan. Partly this is worship of general homage and respect, partly it is for specific benefits, of which female fertility is important.

No Sati has occurred in Ramkheri since the incident of the Brahman headman's wife which I have recounted (see p. 18). But there are enough instances of immolation in recent times to keep the tradition alive. In 1951, for example, the wife of a senior Army officer became a Sati in Jodhpur. Several houses in Ramkheri were decorated with coloured lithographs portraying this scene. In them the wife sits on the pyre, her husband lying with his head in her lap. Around is a vast crowd, among whom can be distinguished minor gods such as Ram Deoji Maharaj, and leaders such as Pandit Nehru. Again, a few years ago, an Oil-presser woman in a town some twenty-five miles to the north of Ramkheri prophesied that her husband would die on a certain date, and that she would become a Sati. News went round the province, and a large crowd gathered on the day. A family of Farmers went from Ramkheri, and described the size of the gathering by saying that the villagers were selling glasses of water for four annas each. The husband did not, in fact, die; the crowd had to return home, but belief in Sati was not, of course, diminished by this.

There are two Sati memorials in Ramkheri, for a Brahman and a Weaver. The latter is worshipped by Weavers like a Bheru shrine, and is repainted each year. There is no fixed date for the Sati rite, and it frequently takes place at the same time as Bheru is worshipped. Every clan is thought to have a Sati in its history; the location is known by the genealogist, and is one of the distinguishing features of the clan. But there is no need to make annual worship if one is not at the place of the shrine, and shrines are not copied in different villages like they are for Bheru. In contrast to the rites of the Clan Goddess, worship of Sati can be made publicly, and women of other clans and castes can also ask a Sati to cure their barrenness. Sati worship is a cult with a local basis even more marked than for Bheru, and a correspondingly lesser theoretical amount of participation by agnates.

A man dying a violent death is commemorated by his agnates through the institution of a *Paliya*—a stone which, like Bheru and

Sati, is painted red, and before which an annual rite is performed to propitiate the spirit of the dead person. The Paliya can be set up on the spot where a man died; thus, a Weaver youth was gored to death by a buffalo in the fields, and his Paliya is there. Or it can be instituted in the village, as in the case of a Mina who was killed in a fight in the fields, but whose Paliya is in the ward in which he lived.

There are four Paliyas in Ramkheri; two have just been mentioned, and the others are of a Bhilala who was shot to death in a brawl, and of a Rajput headman who was killed many years ago because of a dispute with a neighbouring village. At that time the people of the other village were cultivating lands claimed by Ramkheri people to be within their village's boundaries. There had been several fights, but these had simmered down into a wary truce between the headmen of each village. At the same time an issue arose about the State boundaries between the Dewas Senior Maharaja and a powerful landlord in neighbouring Gwalior territory. These notables asked the Ramkheri headman to come and help settle the matter. His way to the spot lay through the rival village's land, and as he crossed the Ramkheri boundary the enemy headman, deciding that he had broken the truce, shot him. His Paliya stands in the main square of Ramkheri, and men of his descent group perform a small rite there annually. These deaths are only commemorated at the Paliya itself, are not incorporated into clan history by the genealogist, and so concern fellow-agnates of the dead man only as long as they live in the same village. If they move, the Paliya may well be forgotten, for it is not transferable to another village. The village headmen may continue to include it on their annual round of village shrines, but it may lose its identity, and even be given another name if enquiries are made. Several shrines now visited by the headmen were not given the same names by them all.

There are other rites reserved for clansmen besides those I have described. But these are only parts of wider agnatic responsibilities in a larger kinship ritual. Thus, the worship of the Clan Goddess at a wedding is only part of the activities of the spouse's agnates. I shall therefore mention these rites during the later discussion of the ritual aspect of kinship.

FUNCTIONS OF THE GENEALOGIST

The genealogist has appeared frequently in this account as one who maintains the essential knowledge of the Clan Goddess, the Bheru, and the more remote patrikin, without which the pattern of descent could not exist in its present form. More detailed account of the work of these men is based, first, on the things told me by the people of

Ramkheri about their genealogists and, second, the information given me by genealogists serving Farmers, Rajputs and Carpenters.

Genealogists (generally known as *bhat*) form amongst themselves a microcosm of the wider society. To a considerable extent they are divided commensally and endogamously by the status of the castes they serve. Thus, the Farmers' genealogist said he was descended from Brahmans; there were a dozen or so clans, of which only one had the right to practise the profession of genealogist. These clans neither ate nor married with any other kind of genealogist, nor did they eat from any caste save their Farmer patrons (*jajman* or *battandar*). Again, the genealogist of the Rajputs maintained that he was not called a *bhat*, but was a higher grade genealogist, known as a *barva* or *raoji*. There were forty-six clans of Rajputs' genealogists which formed an endogamous unit, eating from Rajputs and a few other genealogists. He estimated that a quarter of the members were carrying on their traditional work, and that the remainder were now farmers. In general, the genealogist ranks lower than his patron; the latter will eat only *pakka* food from his hands, whereas he will take *kacca* food when visiting the villages. There are said to be genealogists of the genealogists, who are similarly placed. The Warriors' genealogist said there were three links—i.e. the genealogist of a genealogist of a genealogist did not himself have a genealogist; presumably he keeps his own records![1]

In many cases a clan of genealogists will have a single subcaste as patrons. Thus, I was told that the Darshana clan of the endogamous Bhuma division of genealogists serves the Mewara Carpenter subcaste only. About 15 per cent. of genealogists' clans were said to serve more than one subcaste. All clans of a subcaste are served within a given area. The right to this work is heritable property (*jaydad*), and the areas are sometimes divided in a family partition if more than one brother wishes to follow the traditional occupation. Often, however, some of the brothers take to farming, and let one or two trained men carry on the genealogies.

There are exceptions to this pattern of division. The Farmers are a localized caste, and have four genealogists each of whom covers the entire caste, it is said. There may be an informal division of the area by each genealogist family, but there is no formal arrangement for division into sectors. Again, the Rajputs' genealogist maintained that, though the original division of patrons was on a territorial basis, a man was now the permanent patron of a certain genealogist and did not pass into the records of another if he changed his residence. He cited as example the case of the Dewas Maharajas. As Ponwar Rajputs they had had genealogists in Malwa before they emigrated

[1] See Dave 1951: 171.

195

to Maharashtra. The great-great-grandfather of the first Maharaja of Dewas Senior was granted the headmanship of the Maharashtrian village of Supa by Sivaji. And this post is still held by the senior branch of the Maharaja's family. Though all notables live in Dewas, there are still descendants resident in Supa, and the genealogist has the right to visit them and register them in his records; their names cannot be inscribed in a more conveniently placed genealogist's books.

Genealogical records take either of two forms. One stresses the local groupings, and the other the ties of descent. The records of the Mewara Carpenters' genealogist provide an example of the former; and this was the pattern for most of the subcastes I knew about (e.g. Rajput, Malwi Weaver, Malwi Potter, Rajguri Nath, Purviya Tanner, etc.). The genealogies are enshrined in two thick books of perhaps 400 foolscap pages. They are divided into a section for each clan. At the start, the name of the clan is followed by the names of the Clan Goddess, the wood of her platform, and details of the way her worship is to be made. The name and original site of the Bheru is then given, and the time and place of any Sati. Then come the date and place of the clan's arrival in Malwa, together with the name(s) of the kings under whose protection members settled. An abbreviated genealogy of the most ancient ancestors of the clan in Malwa follows. In this book, thirteen generations were given, stemming from three brothers. Not all agnates were included, only the eldest sons; they formed three large paragraphs, and took up about two pages of the book.

Lastly comes the real substance of the genealogy—the account dealing with up to the eighth to the tenth ascending generation from the present. This is organized by villages. Under each village's name are written all the names of clan members residing there, with the names of their wives, wives' fathers and their villages and clans. Marriage with the wife's close clan mates is prohibited, and her clan and village names are presumably recorded in case the patron or his descendants forget them. A note is made if a man leaves the village, and his name is added to the records of the new village, with a cross-reference to his former settlement. The occasions of the genealogist's visits are also written down, with the names of the village headman of the time, and details of any large gifts (*bidagari*). In former days, it is said, he was given presents in kind—a horse or a cow—but now cash is paid. There is also an occasional note of those in whose presence the genealogy was read (this, I suspect, is when a larger payment is made).

The type of organization in which there is more emphasis on descent is provided by the Farmers' register. Here, again, the books are divided into sections for each clan, at the beginning of which come details of the Clan Goddess, Bheru, etc., and a short genealogical résumé of the first members of the clan. The account differs when it deals with recent descent links. For the agnatic progression is followed through without regard for the particular place in which individuals happen to be living. The names of the villages which are and have been inhabited by the members named are written at the top of each page; but if a man transfers from village A- to village B-, his place in the book does not change. There is a note that he has moved, but the agnatic line, and his place in it, is the major consideration. Again, only the names of men are given; there are no details of the wife's name, her clan and village, though the Farmer system of exogamy is the same as that of other castes.

The difference in the organization of the books is significant. One emphasizes descent at the expense of territorial segmentation; and that this is in the Farmers' book is because the caste has a small territorial compass, so that the genealogist can cover the entire caste. He need therefore take little notice of village, since no Farmer moves out of his territory by change of residence. The Carpenters' genealogist, on the other hand, has a definite section of the subcaste's territory to cover,[1] and if the people move out of it, they move into another genealogist's records. Further, any division of the work among heirs is made on a territorial basis, and is easier to make if the genealogies are already arranged by villages.

Another consideration stresses the similarity of the books. In particular, both have the 'gap' between the accounts of the earliest genealogies, and the present records of the much nearer past. Each book has the early history in a standardized form, and when genealogists divide up a district, these are copied into the new books. But no descent ties can be traced between the last names in these accounts and the first names in the recent genealogies which, as I have said, go back up to ten generations, or some 250 years. It is not, in fact, true to say that the genealogist can trace the relationships between any pair of men of a specific clan, as many villagers believe. But he *can* trace the links within what I have called the lineage of recognition.

The process by which this genealogical gap is created is as follows. A book when new consists of the initial clan history and genealogical summary, after which sections for each village are left blank, save for the most recent names to have been inscribed in the previous book. Slowly, each blank section gets filled up until, after about ten generations, the spaces are complete (and where a village has had an exceptionally rapid increase of the clan, extra pages may have to be

[1] It included the districts of Sonkachch, Dewas, Indore, Ujjain, Ratlam, Mandsaur and Jhabua—an area of about eighty miles square.

stuck in). When the book is full, a new one is prepared and the process starts again. One book I saw was at this stage; it was crammed, with names added in the margins and between the lines. The genealogist was writing a new book, but had delayed this arduous task as long as possible.

The old books are seldom used for more than several generations after the new book is in operation. And they are obsolete by the time the new book is half full. In some cases, it is said, the old books are 'cooled' by being ceremonially sunk in a lake, but in other cases they hang around the house and gradually fall to pieces through the attrition of time and the attentions of small children and vermin. The current books, on the other hand, are greatly treasured; they constitute the genealogist's livelihood, and he will never be parted from them, nor will he open them lightly and without due payment. In only one case are the old books not put aside. The genealogies of noble families are maintained without gaps, as well as being recorded in considerably greater detail. The genealogy of the Maharaja of Dewas Senior, for example, takes up an entire register, and all major events in the lives of each Ruler are recorded.

The reason for this disregard of the older books will be clear when we consider the purpose for which the genealogies are used. One is in connection with inheritance problems. If, say, a man dies without issue, with his wife and parents both dead, and without near collaterals (to list the immediate heirs in order), the claimants for his property may then be related through more than two or three ascending generations, and the actual relationships be open to doubt. The genealogist will then be called to the court, to say whose tie is the closer; his evidence is assumed to be correct by the judges unless specific proof to the contrary can be brought.

A similar function exists over marriage rules. As I shall describe, a person cannot marry into several other clans, and the prospective spouses may not be able to recall their names. A genealogist should then be consulted, though this may not always be done. It is interesting to note that, as I was told, a genealogist does not knowingly enter any irregularities (*aib*) in his book. If, say, a marriage is made with a man who has the blood of a forbidden clan, the genealogist will refuse to enter this in his book. Whether this rule is evaded, it is impossible to say; but it means that genealogies cannot be consulted to see if any person's ancestry is 'irregular'. Legal enquiries about inheritance and marriage do not concern ancestors of even up to eight or ten generations, say the genealogists; and since 'the people often do not even know the names of their grandfathers', their own enquiries will not go so deep. Hence, the old genealogies can be 'cooled'.

The second purpose of the genealogy is to keep green the memory of the ancestors, and to enhance the reputations of the living members of the clan. The frequency of the genealogist's visits varies. The Farmers' genealogists appear to come most often, every two or three years; others, on the other hand, serving widely scattered subcastes, visit less regularly and may arrive in Ramkheri every five or even ten years. A death in the genealogist's family may also postpone the visits. In a village of Ramkheri's size there are visits by half a dozen genealogists each year, mostly during the hot season; for travel is easier, and people are less occupied with farmwork and can more easily entertain such a guest.

The main part of the genealogist's work is the entering of new names in the register, and an important subsidiary is the reading of the clan's history. The genealogist of a small clan group may stay only a single night, accepting payment of about Rs. 5 (laid on the book as a mark of respect, rather than given directly to the genealogist) for each name. Next morning he will mount his horse, his books tied on the saddle behind him, and ride to the next village. If the caste group is large, the genealogist may stay a week or two. Each day he will visit a different household; and after entering new names, he will tell of the clan's history. This is partly taken from the data in the books, and partly from the general knowledge of the clans and the subcaste which is handed down from one genealogist to another. Clansmen may also ask him where there are representatives of their clan living in the area outside the immediate region and in this way add to their knowledge about more distant agnates. Genealogists may also tell stories from the classics, and such general tales as that of the Golden Age of Vikramaditya. Such recitations are bardic; but I have not called the speakers bards because their main function is the registration and exposition of genealogies. I would prefer to designate as bards those known as *caran*, who sing the exploits of the clan's famous men before the marriages of notables, mostly Rajputs. Such people have no books, and their work is purely to recite these laudatory lays.[1]

The visit of a genealogist is not always smooth. He may demand too much money to write the name. The Balecha Chauhan Rajputs were visited for the first time in seven years, and the genealogist asked for Rs. 100 to inscribe the name of the headman's son; this was refused, and the genealogies were not opened at this house. The position of the patron is an ambivalent one. On the one hand, the genealogist is the servant of the clan; he is considered to be slightly lower than they, and does them a service. But on the other hand, he has a specialized knowledge and his books are unique. His is really

1 Some writers have, however, called both *bhat* and *charan* 'bards' (Dave 1951: 168-9) though recognizing their different functions.

the more powerful position, for his refusal to inscribe the name means that the man will not live for his posterity.

This strikes at one of the most dearly held values of Ramkheri people. Not only prestige in this life (*ijjat*), but also fame in the future (*nam*) are important motives for action. Present prestige is a complex value, bound as it is with both the ideal patterns of behaviour, and with wealth which may be gained in ways far from prestigeful. In comparison, ways of gaining posthumous fame are simple. They include the performance of work of public, rather than private benefit (building rest-houses for pilgrims and guests to the village, constructing public wells on the roadside). Again, to have a large feast in honour of a dead agnate is a worthy act; it lives in the future for as long as the participants remember it. But these means are out of reach for all but the wealthy. The genealogist's register provides for the average man the only way in which he can exist for descendants who, though in practice they do not bother to worship specifically any but near ancestors, could in theory look up their ascendants in the genealogy, and honour them individually. Hence the importance of the inscription of one's name, and hence the respect which is given to the genealogist. People may say behind his back that he does not give them anything tangible in return for the presents they make him (in much the same way as they talk of the village priest); but they would not imply such a thing to his face and are concerned if there is any difficulty in getting the names of their progeny written down. For villagers believe that all clan members are traceable by the genealogists; and when their own name is written in the book, they imagine it will remain there forever.

The genealogist's work reflects the general influence of unilineal descent. His books clearly distinguish the clans, with their own Clan Goddess, tales of origin, etc.; and though he may seldom be questioned about forgotten clan affiliations at the time of marriage or, say, about details of the Clan Goddess worship, people are satisfied that these are known to someone, and I have constantly referred to this sustaining role. Below the clan, however, the emphasis is on shallow lines of descent. In most cases the organization of the books on local, rather than genealogical, lines makes it easy for villagers to keep in mind a lineage of recognition within a radius of some twenty or thirty miles of the village. (If the agnates are much further away, people will say that they are not of the *bhaibandh* but have 'gone into' the *gotra*.) In this way the genealogist's books help to define the descent group in a local region.

The *bhat* is the most important of the genealogists. But I must, in concluding, mention those genealogists who live at pilgrimage places, and are known as *gangagaur*. Ramkheri people make their Ganges pilgrimage mainly to a place called Soron, on the Mathura–Bareilly branch railway line. As soon as they change trains at Mathura, they are accosted by agents who ask them their subcaste and the place from whence they come. They direct the villagers to the appropriate *gangagaur*. He conducts their offerings to the ancestors and supervises their bathing and collection of Ganges water, which they take back to the village. Before they leave Soron, their names and family details are written in the *gangagaur's* book. He, in turn, tells them of all the visits which their ancestors have made. I was not able to see these books and do not know how they are organized; but there is no reason to doubt that if they are arranged by villages, the details of at least two or three generations are available. The rest may be concocted, as I have heard it said by townspeople, but the villager certainly does not believe this.

People told me that there are similar genealogists at Allahabad and Banaras, but nobody from Ramkheri has ever been there. Recently, a Rajput woman went to Badri Narain in the Himalayas, the first Ramkheri resident to make the pilgrimage. She said that the genealogist there asked about her family and the extent of its landholding (possibly with a practical view of his fee in mind) and wrote down these particulars, as well as a general note of the size, composition and headmen of Ramkheri; on parting, he asked her to send other Ramkheri pilgrims to him.

The offering of oblations to the ancestors is the major object of these pilgrimages, and explains why they are mainly undertaken by older people. In the last few years, several groups of young men between twenty and thirty years old have gone to Dwarka, on the coast of Kathiawad. As they put it, 'We go there because we can have a look at the sea; there are no *gangagaur* there, nor do we offer oblations (*pind*). But we are not yet interested in our journey to Rampura [e.g. Rama's abode, or heaven] like the old people who go to Soron.' Journeys to the latter place seem to occur every generation, and are made in large groups.[1] Some forty men and women went in 1944, and it is said that about eighty people went some thirty-five years ago. The pilgrim-genealogist is very rarely in contact with villagers, then. But he also provides a reflection of the unilineal structure of the society, since he is believed to have records of the agnates to whom worship is at the same time made.

[1] The exception is when a man goes to get Ganges water to use at the marriage of his child, in a ceremony giving extra prestige and merit.

X

THE PATTERN OF MARRIAGE

I HAVE drawn the picture of the territorial and genealogical extent to which agnatic ties link people. The spread of affinal relations and the resulting kin ties can be gauged from an analysis of the pattern of marriage. This includes both the criteria for selecting spouses, and the spatial distribution of affinal links that result.

CRITERIA OF SELECTION

There are three bases for match-making within the endogamous groups (most of which are the subcastes themselves). The first two are restrictive—the degrees of prohibited relationships, and the quality and reputation of the person's ancestry (*khandan*). The third is of a different order, being the pattern of marriages possible within these rules, given the restrictions imposed by the factors of demography and distance. There are no positive regulations about whom one should marry, and so the question of marriage alliance[1] does not enter the account.

It is generally agreed in Ramkheri that one should not marry a girl if any pair of the following eight clans are common—the boy's and the girl's natal clans, their mothers' natal clans, and both their maternal and paternal grandmothers' natal clans. But these prohibited limits are sometimes transgressed. It is impossible to assess how often this occurs, though I believe it is rare. Such information is not freely given, and the genealogies do not prove anything, since the clans of ascendants can be changed to hide any such correspondence. It seems clear, however, that more exception is taken to a correspondence of clans of the first ascending maternal generation (i.e. clans to which the subject is sister's child or *bhanej*) rather than to those of the second ascending generation (to which the subject is a sister's son's (or daughter's) child, or *tanej*). I have never, for example, found a case where the clans of which the pair were *bhanej* were the same; but cases have been cited where the *tanej* clan of one and the *bhanej* clan of the other, or the *tanej* clans of both, were identical.

It seems unlikely that such matches could happen unknown to the contracting parties (save in exceptional cases of orphans with no

---

[1] See Dumont 1957*b*: 24.

other near relatives). For, though some people do not know all their grandparents' natal clans, they need only have the names of their wife's and her and their mothers' natal clans for the marriages of their children, and these are almost always available, and are asked for by the prospective spouse's parents. The fact seems to be that not too many questions are posed if the marriage is especially necessary —as I was told, people do not wait for the genealogist to come round and give them the information, when this may take two or three years. Such matches usually take place between the very poor (who may not be able to find another mate) or the rich (where financial considerations are paramount). There is also a general shortage of girls, I was told (see p. 21), and the boy's family may often be tempted to simplify the rules of exogamy.

The marriage is not dissolved when such an irregularity is discovered, if the parties can show that it was unpremeditated. They are merely fined by their subcaste council and allowed to carry on. This indicates that marriage within the more distant prohibited clans is not the height of unforgivable behaviour. And there are a few cases known to some people in Ramkheri where no steps have been taken. Only the marriage of a couple from a single clan is held to be extremely grave; and I believe that anyone knowing of such a case, whether premeditated or not, would feel bound to bring it into the open. I heard of no such marriage; in one case parallel cousins became lovers, and they had to flee the village into distant anonymity.

Besides this 'four-clan rule'[1] a wider circle of kin is also forbidden to a prospective bride or groom. Traditionally, the *sapinda* rule prohibited marriage between people who could trace a common ancestor to the seventh inclusive generation on the male, and the fifth generation on the female side. In practice, however, the limits were set at the fifth and third generations respectively by many in India.[2] And this may contract still further in Ramkheri, for it is said that it is enough if no relationship can be recalled; and the memories of most people do not go beyond the second or third generation.

Though marriage is forbidden with, say, the daughter of the father's sister, it can take place with more distant members of the father's sister's husband's clan. The explanation given is that the father's sister (and mother's sister, etc.) have the same blood as one's parents, and so marriage is impossible with their daughters. This is inconsistent with the idea that the agnatic kin alone have blood in common. There are, in fact, two ideas about the blood line. The one is strictly agnatic, and in it the woman is merely 'the field in which the seed is sown' (the most frequent metaphor), giving nothing of

---

[1] See Karve 1953: 117–23.   [2] Trevelyan 1929: 46.

her own blood and qualities to the offspring. According to this theory, villagers say that the child looks like the person first seen by the woman immediately after conception (i.e. the husband, it is to be hoped)—the mother being in this way a passive recipient of outside influences. The other idea is that the line is a family matter, both parents contributing towards the procreation of a child.[1] But though Ramkheri people acknowledge that a tie exists between siblings of either sex and their children, they maintain that the matrilineal descent tie fades when it extends beyond the immediate group of kin. There is a proverb: 'The support of the milk is over, the support of the semen remains.' This applies to ties with the second descending generation; it shows that links through women are transitory, lasting only for the generation where the 'milk' has been in common, or is remembered—but that agnatic links through the progenitor endure. This means that only a limited group of closer cognates are debarred from marriages, and I have recorded instances where men have married into the clans of their father's brother's wife's brother, or father's sister's husband.

There is no rule which forbids marriage to affines, but matches with closer relatives by a close kinsfellow's marriage are discouraged. Thus, two brothers occasionally marry two sisters, or a brother and sister marry a pair of siblings.[2] The danger in the latter is that quarrels between one couple will spread to the other married pair, and so break up both families; and bad feeling between the two sisters can also estrange their husbands. The same danger exists in marriage with other near affines; e.g. in one case a man's brother's son married his wife's sister, and in another a man and his mother's

[1] The analogy of the seed and the field is very old (see Manu IX. 33). But at the same time, though the 'seed is declared to be more important' (IX. 35), Manu also writes (IX. 34) 'in some cases the seed is more distinguished, and in some the womb of the female; but when both are equal, the offspring is most highly esteemed' (quotations from Bühler 1886: 333). Hence, either theory can be held by the villagers of Ramkheri with traditional justification.

[2] In only one case did I find a three-link marriage, as shown in this diagram:

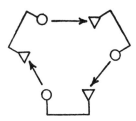

I have no examples of a four-link match as described by Hu (1956: 116–29).

brother married sisters. These matches are rare for social, rather than exogamous reasons.

Another limit to the selection of spouses is ancestry (*khandan*), the moral, physical, and sometimes economic state of their ascendants, and to a lesser extent of the parties themselves. Physical disabilities are called *aib*, and include epilepsy, leprosy, eye pupils turned white by smallpox, albinoism, and reverse or double hair whirls (*bhaunra*). A youth in Ramkheri over twenty years old had not married because his feet were deformed, having no instep and missing several toes. He came from a good family, with moderate wealth, but was faced with the choice of marriage with an inferior line or, what appeared likely, bachelorhood, for his elder brother refused to countenance the former course. The shade of the skin must also be approximately equal, for a very dark girl will be taunted by her affines at times of dispute.

Immaterial ancestral qualities include witchcraft—an involuntary power said to be inherited by a daughter from her mother, though not necessarily manifesting itself in successive generations. Other personal qualities are considered—the temperament of the prospective mother-in-law, signs of drunkenness or improvidence in the family, or positive qualities of thrift, good management and popularity in the village. The personalities of the candidates are not a major consideration; they are usually too young, it is said, to have sufficiently firm characteristics to be judged.

Finally, the ascendants are checked for evidence of an irregular match—outside the subcaste or with someone who himself had an 'unequal' ancestry, or a remarriage of either man or woman in those higher castes in which this is looked on as demeaning.[1] Some say that wealth is not a feature of ancestry, which is purely a matter of reputation, and there are instances of poor but reputable men making as good matches as people with more money but less prestige. Others maintain that ancestry does include economic position. But all would agree that wealth is extremely important, sometimes over-riding irregularities in ancestry. On the whole, people of more or less equal wealth will marry their offspring together. If there is any marked inequality the greater wealth will be on the boy's side. For if it were on the girl's, the boy's parents would have to give costlier jewels and organize a larger marriage party (*barat*) than they could afford; whereas a wealthier boy's parents do not mind having a small wedding, since they are gaining a girl in the process. This is a reason

---

[1] The *vivah*, or full marriage, can be made several times by a man but only once by a woman. I shall call it 'marriage' or 'second marriage'. The short *nathra* rite can be performed an unlimited number of times by each sex. This I shall call 'remarriage'.

why wealthy landed families of Rajputs marry girls from the petty headman level of Rajputs, but give no girls in return; and the former through this hypergamy become a sort of separate subcaste, though this is not formalized by the population.

The quality of the ancestry of each side is usually roughly balanced, however. If there has been an irregular union on one side, there will be a disability of similar degree on the other; for people without such a slur will not give their offspring. Thus, a man born of an informal union could only marry, after a long search, a girl who was well past puberty—and even then had to pay a large sum to her father. Again, a man born of a Brahman–Rajput union married a woman who was privately said to have the same mixed ancestry.

The ascertaining of another's ancestry is a matter for diplomacy. One cannot, of course, directly approach anyone and try to find out about his ancestors. Rather, the match is arranged by a middle-man (*madad-gar*) or matchmaker who is usually a relative, though a member of another subcaste is not disbarred if the candidate has nobody 'to speak for him'; but the traditional role of the Brahman and Barber as matchmakers no longer exists. A matchmaker can be a cognate or an affine (often he is the mother's brother of one of the parties). He may live in the same village as a candidate, or may merely have ties in both villages. Anyhow, he is in a position to know or find out such details as are relevant. The parents inspect their future affines, but this is more of a formal visit when the affair is well advanced; and any open refusal at this stage would cause a great deal of ill-feeling.

It may happen, of course, that an unfavourable feature comes out after the formal engagement (*sagai*) and before the marriage, and in such cases the match can be broken and any gifts returned. If it is only found after the marriage there is no refunding of expenses, and the only course for a husband who discovers that his wife has developed, say, leprosy during the engagement period is to cast her off and marry again. Usually, however, such things cannot well be hidden; a Carpenter, for example, broke off the engagement of his son on hearing that the wife-to-be was an epileptic. Only those who are prepared to overlook at least minor inequalities in ancestry pay no attention to the talk that surrounds all matchmaking.

The influence of the matchmaker is considerable, for he is primarily responsible for the marriage, and can suggest to various kin where their children would make a good match. This may not always work out well, though. In one instance, a Rajput told me that he had left the selection of a husband for his daughter to his wife's brother. But the man had selected a suitor from a village in the 'wrong direction' (see p. 211). In theory, the Rajput could have refused this match, but he had felt impelled to follow his matchmaker's suggestion (perhaps to keep peace with his own wife, whose brother the latter was), and married his daughter there. The matchmaker is also important in smoothing out any last-minute difficulties. In one case, a son of an informal union wished to marry. Since he was twenty-two, the prospective bride's father asked why he had not married already, and the matchmaker replied that it was because he had been too poor to do so. 'I was not lying,' he maintained, 'for X- *is* poor. I merely did not say something else [e.g. about the irregular birth] which the girl's father would not have wanted to know, anyway. If he is very eager to find out about X-, anyone will tell him the facts of his ancestry.' In this way, the matchmaker may suppress features of ancestry if he thinks the situation warrants it. In this case, X- was hard-working and of even temperament, and the matchmaker evidently considered he would make a good husband for the girl.

The matchmaker is not the only one to have an interest in the course of the marriage. All members of the kindred of recognition are concerned to have kin ties with people of good ancestry. For even the remotest link may stand them in good stead. As an example, a man went to a town some forty miles away to negotiate for a second marriage. As he put it: 'Her father was not sure of my ancestry and said he would think it over. We went into the town for some tea, and got into conversation with one of his friends. He asked my village, and established he was my wife's sister's husband [classificatory, of course]. I had never seen him before, but the father at once gave his consent to the match; for he knew that this man's wife's ancestry was "equal" (*barabar*) and that she would not be related to one whose line had any inequality.' This, of course, applies to the ancestry of the individual, and not to his physical constitution; he should still be examined for defects. But it shows how marriages affect distant kin.

The term *khandan* when it refers to ancestry is therefore used in a special sense. We have seen above that one meaning of the word refers to unilineal descent groups of up to the clan in size, though with a tendency to denote the shallower lineages (p. 169). But a person's qualitative, as opposed to his genealogical ancestry, is very much shallower and is also bilateral. The reputation of witchcraft, physical disease and other attributes of poor ancestry are rarely recalled for more than the memories of the oldest people. And ancestry stems from both parents, since the stigma of inequalities is not essentially patrilineal. An individual's ancestry contains his immediate bilateral ascendants; but the extension of the concept can link distant affines, and so provide a clean bill of health for people within the lineage of recognition.

The Pattern of Marriage

Underlying the criteria of choice lie the demographic facts of the density and distribution of the subcaste and its clans. These play a major part in the pattern of marriage links between villages. I base this account on an analysis of 446 matches (of which 16 are re-marriages) of people of Ramkheri, in the 19 largest subcastes. The majority concern matches of living people, but those of ascendants are also included.

The figures first show that there are few repeated marriages with other places. The 446 matches took place in 219 villages and towns.[1] There are four villages into which between 10 and 13 matches have been contracted, the rest being less, usually not more than one or two. Why is there this wide spread? An obvious answer is that there are too few clans in the subcaste populations of most villages to allow repeated intermarriage. In Ramkheri, for instance, 14 out of 28 subcastes contain not more than two clans. Any marriage into these subcastes from other villages is very limited, unless the other village's subcaste has many clans, which I see no reason to suppose exists in a greater proportion of instances than is the case in Ramkheri. To support this, it can be shown that repeated marriages between two villages usually take place in numerically large subcastes with many clans. Thus, villages linked with Ramkheri by four or more marriages are distributed among castes as follows:

TABLE 1

Subcaste	Number of Villages
Farmer	7
Rajput	5
Cotton-carder	5
Gujarati Gardener	1

The first three subcastes are the largest in Ramkheri, and also possess the greatest number of clans. There is only one repeated link with a town—the Gujarati Gardeners have had more than four marriages into a small town nearby.

A further aid to the wide spread of marriage ties is the fact that a village may be put out of bounds to a kin-group because of a re-marriage there. For remarriage is looked down on, and the relatives of a first husband will not wish to meet the second husband of his

---

[1] Of these only 20 were made in recognized towns like Dewas, Indore, Ujjain and Sarangpur. A further 22 were in smaller towns whose population I estimate to be above 3000 but under 10,000.

divorced wife or a widow. Now, if these relatives have other kins-women already married into such a village, their dilemma is plain. Either they must break with their relatives through marriage, or they must keep up these ties but also come into contact with the new relatives through remarriage. People try to avoid this problem by not making more than one marriage into any village. An instance of this difficulty concerned a Rajput's widow who was given in remarriage by her parents to a man of village A. Later, a Rajput of Ramkheri engaged his daughter to another man of the same village A. The other Ramkheri Rajputs held a council, and decided to boycott the offender. 'We cannot eat with the people of the house in which our kinswoman was remarried,' they said; 'and yet they should come to your daughter's wedding, since they are her fiancé's fellow-villagers.' Negotiations were started to break the engagement or to find a compromise. Finally it was decided that the man in whose house the widow had remarried would not come to any function at which Ramkheri men were to be present. People com-plained of the 'weakness' of the time, when such solutions were deemed possible.

Another factor is village exogamy. In areas further north, the village is not only exogamous, but no marriage is allowed into those settlements with common boundaries.[1] In the south, on the other hand, intra-village matches are quite normal.[2] Malwa occupies a position socially as well as geographically between these two poles. Marriage within the village is allowed, but it is uncommon and not very well regarded. The main arguments against it are that the people are of one village (and thus have a sort of fictitious kinship) and that the presence of affines will exacerbate any friction between husband and wife. Such matches are contracted by people too poor to find wives elsewhere. Ramkheri contains two such couples; and people try to find excuses for them. Thus, one marriage was between people living in different wards of the village, and this was said to be 'almost as if they were in different places'. The other, however, was between a couple living in the same street. Here it was said that the marriage was only made when they had grown up, and so was all right; only marriages between children should be avoided, for they live in the same place, and call each other 'brother' and 'sister' in the way that other children do, without knowing what they are saying. People try to justify intra-village marriage in these ways, though they dislike it, and will not admit that it has occurred if they think the enquirer does not already know.

Marriage into adjacent villages is not stigmatized in this way. It is,

[1] Karve 1953: 119 (this data is given for one caste, but may apply to more).
[2] Ibid.: 183.

however, considered preferable to marry at some distance, so that the wife's parents are not too close, and cannot control her when she should at least overtly be ruled by her husband. The six adjacent villages to Ramkheri account for only 12 of the 446 matches recorded. And the average distances to which Ramkheri girls go, and from which girls come to the village, are shown below for the largest subcastes.

TABLE 2

Subcaste	Girls go from Ramkheri		Girls come to Ramkheri	
	No.	Distance*	No.	Distance
	Matches	(miles)	Matches	(miles)
Rajput	38	12·8	48	17·0
Farmer	45	12·5	51	11·8
Bhilala	20	9·4	19	10·7
Cotton-carder	16	18·6	38	19·7
Malwi Weaver	20	7·3	23	13·7

* Distances are approximate, being based on the estimates of informants.

The table shows that the distances to which girls go and from which they come are equal for the Farmers, Bhilalas and Cotton-carders. Villages into which Rajput girls marry are nearer than those from which brides are sought; and this is explained by the marriage chain, to be described below. The Malwi Weavers have the same pattern, but I have found no specific marriage chain there and cannot thus explain the figures, which only became apparent after I left the field.

Some castes go further than others for marriages; e.g. the Bhilala spouses live only ten miles from each other, whereas the average for the Cotton-carders is nineteen miles. This may be because some subcastes have a more scattered population, or because their main centres happen to be further from Ramkheri. The details of the pattern vary for each subcaste, but the outlines are the same.

The only exception is when there is a marriage chain; by this is meant a distinction between villages from which girls come in marriage and those to which Ramkheri girls are given. It differs from what I call a marriage direction—i.e. when both the giving and receiving villages tend to lie in a particular direction. Table 3 gives details of data collected for the two largest endogamous units in the village.

There is no appreciable distinction of girl-giving and girl-receiving villages among Farmers; that is, girls come and go between any pair of villages. The Rajput figures, however, show a trend towards receiving girls from the south and east, and giving to the northwest. Exchange with western villages is fairly even, largely because most of

TABLE 3

Direction	Farmers		Rajputs	
	Girls Come	Girls Go	Girls Come	Girls Go
North	2	3	2	1
Northeast	10	8	—	—
East	—	1	13	5
Southeast	—	—	4	—
South	10	8	1	—
Southwest	19	19	15	3
West	9	5	11	7
Northwest	1	1	2	22
Total	51	45	48	38

the villages in this category form part of one inter-village subcaste council with Ramkheri, and so are considered 'equal'.

There is a feeling among most castes that people from the east are rather inferior—the east including the Uttar Pradesh which is north-east. People talk about immigrants from these parts as being less cultured. In a few cases the same attitude exists towards people of the immediate south; thus, the Weavers of Malwa look down on those of Nimar, who are 'below the hills'—that is, do not live on the Malwa plateau. But these attitudes are not reflected in marriage chains, and may only be verbal attachments by other castes to the Rajput custom.

The Rajputs at first did not admit to me the existence of this chain; indeed, it is not an explicit rule, and there are cases of girls coming from unfavourable directions. Nevertheless, they were forced to admit from the evidence that they did not like to give girls to the south and east; their reason was that the people there were not true Rajputs, since they practised remarriage. But this is hardly a valid distinction, since the Ramkheri Rajputs themselves make remarriages. The idea that the better Rajputs are to the west is general over the whole of northern India and stems from the existence of the major Rajput States in the west.[1] Rajputs in Ramkheri appear to feel it as an unformulated principle of the caste, for which they must find reasons only for the anthropologist.

Village subcaste populations may tend towards marriage in a given

[1] A theoretical question which my data cannot answer is 'what happens at the boundaries of Rajput habitation?' Is there any chain in Rajasthan, the furthest west of all, where there should then be a surplus of unmarried girls; and what happens in the south, where there is presumably a shortage of girls? It would be interesting to see whether the principle of a marriage chain has a force at the periphery equal to that in the centre of the area of habitation.

direction, rather than having a chain, because of the location of middle-men. For these will inevitably be able to give more information about people living near them, and so will tend to arrange matches within their own locality. This may be a reason for the fact that 13 out of 25 Tanner marriages have taken place in the north and northwest; again, Bhilalas tend to marry towards the south and west; and Table 3 shows that Farmers marry more in the south and west, too. This may also be a function of the subcaste's greater density in that area.

I have already pointed out that the subcastes are not spread evenly over the province. There are several subcastes of each caste in this part of Malwa, and these rarely live together in the same village. Either of two patterns may therefore exist in a region; each subcaste may inhabit separate 'clusters' of villages, or there may be a 'random' distribution of different subcastes in neighbouring villages. This study has not covered enough villages to enable me to say which is generally the case. People when questioned tended to see their sub-caste in clusters. 'All the villages around X- are of my subcaste,' they will say, 'whereas we are not found anywhere to the north of Y-village.' But this may easily be a simplification of the distribution, just because distant villages without one's own subcaste in them may be forgotten. A regional study is needed to clarify such problems, and this is clearly wanted for any further work on kinship and subcaste structure.

The rules of marriage and the demography of the subcaste combine to produce the following features. First, the affinal links of a village subcaste group stretch out for an average of twenty to thirty miles, with the most distant up to fifty miles or so. The kin in each of these villages usually contain a wide range of relationships. Only when there is a marriage chain does one find, say, that there are sister's husbands but no wife's brothers in another village. Second, these affinal links and the cognatic ties stemming from them cover all or nearly all of those villages in the area which contain the subcaste. And, since a man is usually related to the other members of his village subcaste group, he himself participates in this network of ties. He has links with a certain number of settlements which are based on his own near kin, from which stems his kindred of co-operation. And he is also related to other villages' subcaste groups through his more distant kin, and the kin of his fellow-village subcaste mates, and these comprise his kindred of recognition. Together, these kindreds compose the marriage area or the 'region' of the village subcaste group.

This region comprises only the villages inhabited by that particular subcaste, of course. It is a subcaste's region; a village's region would in theory include the regions of all constituent subcastes, e.g. the 446 villages I have mentioned above, at least. This region is never made manifest, for the village as such never invites guests or acts as a body in this way; the Smallpox Goddess Worship (see p. 249) is the nearest approach to this. Nevertheless, the village region to some extent exists because villagers do think of an area in which they are at home, where people are not felt to be strangers. In the same way as a subcaste member coming from a distance is not admitted until he can claim some connection with 'recognized' relatives, so villagers see the people outside their region as strangers, with different customs, different ways of speech, etc. I was often told, for instance, how the people east of Ashta in Bhopal (some forty miles from Ramkheri) chewed tobacco instead of smoking it, and Ramkheri men amused themselves by imitating their accents. Now, it is doubtful that there are miniature 'culture areas' so clearly marked, and more probable that the changes which one can observe in going from one part of Malwa to another are gradual. But the villager conceptualizes these as taking place outside the area in which he and his fellow-villagers have most of their kin. One only marries people like oneself, and kinship and common customs should coincide. The boundaries of both subcaste and village regions cannot be precisely defined, of course; and sometimes a subcaste group which is part of a scattered population will have a region wider than the average region (e.g. the Tailors had relatives in Ashta). But there is a general recognition of common features which make a limit to the villager's world.

XI

INTERPERSONAL RELATIONS
BETWEEN KIN

I T is not enough to know about the territorial aspect of kin ties. A description of the attitudes, rights and duties which kinsmen have to one another, and the degree to which these are fulfilled will give us a picture of the constitution of the effective kin-group. There are four rough classes of interpersonal kin relations—those between kin living in the same household, between agnates living outside the household though usually in the same village, between other cognates usually in different villages, and between affines.

IN THE HOUSEHOLD

The dominant note in the formal pattern of relations in the household is that of restraint. There is restraint between people of different age, and restraint between those of opposite sex. The rules that I shall describe may make the household seem a place full of restrictions, of prohibitions and of autocratic authority. Yet, in a happy household this is patently not the case. Authority on the one hand and respect on the other mix in an easy carrying out of duties, and the reticence of the women is one of modesty, not fear. Where there are tensions in a household, this changes and the barest features of the domestic hierarchy emerge. The rules may be followed equally closely in each case; but the spirit in which they operate makes a difference which can be clearly felt by the observer.

There are several more or less well-defined stages in the lives of men and women. Until the baby first eats solid food (at about one year, over which there is no ceremony), it is hardly counted as a member of the community; if it dies, it is buried rather than cremated. After weaning it is cremated and minimal funerary rites are carried out. The child is spoilt by its family until it is five or six years old. Vows made to Bheru or the Clan Goddess for the preservation of sons are redeemed at this age if the parents are financially able, and this can be seen to mark the end of early childhood. From this age the child starts to have duties around the house (herding the cattle when they come home or, if a girl, doing minor housework and baby-minding). Still, until about ten years, the child is not really

214

considered responsible for its actions, and can therefore do things for which it will be punished when older (e.g. eating with the left hand instead of the right).

After this, boys go through a period of rather indeterminate status. They are accounted as youths and should obey all rules of etiquette, respect for their superiors, etc., and some older men are especially hard on them if they are slow to change from their previous carefree existence. They may be married before or after puberty,[1] though puberty itself is not marked as a stage in their lives. Marriage is a major change in status, but often only a formal one. People who do not get married are not respected as full adult males (there are no spinsters): for those who do marry, the occasion has a primarily ritual significance, for the full funerary rites must be performed for a married person.[2] Otherwise, since marriage is usually early, and takes place several years before cohabitation is possible for the girl, there is not much change in the attitudes towards a youth. This is reflected in the different answers to the question of when a youth becomes a man (*admi*). Some said it would be from his marriage, whether before or after puberty, others gave the start of cohabitation or fatherhood as criteria, which would mean that manhood starts at around nineteen years. From that time, the person will be called by his own name, unless a kin term is used—before, he is usually called 'child' (*coro*).

Parenthood, especially the production of a son to perform the propitiation of the father's and other ascendants' spirits, is most important. A man known to be impotent is, like a bachelor, treated with only outward conformity to the rules, and has little influence. A man who produces only daughters, or whose children die, is not at any disadvantage, though. He is seen as a victim of his fate; people may be sorry for him, and his adversaries may speculate on the sins which have brought this divine reckoning. But he can have just as much authority as can a man with a large family. Though not entailing as much expense as a marriage, the birth of a first child or a son is the occasion for gifts from uterine kin and affines, and marks a stage in the father's life.

The corresponding stages are more clearly marked for a woman.

[1] Data about the marriages of 46 of the 257 adult males, which includes information from all caste groups, shows these ages:

	Age at:	
	Engagement	Wedding
Men	11·9	15·2
Women	6·6	9·9

[2] A bachelor of ripe age will have these rites too, it was said, but as a concession rather than a right.

Marriage usually takes place earlier than for a boy, and is more a ritual status than a behavioural change, since it is almost always before puberty. But for the woman puberty marks an era in life, for shortly afterwards the wife will start to live in her husband's village. There she will have the status of a married woman. Little by little her influence will grow, especially after the birth of a child. The prime ages of the couple are between thirty-five and fifty years. At that time the wife has her children's wives under her control (afterwards they tend to leave the joint household); and this is usually when the husband's vigour and authority in the kin-group is greatest.

Old age is both a physical and psychological stage. When a man's teeth drop out and his hair goes grey, whether sooner or later, he will be called old (*dokro*). One theory is that a man without teeth cannot digest his food properly, and so loses bodily strength and becomes old. Others say that a man is old when he relinquishes control of his household, and his voice is silent in village and subcaste affairs. One is not old, in fact, until one feels old. Because this theory depends on the diminution of influence, people do not like being called '*dokro*', but should rather be addressed as *baji*, a polite way of speaking to all older men. Much the same would apply to women, who retire from active management when they feel they are too old for it.

Even though there are few formal acknowledgements of increasing age, relative age differences are marked in many ways. The kinship terminology, for example, distinguishes between father's elder and younger brothers (*ba* and *kaka*), between people of the same generation older and younger than oneself (the former called by the kin term, the latter by name), between wives of elder and younger brothers (*bhabhi* and *lari*), and wife's elder and younger sisters (*barsas* and *sali*). Again, marriage should be contracted in descending order of age, the elder brother being married first and this is rarely contravened. Another example concerns formal greetings of kinsmen, when the younger men touch the feet of the elders, the latter putting their hands on the youngers' heads (the form of greeting between equals varies, being either an embrace (Farmers) or a handclasp followed by the joining of one's own hands (Rajputs)). Further, sociological age has precedence over actual age, if the two conflict. A father's brother may be younger than his brother's son; but the required behaviour is for him to be treated by the latter with respect.[1]

Age differences in the household are, of course, chiefly centred

[1] I regret that I have not seen whether this exists in practice, and a personal communication from Sri K. S. Mathur indicates that they treat each other as good friends or as brothers.

around the relations of parents to children. To a lesser extent they exist between elder and younger siblings, the wives of elder and younger brothers, etc. But age is only one of the factors on which behaviour is based. Another is differentiation between the sexes, and the third stems from the theory of procreation. Under these influences, the father is the disciplinarian of his sons, and the mother has the dual role of being the centre of affection for her children, and the disciplinarian of her daughters as well as of the sons' wives.

As I have said (see p. 204), both parents are seen to contribute to the procreation of a child. But, as one man told me, each person has seven qualities (*gun*); a daughter receives four from her mother and only three from her father, whereas a son gets four from his father and the balance from his mother.[1] Hence, the mother transmits more of her character to her daughter, and has more affinity with her than with the son, and the father is paired with his boy. If there is any difficulty, the mother should deal with the daughter, and the father the son. In most cases this works; for minor issues usually engage the attention of one parent only. Thus, if the son does not work hard in the fields, the father speaks to him; whereas the daughter is more under the mother's eye at home. But even when the son does something very bad, under the eye of the mother, the latter will find it hard to reprimand him. I was told a story about a widow, whose son once stole a grain of wheat. She was not able to punish him for this, and the son gradually increased his ambitions, and finally was brought before the King on charges of stealing large amounts of jewellery. Condemned to death, the son asked to see his mother, and reproached her for her initial mistake in not punishing his first theft. The King, on hearing this, remitted the sentence, saying that the deed was not the son's fault; neither did he punish the mother, for it was not her fault, but Fate that had made her a widow.

Some people are uncertain about this theory of transmitted qualities, saying that the woman is merely a passive agent in reproduction. I have noted the oft-used analogy of the seed and the field (p. 203); according to this, the qualities transmitted to both sons and daughters are those of the father. Thus, a man born in adultery is said to be inherently quarrelsome and to have little loyalty to his half-brothers though they are of the same mother, and though they may think they are all of the same progenitor. The qualities transmitted by a man to his daughter are of little importance, since she leaves the household early on; but the father and son should co-operate closely, and this theory of procreation also reinforces the requirements of a patrilineally oriented household.

[1] This is probably an adaptation of the Sapta Dhatu, an Ayurvedic theory of the constituents of the human body.

Many women in Ramkheri insist that they have equal affection for sons and daughters. They say that the bond which common sex gives is counterbalanced by pride in her husband's heir, and the fact that a son looks up to her and honours her. For men say they feel warmer affection for their mother than they do for their father. They know that she has brought them up, and shown infinite patience with them. As one person put it, 'If an infant defecates when sitting on his father's lap, he will be pushed off at once, and the father will go to wash himself. But if the mother is holding him, she will first go to wash the infant, and only then clean herself.' The health and domestic well-being of the household are in the mother's hands, and indeed the deity which presides over the fortunes of the lineage is a woman.

Perhaps because the mother is not so responsible for the son, she will forgive him more easily than will his father. Several men told me how they had thought of running away from home during their adolescence, being unable to stand their fathers' strictness. And during my stay one boy of fifteen years did, in fact, abscond. He went to stay with relatives, and then gravitated to the town, where he lived off friends and made petty thefts. His father was very worried, and went into town to fetch him; several times he brought him back, but on each occasion the boy escaped. The general feeling was that the father was to blame; he had beaten the boy too much, and had started a rebellious attitude which he was now powerless to overcome. This is an extreme incident, for generally the father does not have to resort to such measures to get obedience. The ideal pattern is sufficiently closely followed in most households without being enforced by corporal discipline.

This ideal pattern is based on restraint between a father and his sons. A man does not talk freely before his father, nor will he joke with his contemporaries if the old man is there. In one large joint household two sitting-platforms faced each other across a narrow alley. The youths almost always sat on one side, and the older men on the other. The latter comprised the father, any visiting contemporaries, and the eldest son. Again, it is not considered fitting for a son to smoke in front of his father, and this rule still holds in the case of the more orthodox fathers. In one instance, a son of about thirty-five years had a long discussion with his old father about their farming problems whilst sitting with his back to him, so that he could at the same time smoke. More widely followed is the restraint on a son fondling, or even noticing, his child in front of his father. He would feel very shy (*sarm*) to do so, and I only once saw this contravened, in a house of urbanized people; even here the son was rather nervous and held the child with no attempt to be tender or

218

play with it. With this submission to the father should go a willing-ness to take orders from him, and this is indeed often the case, though there are instances where its denial leads to divisions of the household.

I have already outlined the relation of son to mother as one of respect with less formality than towards the father. Some people talked approvingly of a man who had sent away his wife because she had insulted his mother; this was right, they agreed, the son should put his mother before anyone else. One might question whether there were not other underlying reasons for the man's action, and certainly there are enough instances of men leaving a household because their wives have quarrelled with their mothers to show that a man does not always stick by his mother. There are, however, more histories of sons abandoning their fathers to live alone than there are of mothers being left without filial support.

A man's tie with his sister is accounted very close. The two have grown up together, at an age when there is no distinction made between the sexes. And later, when the sister marries, the brother is seen as her main protector, for when her father has died to whom else can she turn if there is trouble in her conjugal household. In return, the sister bestows ritual protection on the brother at the Raksha Bandhan festival. In fact, of course, the relations of brothers and sisters vary after marriage. If the mother is alive, there will usually be closer links between them. For she will wish to keep in contact with her daughter, and the son will be the main means of doing this. The tie also depends to some extent on the distance of the sister's conjugal from her parental household, and on her relations with the husband's family; for both of these will influence the frequency of her visits to her parental household. If it is near, or if she is badly treated, she may come often and in the latter case not wish to return. The brother may then have to take a strong stand on her behalf, and even risk an open rupture with her husband's family. There is more informality between a man and his younger sisters than with his older sisters, as might be expected from the general importance of age distinction.

The expected pattern of behaviour between brothers is one of close friendship and mutual support, coupled with the respect of the younger for the elder. This seems to be followed until early manhood, before divisive forces become important. After marriage, there are various contexts in which rivalries can develop, and these may estrange brothers even after they have divided the ancestral property and gone to live separately to evade them. Like most agnatic relations, the tie between brothers tends towards the formal, and the examples of really close friendships in Ramkheri do not involve brothers for the most part, but are between more distant kin and people of different caste.

A grandson is said to be 'not as a son'. Though he is expected to hear the grandfather with the deference he would give to other older agnates, it is said that the grandson does not greatly heed his grandfather's words. Perhaps it is because they come from an old man who has largely or wholly relinquished authority; perhaps it is because, in these times of change, the gulf between the values of the orthodox grandfather and those of the 'modern' grandson are too great to be bridged by a formal observance of subordination. When he is not in control of the household, the grandfather may intervene on behalf of the grandson to the father.

Two categories of affinal relations are found in the household; the first are the wives of the agnates living there. A wife (*lari*) at first talks to nobody when she enters the conjugal house, save to her husband privately. She keeps her face veiled, is given little work to do, and conversation with her takes the form of commands or requests. The first people with whom she talks are her mother-in-law (*sas*), her husband's sisters (*nanand*), and her husband's elder brothers' wives (*jethani*). Even then, there is little freedom of conversation. After about a year she is doing work equal to that of the other women in the house, and the relation with the *nanand* and the *jethani*, as well as with any younger brother's wives (*devarani*) who may have arrived, is increasingly familiar. This may be of growing friendship; or the *nanands* may take advantage of their established position in their own household to tease her, and the *jethani* may bully her in compensation for the orders which she herself receives from the *sas*. The younger wife should suffer all this, but sometimes she gives as good as she gets, with a running battle in the household as the result. Once, for example, two brothers' wives were working in the field. The *devarani* went away, and on her return was scolded by the *jethani* who said 'you have gone for so long that I thought you had run away home'. The *devarani* replied 'it is not for want of food at my parental home (*pihar*) that I do not go there [e.g. she implied that the *jethani's* parents were poorer than her own]'. At once a quarrel started, which ended only with the *sas's* appearance.

Gradually, the wife becomes established in the household. The change in her position is symbolized in the eating pattern. At first she will eat after the other women; then at the same time, but will not face them. Later they will face each other, or eat side by side. And in cases of great friendship, it is said, the *sas* and her *lari* will eat from the same dish.

The first men to whom the *lari* will speak and show her face are her husband's younger brothers (*devar*). With these she has an informal relation. Some said that one could joke with the elder brother's wife (*bhabhi*), though not too broadly; others said that she was to be considered a mother, and so a relation of informal respect was required. I think the interpretation of the word 'joke (*dillagi*)' may differ. It is certain that there are none of the broad jests to be found in other parts of India. This may be because there is no levirate in Malwa; in other provinces the *bhabhi* is a possible spouse, and this underlies many of the jokes. It was noticeable that the men joking most freely with the *bhabhi* were Dairyman immigrants from north India, amongst whom a leviritic marriage had taken place in the last generation. Among the people of Malwa there can be free speech between the two, though this is limited by age differences.

The relation contrasts with the complete restriction between the wife and her husband's elder brother (*jeth*). Here no speech is allowed and the wife must always keep her face veiled. A similar restriction exists for the father-in-law (*sasur*). In some cases this had never lifted; in other families the conversation was limited to straightforward requests, and the wife still kept her face covered.

At first husband and wife do not publicly acknowledge each other's existence, and, in fact, are rarely together during the day. After several years, especially if the wife has borne a son, the couple may talk in front of the elder women of their generation, then before the younger brother and mother, and lastly, if at all, before the elder brother and the father. Four old men were said never to have talked publicly to their wives, even in front of small children. If the household is large the husband will eat with other men, and the wife afterwards with the women. I have seen husband, wife and children eat at the same time, but this was in an elementary family household, and after some twenty years of marriage.

The wife should treat her husband as master, thinking only of his welfare. The traditional pattern demands it, and even now there are Satis who perform a last act of submission to their spouses. This kind of behaviour is by no means always the rule, however. In lower castes, the women go out to work and thereby gain economic independence and a knowledge of the ways of the outside. They do not always treat their husbands as leaders; nor do the women of higher castes, though these have less opportunity of showing this. But in all households the woman's role changes from that of a wife, in a weak position, to that of a mother in a much stronger one. In the latter she learns how to run the family; some women 'manage' their husbands from behind the scenes, others are more open, and in some cases control the affairs of the household, deciding the shape of the budget and controlling funds.

There are few cases of men living in the parental households of their wives. These are known as *gharjamai*,[1] and are distinct from the men who live in their wives' villages but in their own households, being known as *jamai* (guest). The *gharjamai* usually lives in a house which is without an adult male; the property does not pass to him, however, but to his wife and sons. He is in a weak position, therefore, in this respect as well as because he does not have agnates in the village to stand by him in crises, and people laugh at the *gharjamai*. He himself has a very formal relation with his wife's parents (his *sas* being veiled before him). On the other hand, his wife is on speaking terms with the men of the neighbourhood; for these are real or village brothers and uncles. She need not veil to them, and this is also a reversal of a married couple's usual behaviour after a virilocal marriage.

The *jamai* (of whom there are six, as opposed to two *gharjamai* in Ramkheri) is like the *gharjamai* in having no agnates around him, and in the freedom his wife enjoys; but he is at least master in his household. The verse illustrates the position of these affines:

> Far off *jamai* like a god
> Village *jamai* ordinary:
> *Gharjamai* like an ass,
> Load him with what you like.

OUTSIDE THE HOUSEHOLD—FATHER'S AND MOTHER'S BROTHER

Many households contain a single elementary family. This means, of course, that some of the typical behaviour I have just described will less often exist or may be affected by previous quarrels at the division of a household and its jointly held property. It also means that any other agnates in the village live in separate households. Uterine kin, of course, reside mostly in other villages. The key relationships in each of these classes are those of the father's brother (*ba* (elder) and *kaka* (younger than the father)) and mother's brother (*mama*), and these are worth comparing.

The expected behaviour of both kinsmen is based on socio-religious duty (*dharam*), but the connection with the father's brother is one of inescapable agnatic descent and frequently physical proximity, whereas that with the mother's brother has an emotional rather than an authoritative basis. The first is characterized by the statement of a man who had split from his brother's household. He did not attend the festivities previous to the wedding of one of his brother's

---

[1] I heard of only one case which could be called marriage by service, in which a Weaver lived in the house of his father-in-law and worked to pay for the cost of ornaments for his wife.

sons; but he went with his nephew to the bride's house for the actual marriage rite. 'If the father's brother does not go, who will go?' he asked. 'Can you divide a pool of water with a stick?' Whatever the internal relations may be, the group of agnates is expected to present a solid front to the outside, and the father's brother should help the nephew.

The relation of the mother's brother is best expressed in the proverb, 'One hundred Brahmans, one sister's son.' This means that there is more merit in helping the latter than there is in performing the ordinary run of almsgiving. The mother's brother should give to the sister's son without thought of return and count it a meritorious (*punya*) act. The relation is closely connected to that of a man with his sister. Here, the brother regards himself as his sister's protector and gives her more than she or her husband will give in return (in many cases the brother will not accept anything from his sister, and gifts must be made to his children instead). It is, in fact, an extension of this tie which covers the sister's son. I was told several times that the mother's brother takes more interest in the nephew whilst his sister is alive. 'When she is dead,' it was said, 'who is there for him to ask "how are your little ones?" ' The primary interest thus lies in the sister rather than the people of her conjugal household. In this sense the mother's brother has the interest of an agnate, but shows it in terms of a uterine relationship. For the material expressions of the relation occur mainly when the nephews and nieces are married, and have children.

The sister has a firm attachment to the brother, but this does not extend to such an extent to his children. Gifts and aid from the father's sister (*phua*) carry some merit, but are not seen to be so necessary, and a man will expect aid from a mother's brother sooner than from a father's sister's husband (*phupha*). The mother's sister (*masi*) also takes an interest in her sister's family, especially if the two sisters have married in fairly nearby villages; but failure to attend ceremonies and make gifts is not very severely criticized. As the description of weddings will show, the mother's brother is set apart from all other relatives by the type of present he gives, as well as by its size.

The father's brother and the mother's brother play parts which can be compared, but not assessed as stronger and weaker, or as closer and more distant, because they are so different. The former usually lives in the same village as his brother's son (*bhatija*) and so is involved in subcaste disputes and other minor village matters in a way which the mother's brother is spared. The outline of factions shows that these sometimes divide brothers (see p. 241) and involve the father's brother and his nephew on different sides. The relation

223

is, in fact, an extension of that between brothers which I have characterized as being 'correct' and restrained as often as it is warm and co-operative, and which always carries the seeds of rivalry and division and of superiority and subordination. The mother's brother, on the other hand, avoids the more mundane types of kinship obligation since he lives in another settlement, and usually appears only as a gift-maker or as a helper in time of financial trouble. If he is not willing to fill this place he does not come at all. His is either a positive or a neutral, but not a negative role; and distance enables him to cast a cloud of excuses over his actions if they contradict the ideal pattern.

What of the subcaste groups in Ramkheri which contain both agnates and uterine kin? Here, a man is frequently both mother's and father's brother to different villagers. Which role wins if they conflict? An example concerns men who were in this relationship:

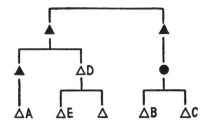

D's position was ambiguous when A quarrelled with B and C and struck B with a staff, for he had obligations to both sides. In the event, as might be expected, he did nothing. In fact, he refused to discuss the affair, and neither side counted on his help in the fight of revenge which B and C were expected to mount. E's position also produced a conflict of loyalties, and could not be shrugged off so easily since he had been present at the time of the incident. It was generally agreed that he had tried to stop the dispute before the blow was struck, and had roundly condemned both sides. A witness said that he had spoken more harshly to A, his agnate, and this would be consistent with the stricter role towards him than towards the uterine kin. But later, I observed that E was talking in a more friendly fashion to A than to the brothers B and C. This could be linked with rivalry between B and E for the leadership of the subcaste group, a rivalry based on personal ambition to lead which had nothing to do with their relations as kin and which would no doubt have arisen even if they had not been related. In this way, kinship roles can become factors in, or be affected by, the intrigues of the village subcaste group.

OUTSIDE THE HOUSEHOLD—AFFINES

Relations between affines start after the engagement has been made. A survey of forty-four matches put the interval between engagement and wedding at three-and-a-half years.[1] During this time the parents of the couple may meet at other people's houses, and the boy's parents must make gifts of clothes and, if possible, ornaments at the Holi and Raksha Bandhan festivals. (Few make two gifts annually, but most give once.) The behaviour I observed was one of friendly respect; but I imagine that there can be a certain tension, since the engagement could still be broken at any time. The party making the break does not suffer, but the reputation of the other side is naturally lowered and a second engagement is harder to make.

A further reason for tension between the fathers of the prospective spouses (*byahi*) is the uncertainty connected with some of the major economic aspects of the wedding. I was assured that the size of the dowry was never fixed between these men, nor the exact value of presents given by the groom to the bride. So there is always the danger that if too much or too little is given, either dishonour or economic competition with insufficient resources will result. Again, the fathers of some girls may demand a sum 'for their expenses' (see p. 233) when it is too late for the boy's father to withdraw, or may raise the size of the sum already agreed on. One Brahman father had arranged the marriage of his son with Rs. 150 to be paid; but a month before the wedding the girl's father forced an extra Rs. 100 from him.

There is also no agreement over the size of the groom's party. A party of only twenty men came to a wedding at a Ramkheri headman's house, and everyone there felt insulted at the paucity of guests, for whom a large supply of food had been prepared. On the other hand, a Farmer's story illustrates the other extreme. As an engagement party finished, the girl's father said jestingly to his *byahi*, 'Mind you bring a good marriage party, though you live in a small village.' This stung both the man's family and his local pride, and he came to the wedding with a party of 200 bullock carts. The girl's father had to send out for more food, and in revenge came to fetch back his daughter after the wedding with 250 carts. The boy's father should have made a gift of welcome commensurate with the size of this party, but was unable to do so. Later, a Farmer council

---

[1] In seven cases there was a gap of less than six months, sometimes of no more than a week. This appears to be correlated with caste status and wealth. For a shorter engagement means fewer expenses to be met, and those marrying soon after included people of the Tanner, Nath, Drummer and Mina castes, all from divisions 4 or 5.

considered the matter, and called unsuccessfully for a limit to the size of marriage parties. The costs of weddings and their associated gifts are still a source of worry and potential friction between prospective Farmer affines.

After the wedding, the fathers of the spouses have an informal joking relationship. On one occasion, for example, a man arrived at his daughter's conjugal house to fetch her, and the boy's father teased him about his temerity in leaving his wife alone in his village. This sort of joking is only done when both parties are quite sure that no offence will be taken. I have known occasions where quarrels have flared up over such chaff, and the relation is tailored to each situation. A man can make small jokes to his son's wife's mother (*byahin*) and the mothers joke more broadly among themselves. Relations with the more distant affines are the freest of all; one man, for example, said that the person with whom he joked most was his brother's wife's father, and another mentioned his wife's sister's husband's father; such relations are *byahi*, but may seldom be encountered.

This freedom contrasts with the relation between the groom and his wife's parents and others in that household. Most men do not talk with their wife's father or mother, nor go to their house, for at least three or four years after the marriage. They are, in general, shy of talking about their wives or anyone connected with them; and they hesitate to tell the name of their wife's village or clan. If someone must go to fetch the bride, for instance, the groom will not be included, but will send his elder brother, or his father's brother, etc.

Though restraint exists between some of the principal actors, the first years after marriage is consummated see the most contact between the two households. If the bride is not mature at the time of the wedding, she will live with her parents, going only for a week to worship her husband's Clan Goddess on at least the first Nine Nights of her marriage. After puberty the girl comes to live with her husband (*ana* or *gauna*). But for several years she will spend an almost equal time in her parental house. At Raksha Bandhan and Divali she may return for up to a month; and she is also required at the first Holi festival after the death of any member of the parental household, and during the marriage season she acts as bride's aide (*khvansi*) to girls of the parental kin-group.

Each time, the period of a few weeks at home can be spun out if the parents wish it. The father will make excuses when the husband's relatives come to take her back—she is ill, or her mother is sick and she is needed for the housework, or simply that the time is inauspicious. The groom's representatives do not press too hard for her return, for this would imply that they cannot manage the household without her, or that the groom has an unseemly eagerness to see his wife; and so they often return empty-handed. If the two villages are far from one another, and if the groom's household is not wealthy, it may be a month or more before they can spare the time and money to make another expedition to fetch her.

As time goes by, the bride's responsibilities in her conjugal household will increase. She finds it less easy to return to her parental home and is less willing to do so. Little by little the loyalties of the girls are changed, until they come to the parental village only after several years at a time, and for major occasions alone. The links between the two households can vary at this time. They depend on the degree to which the woman's brother fulfils his duties towards her children—and to a lesser extent on the way her husband regards her brother's children. If these roles are filled as they should be, relations between the spouses' households will not only continue but may become more and more informal. For it is possible that the parents of the wife will die around this time; and the husband will then find at the wife's household only people of his own generation with whom he is on easier terms—the wife's brother, etc. He may also have occasion to use such people as go-betweens for the marriages of his children, and this can cement a tie of mutual aid and friendship.

This account of affinal relations does not include the occasions when a marriage breaks up through quarrels of the couple, quarrels of the wife with her conjugal kin, or quarrels between the kin of the spouses. I hope to publish an account of this elsewhere; here, it is enough to say that such quarrels can occur on a variety of topics, and will break contact between the two households; if the wife's remarriage is made, each village will be out of bounds to the respective affines.

BEHAVIOUR OF KIN—AT WEDDINGS

The part played by the various relations may best be illustrated by descriptions of the ceremonies in which they have ritual and economic duties and prerogatives. Weddings and funerals are the main occasions for the display of these.

Marriage (*vivah*) is one of the sixteen classical stages (*samskara*) in a person's life, and is by far the most important in its economic and social aspects. Economically, a wedding is for most people the largest single expense of their lives, costing on average from six months' to over a year's income. Socially, it inaugurates a new series of relations, and it also reflects existing ties in the behaviour of the wedding guests. Ritually, it is a prerequisite for the son who will propitiate agnatic ascendants and so prevent their being denied the world beyond,[1] as well as marking major changes in the ritual status of the partners. There are no spinsters in Ramkheri, and only six bachelors over twenty-five years. Some of these have remained single because of a gross physical defect (which does not prevent a girl's marriage, because of the shortage of brides). Others belong to upper castes where possession of land is a requirement for a suitor; being landless, they have failed to get a partner where brides are at a premium. A few later make a remarriage but this is not a *samskara*, and ritually they remain bachelors nevertheless.

The wedding provides a complex of rites which lasts for a week or more, and many variations of content and timing exist in different subcastes. Here I wish to concentrate on the kinship aspect only, and so will describe the ceremonies in only the broadest and so most comparable terms. The wedding starts with an invocation to Ganesh, the deity who attends the inauguration of all important enterprises, with the worship of the potter's wheel, and with the installation of the spouse (*bana baithana*—the seating of the spouse). Then follows an average of a week during which the spouse is rubbed with purificatory turmeric (*haldi lagana*), and is taken round the village in procession and regaled with sweets and sometimes food at the houses of friends and relations (*bana jhelna*). These preliminaries end with the erection of the marriage booth (*mandap*) in front of the main doorway of the spouse's home. There, the Clan Goddess is worshipped and her blessings on the match are invoked.

Next day is called *gharviyah*. The significant acts are the worship of the Mother Goddess (Mai Mata) by the groom, and the giving of presents to the groom's family by his mother's natal clansmen (*mamere*) and by his agnates and others (*ban*), after which his father gives a large feast. On the third day the groom leaves for the bride's house with his party (*barat*) of kinsmen and male fellow-villagers.[2]

The crucial rites of the wedding start in the evening of this day (*lagan*), with the arrival of the *barat* at the bride's village, where the *mandap* has been erected during the day. The first acts are the welcome of the *barat* by the bride's village priest and the washing of the groom's feet in milk by the bride's father or other agnate. At this time the bride is being anointed in oil, and then washed by her female attendants. Later (often in the early hours of the morning) the groom comes to the bride's house from the reception hall where the *barat* is housed and strikes a carved wooden frame (*toran*) outside her door with his drawn sword. Her mother comes out and welcomes him. He enters the house and sits with the bride in front of the Mai

---

[1] Kapadia 1947: 88, quoting classical authorities.
[2] A few castes also take women (e.g. Oil-pressers), though there is now a tendency to conform to the majority custom.

Mata (a drawing on the wall). The priest chants Sanskrit verses and then, after tying their clothes together, places the horoscopes of bride and groom in the bride's hand, and at the auspicious moment (*lagan*) puts the groom's hand over them. This is accompanied by clapping and shouting, and provides to the observer the most dramatic moment of the wedding. The bride and groom then worship Mai Mata together, and in some subcastes play games together to the accompaniment of broad jokes by the bride's women kin. After, it is usual for the groom to return to the *barat's* house.[1]

Next day is called *caunri*, after the name of the most important rite. This is the pair's seven circumambulations of the sacred fire, blessed as they go by the village priest. It is the rite which seals the marriage. After the *caunri* (also called *phera*), there is gift-giving by the bride's kin. The *mamere* and *ban* are made to the bride's family, and in addition there are gifts of ornaments for the bride (*sivcauni*) and the presentation of the dowry (*dahej*) by the bride's father to the groom's father, and gifts of clothes from the bride's people to kinsmen of the groom (*paharavani*).

The groom departs with his bride on the third day (*bida*), after a final worship of Mai Mata and obeisance made by the bride to the threshold of her parental house. On their arrival back at the groom's village the couple worship the groom's Mai Mata, and the bride 'cools' the marriage booth by taking leaves from it and sinking them in a well.[2] She then brings water for the first time to her conjugal household, and the couple make obeisance to the major shrines in the groom's village.

This is an extremely bald chronology of what is a very complex series of rites. Having given the reader an idea of the overall programme, I discuss each step in more detail, from two aspects—the parts played by the various actors in the main rites, and the nature of the ceremonial exchanges of gifts (presentations) which take place. It is simpler if I divide the account into the parts played by agnates of the couple, by uterine kin, by affines, and lastly by fellow-villagers and other such outsiders.

Agnates pay homage to the Clan Goddess when the marriage booth is erected. This booth is made of four bamboo poles or plough shafts, on which a framework is constructed and leaves placed. The actual building is made after a rite in which each post is held by an agnate, and it and he are blessed by the village priest. On three of eight occasions I saw that either a sister's son, a daughter's husband, or a fellow-caste man who was 'as a brother' held one of the posts.

[1] If the *lagan* has taken place during the day, the further rites and gift-presentation may take place at once.
[2] The bride's booth is cooled by her kinswomen.

This shows that the affair is not entirely exclusive, for these could have been replaced by real or classificatory brothers.

After the booth has been constructed, there is worship to the Clan Goddess by all agnates present and their wives. The sister's son, etc., who had held the posts did not take part in this—being directly addressed to the Clan Goddess, it is very exclusive (see p. 186). On two occasions at the booth of a Farmer an aged agnate called out the names of as many male ascendants as he knew; people of other castes said they asked the blessings of all ascendants for the wedding by worshipping the Clan Goddess, so did not need to do this. This worship is seen as a duty for all members of the descent group, as this instance shows; a man had fallen out with his father's brother's son, and the latter did not attend any of the various feasts at the wedding of the man's son. But he came for the Clan Goddess worship, not talking to his host and leaving soon after. I was told that he needed no invitation to worship, and that in fact he should have come whatever his relations with other agnates. The men taking part are usually of the village only. The ceremony occurs one or two days before the wedding for the bride and groom respectively, and agnates tend to come from other settlements only on the day itself. Again, as I have mentioned, weddings tend to be bunched together on certain auspicious days, and a man cannot come to the weddings of all agnates. Finally, of course, not all agnates in more distant villages come, because of the fairly short time during which such ties remain effective.

The unilineal descent group is also made manifest at the worship of the Manure Heap Goddess (*Unkaldi Mata*) which takes place on the morning after the marriage booth has been erected. The groom or bride goes with kinswomen to the household's manure heap at the edge of the village. There the mother (or father's brother's wife, etc.) of the spouse-to-be makes offering for the prosperity of her conjugal descent line; and sometimes a woman calls out the names of agnatic ascendants of her conjugal clan and their wives.

The personnel for the invocation to Ganesh varies from caste to caste; in some women alone worship, in others the men join them. Nevertheless, it concerns mainly men and women of the unilineal descent group (the women being either conjugally or natally affiliated). The main exceptions I noted were sister's sons and daughters—but they have an exceptionally close position since this is their mother's brother's house. Only once did I see unrelated caste mates worship. There is a constant proviso that the woman who takes the image of Ganesh off the stool on which it has been placed for worship, to allow the bride or groom to sit there for purification, must be the wife of an agnate—she cannot be a sister who has returned for the marriage. This rite is not addressed to a deity of the descent group, of course, but rather to the guardian of auspicious enterprises in general; it is not an act of reverence for the unilineal descent group, but a rite with limited personnel.

The remaining duties at weddings do not concern kin-groups but rather individual kin. Thus, the bride and groom stop during each of their journeys round the sacred flame, and the bride's younger brother pours rice over the horoscopes held in the bride's hand. Again, it is the mother's brother's duty to take the horoscope from the bride after the *lagan* rite. Another instance concerns the carrying of the bride from place to place (for she never walks); this is done by a relative such as the father's sister's husband, or an affine such as the sister's husband—these being kinsmen who are usually present —but never by an agnate. Last, the washing of the groom's feet on his arrival should be done by a senior agnate of the bride.

Besides people who act on specific occasions, there are girls who help in the general preparations and management of the wedding. These women (*khvansi*) are mainly real or classificatory or ritual sisters in any generation. They thus include sisters and cousin-sisters of the spouse, and such members of the ascending generation as mother's or father's sister. Only when there is a lack of women do the brother's wife and other affines help. There are also men (*khvansa*) who go with the groom and attend his needs; they are generally the husbands of the *khvansi*, and so are affines (the most common is the sister's husband, but the father's sister's husband, etc., also come). These have less to do than the *khvansi*, who busy themselves with rubbing the spouse with turmeric, aiding the cooking, fetching water, etc.

The above activities, then, mainly concern clan members. The ceremonial gift-giving, on the other hand, brings in all categories of kin. Here the main distinction is between the relatives of the father and mother. The father's kin have three occasions for making gifts. In the *ban* they give cash to the father of the spouse, to help defray his costs. In the *sivcauni* they give ornaments or cows (rarely cash) to the bride, which are then her personal possession (*stridhan*) and are kept apart from the wealth she brings to her husband in dowry. And in the *paharavani* it is the bride's close agnates who make gifts to the groom and his agnates. Of the first two kinds of gift, the *ban* is more favoured; for it is part of an exchange which is carefully calculated. As each man puts his money in the tray, an accountant notes it, so that the groom's or bride's father will know how much to repay. There is no idea that a slightly larger amount should be given in return.[1] The *sivcauni*, on the other hand, does not stay with

[1] For an instance where this unofficial 'interest' exists, see Mayer 1952: 123.

the father's kin-group, for the ornaments are taken by the bride and when she dies are kept by her husband's family. The giver of *sivcauni* may have the same type of gift made to *his* daughter later, from which he derives no monetary benefit. Is is therefore considered to be a more selfless and meritorious gift—but few people make it. Of the Ramkheri castes, the Rajputs give most *sivcauni*, for it befits their ideas of prestige; the Farmers are more severely practical and usually only give *ban*, and the lower castes can hardly afford to give without any hope of return.

Gifts from the mother's relatives are called *mamere*. They are invariably clothes, and are taken round the village in a procession, led by the Drummer and followed by the gifts borne on a brass tray by the Barber with the donors following. These include gifts from such relatives as the mother's brother, wife's brother and father of any married siblings of the spouse, the mother's father, his brothers, etc. The sibling's wife's elder sister's husband is included, though the younger sister's husband gives *ban* and is accounted as a brother. Though both are called brother (*saru bhai*) the elder sister is seen as a 'smaller mother-in-law'—being *barsas* of the younger sister's husband (*sas* = mother-in-law). Hence her husband is to some extent a father-in-law and should give *mamere*. (This is another example of the importance of age difference, and shows how the terminology reflects this.)

The *mamere* gifts are not made to the bride or groom, but to their parents and siblings. Thus the groom's brother's father-in-law will be invited and will bring *mamere* to give to the groom's brother, and perhaps to his father, the mother-in-law giving clothes to her *byahin*. It is, in fact, an occasion for presents to be given to the spouse's close agnatic kin, from the affinal as well as the uterine relatives. It is significant that the gifts made by an affine like a wife's brother to his sister's husband are called *mamere*; for the term itself indicates the relationship which the wife's brother will fill after a few years, when he becomes mother's brother to the children. The situation can be compared to the material set forth by Dumont. Here the point is made that there is often an 'affinal content in terms which are generally considered to connote consanguinity . . .'[1] That is, the wife's brother is not put in a different class as soon as children are born and call him mother's brother. Dumont relates this to the pattern of marriage alliance in the people he studied. But it also has relevance here, where no such alliances exist. For it could be argued that by including both affinal and uterine kin under the collective name *mausal*, and by seeing the gifts of both affines and uterine kin as *mamere*, the people of Ramkheri see the kin through marriage as

[1] Dumont 1957*b*: 25.

being in one category. The difference from Dumont's material is that, because there is no positive marriage regulation linking the two patrikin, the composition of the *mausal* changes after two or at the most three generations.

To say that the *mausal* is not seen as sharply divided into affines and consanguineous kin does not mean that the behaviour of all its members is the same. A man's attitude to his sister's conjugal household is usually formal until there are sister's children there. Especially, the role of the mother's brother is singled out from the rest of the *mausal* at weddings. It is marked by the larger number of *mamere* presents he must make (e.g. to each of his sister's children, as well as to her husband and herself). In addition, he alone of the *mausal* should give *sivcauni*. Again, it is he who takes the horoscope from the bride at the *lagan* rite, and in doing so he must make a present, the most meritorious being a cow or calf, but at least a token gift in cash. Further, the *barat* should be fed at least once by him during its stay in the bride's village; he may either give money for this to the bride's father, or will bring raw materials from his village. Similarly, the groom's mother's brother frequently stops the *barat* on its way home, and entertains it for a day in his village, if it is not too remote from the route.

The gift-giving is not confined to kin, for many fellow-villagers bring presents. If they have a specific kin tie (through ritual kinship) they will bring *ban* or *mamere* accordingly. People who are merely good neighbours will bring *ban* as 'village brothers'. The usual amount for a *ban* collection is between Rs. 100 and Rs. 200 in amounts of between Rs. 1 and Rs. 10. But when a very poor lad got married, the *ban* was only Rs. 25; for there was no guarantee that he would be able to reciprocate the gifts, and people hesitated to give. On the whole, the collections of the higher castes are larger, but the difference is not remarkable.

The comparative expenses of marrying a son or daughter are fairly equal, with the boy's if anything the heavier. In a girl's marriage the largest outlay is for feeding and entertaining the kin and the groom's retinue. Besides this, there is the dowry and the clothes for the relatives of the groom at the *paharavani*. The boy's expenses, on the other hand, start with the ornaments given at the engagement, and continue with annual gifts of clothes during the engagement period. There are additional clothes to be given to the bride at the wedding, as well as the entertainment of kinsfolk before the *barat* sets off. (Both sides engage a band, and wealthier people hire singers and dancers.) Besides, the fathers of some girls take presents of cash from the boy's parents, ostensibly to help entertainment costs. Such presents are regarded as demeaning, since the girl should be given to the groom without any thought of financial gain. But many lower caste marriages are accompanied by such transactions, and even Rajputs have married their daughters in this way. In contrast to the lack of discussion about the size of the dowry (which consists only of furniture, vessels, etc., and is not inflated with jewellery or cash) the size of this payment is the subject of hard discussion, one might even say bargaining, by the prospective affines.

After the marriage, the flow of wealth is reversed. Now the bride's kin have to give more, for the mother's brother is expected to give clothes at all major ceremonies in his sister's house. He gives *mamere* at the weddings of other household members, when his sister produces a child, when there is worship of the Smallpox Goddess, etc. In return, he receives only *ban* from the sister's husband at the marriages of his own children. As one man said, 'To give the minimum clothes costs Rs. 20. But one can give a *ban* of only Rs. 5 in return, and nobody will talk. That is why to have many daughters is an expensive thing for a house.'

Though it is the girl's father who makes the first advances to a prospective groom, though the wedding is held at the bride's house with the consequent extra expense and trouble, and though the bride goes to live with her husband and is thereby delivered by her family as a hostage to fortune, one cannot say that marriage is between highly unequal parties. It does not, for example, result in the groom's village being considered 'high' and the bride's 'low'.[1] For the next match may be of a girl from the former groom's village and a boy from the previous bride's settlement. Again, the kin terms used by cross-cousins are reciprocal. For another thing, there is no large dowry system which impoverishes the girl's side; as I have said, a marriage costs roughly the same for both parents. Moreover, the ancestries of the two parties are usually 'equal'—that is, their reputation is roughly the same, and often their wealth too. And the two sides are often previously related, if not through the matchmaker then through some more devious channel.

All this tends to make relations between affines less graded than may be the case elsewhere. It is only when a girl marries far outside her parents' station that the marriage tie becomes more of a barrier than a link. Thus, a Rajput girl married the son of a landlord, and the groom's family had never allowed her to return to her parental house. Again, a girl whose family had an 'unequal' ancestry was finally married to a boy quite far away. She also returned very seldom, perhaps because her parents thought that their ancestry might be found out with more regular contacts, and so did not go and fetch her home. The fact, too, that remarriage is possible in

[1] Cf. Marriott 1955*b*: 101.

almost all Ramkheri subcastes means that a wife can run away from her husband and, with the support of her natal kin, marry again. Her reputation may suffer, but the fact that this can happen lessens the power of the husband. The wife's family are therefore allowed more variation in the degree to which they fulfil their obligations. And this forms part of a pattern of kin ties in which duties are influenced by individual decisions of expediency or temperament. Again, the relative equality of the affines means that they can mix together more freely, and this is important for the composition and effectiveness of kindred gatherings in which social control is effected within the subcaste.

BEHAVIOUR OF KIN—AT MORTUARY RITES

All castes cremate their dead (except for small children) save for the Gosain, Nath and Sweeper, who bury but whose ensuing rites are similar to those of the majority. Again, people dying from smallpox or leprosy are buried; some cow-dung cakes are burnt on their graves and the ashes used in place of human ashes for the normal rites. The cremation is attended by all close kin in the village, and by other subcaste mates and people of different castes in numbers which vary with the age and importance of the deceased. There is no joint ritual for the unilineal descent group members present. Fire is brought and the pyre set alight by a son of the deceased (or son's son, daughter's son, brother, or brother's son in this order of priority, which is an order comparable with that of the male heirs of the dead person—or by a subcaste mate if there is no relative). This man, after bathing, dons a white turban, and is known by this sign of impurity.[1] He is the main mourner, and just as all agnates are shown as separate from others by growing their hair and beards and eating only the simplest food, so he is even more secluded and should not go about the village (a widow should not leave the house at all). On the third day the ashes are collected and the place of cremation cleaned. The ashes may be 'cooled', i.e. put into a stream by the chief mourner, unless it is intended to take them to Ujjain or to the Ganges.

Ten days after a woman's death, and eleven days after a man's, the main rite of purification takes place (*ganta* or *kriya karam*). Together, the agnates go to the nearby stream; there the chief mourner performs a rite, aided by a Brahman, and all those present shave their hair and beards, those younger than the deceased also shaving their moustaches. Though this mark of respect is said to be confined to agnates, I have also seen a neighbour shave his beard. He said it was his 'neighbourly duty (*parausi dharam*)' and in such ways even

1 For traditional rules of ritual impurity at death, see Kane 1953: 277 seq.

explicit rules of Hindu ritual are apparently flexible in individual cases. If the chief mourner seeks further merit he goes to Ujjain and performs the obsequies there; no joint action by agnates takes place at Ujjain, and the chief mourner goes alone with the village priest to show him what to do (the rituals are monopolized by Ujjain priests) whilst his kinsmen go through their duties in Ramkheri.

A fair number of kin have collected by the time of the *ganta*, if the dead person had any status at all. The funerals I saw indicated no large attendance by people of the co-operating kindred, but agnates of the immediate extended family and other near kinsfolk come. Thus, daughters will return for their mother's or father's *ganta*, and their husbands may come with them; again, sisters will come to mourn their siblings, often with their spouses. The meal after the *ganta* (of sweet rice only) is attended by members of this inner kin-group.

A smaller rite, the *gaurni*, has also taken place at the parental household of a dead woman. Here the main performers are nine men of the woman's natal clan group in the case of Rajputs and most other subcastes, and nine married women of the natal clan group for the Farmers. Afterwards, the village subcaste population is fed. The *gaurni* symbolizes the attachment of a woman to her natal clan, and its scale compared to the *ganta* and the activities which follow in the conjugal household indicate the relative weight of these two descent groups in her life. The *gaurni* does not attract a large assembly of kin. In some cases, it is said, nine appropriate members are not forthcoming and other subcaste members can discharge the duty. Both *gaurni* and *ganta* refer to the type of kin participating rather than the place of death. If a man dies at his wife's village, his affines will cremate him but will not perform the *ganta* rite which will take place in his own village.[1] Again, if a woman dies at her parental house, the inhabitants will only perform the *gaurni*, and her affines will hold the *ganta*.

The *ganta* is the largest mortuary rite centred on the unilineal descent group. The subsequent rites either include a large bilateral kin-group or concern only the sons. The first of these is *pagri*, when the chief mourner is divested of his white turban. This usually follows on the day after the *ganta*; but if it cannot be afforded, or if there are difficulties in gathering kin, there may be a gap of several days during which the chief mourner can move abroad with his turban on,

[1] In such cases the man lighting the pyre might well be an affine. I did not enquire who would be the chief mourner in such a case, but the son would conduct the later rites even though he had not done the first one. If a man is recognized as having left his own village and has been settled in his wife's village for many years, he would doubtless have sons with him; and the *ganta* would then also take place in his wife's village.

and can even go to a wedding, it is said, though he would not have the *tilak* of welcome from the people there. The *pagri* rite is, quite simply, the tying of a coloured turban on the chief mourner by his wife's father, or as second priority his mother's brother or a classificatory equivalent.[1] The fathers-in-law of the mourner's brothers may also tie turbans on the chief mourner among Rajputs, Bhilalas, etc. —and among Farmers these men may tie coloured turbans on their sons-in-law, though these are not the chief mourners. Amongst the Muslim Cotton-carders a similar rite takes place on the fortieth day after death, when after prayers the heirs (*varis*) are given turbans by their affines.[2] Since many brothers may be heirs, several turbans are tied, but the mother's brother of the siblings ties his turban on the head of the chief mourner only.

After the *pagri* rite the guests are fed. If this is to be the final feast, it is called the *nukta*. But, since there is an expectation that a large feast be given, men who wish to invite more guests than can meet at the time will postpone the *nukta*. For example, the death of a Rajput headman occurred during the rainy season. The son was persuaded to delay giving the *nukta* until the hot weather; for people said that were he to give it at once, all would suspect that he had tried to keep down the numbers with the aid of the weather and the fact that it was a time of great activity on the land. The *nuktas* given during my stay in Ramkheri were all immediately after the *ganta*; but one or two men were saving up to give a *nukta* for a relative who had died several years previously.

A delayed *nukta* starts with a turban-tying in the same way as the *pagri*, save that the chief mourner is no longer wearing his white turban. At one large *nukta* I counted over two dozen turbans given by various affines and uterine kin. In addition, any guest can give cash presents; I counted Rs. 165 at this *nukta*, all of which was to be returned in reciprocal gifts. Afterwards, there is a feast. Large *nuktas* are very costly. The entire subcaste populations of many villages may be invited, and Rajput headmen will often bring their Weaver and Bhilala contract labourers to attend to their carts. The guests to a Rajput *nukta* from a village go *en masse*, as for a wedding, and race each other on the way; a pair of really fast bullocks is envied by the younger men. Farmers say that they do not have such large affairs, and I heard no examples of any.

The rites which follow the *nukta* are those of commemoration, and concern the agnates almost exclusively. During the year following a

---

[1] Here, the affinal and uterine relations are seen as interchangeable.

[2] Cotton-carders bury their dead and have purificatory rites on the third day. There are separate cemeteries for each of the two main clan groups in Ramkheri and their linked kin.

death the chief mourner may make propitiation on the eleventh day of each fortnight; and at the first Holi festival agnates will gather at the house of the dead person. The main rite (*sraddh*) occurs in the dark fortnight of the month Bhadon. Here there is both remembrance of the recently dead, and a general propitiation of all ascendants. Some people observe the date of the father's death (e.g. if he died on the fifth day of any bright or dark half of a month, they would worship on the fifth day of the *sraddh* fortnight). The majority of people in Ramkheri only put out food on the house roof for crows (symbols of the dead spirits) during the fortnight, and mark the last day with rites performed for all ascendants. The first *sraddh* may see a gathering of agnates in the village; after this, each man will observe the rite in his own house. If there is no living male descendant a wife can act, or in her absence collateral branches of the kin-group. Last, on the first *sraddh* after their marriage, girls fast for the fortnight and draw pictures (*sanjaholi*) on their house walls. This is only if they are too young to have gone to their husband's house; and it may indicate their continuing connection with the natal descent group, which will later be transferred when they become qualified to perform *sraddh* to their husband.

There is a last rite performed by some people in Ramkheri. This is for Hinglaj Devi, a goddess whose shrine is in Sind and whose worship is especially the task of Naths and Gosains in the village. It does not appear to be a propitiation of the ancestors so much as an appeal for the protection of Hinglaj Devi which, once begun, cannot be left off by the descendants. There is a sect in Ramkheri whose members are committed to the rite at least once after an agnate's death. The proper time is the second day of the dark half of either Bhadon or Vaisakh months. Many stories are told about the rite by people outside it. Meat-eating and vegetarian castes are said to sacrifice goats and to eat in the same line, men and women, high caste and Harijan. But members repudiated this and said that worshippers ate only with those allowed under the rules of their caste; and vegetarian members did not eat meat. I did not see the rite through the special request of its members; the data suggest that attendance is inter-caste with no kinship referent, though the giver is acting as an agnate.

Performance of these funerary rites is a strictly enjoined duty for agnates. Not to do so may even make people feel that the offender is not a true son of his father, as the following incident implies. An old man died in Ramkheri without issue, save for a youth whom he had unofficially adopted (i.e. he had not had the full rite of adoption, but had simply taken him into his house). A few months before his death, the two had fallen out and the old man had gone to live with a collateral of the youth, a man who bore the latter no great enmity but who saw in this a way to possess the small plot of land held by the old man. When he died, the collateral maintained that he had disowned his half-adoption of the youth and had named the collateral as heir since there were no other known relatives. In the ensuing days, both contestants performed all the mortuary rites. The youth was not able to put on the white turban, since the old man had been cremated from the house of his rival. But he went to Ujjain to perform the *ganta*, and both men gave a *nukta* feast. The collateral thought that he need not do the rite for Hinglaj Devi, not being a sect member. But soon after he saw a snake slither across his path, and decided that this was a way used by Hinglaj Devi to change his mind. He therefore went to the Gosain officiant and after some bargaining arranged to feed the sect for Rs. 30. The inheritance case was not decided when I left; but the incident shows that villagers consider the performance of the rites to demonstrate a filial tie—or, in the case of the collateral, to show that nobody else has one.[1]

BEHAVIOUR OF KIN—IN SECULAR MATTERS

As in ceremonial affairs, there tends in other matters to be a division of roles between agnates and other kin. One reason lies in the residence pattern. The fact that agnates tend to live in the same village, whereas such kin as the mother's brother and the father's sister's husband usually live at some distance, means that often agnates alone can provide support in disputes within the village, for example.

In most divisions within subcaste groups in Ramkheri, one finds the co-operation of agnates to be an important, if not the main feature. A detailed analysis of factions within the village would be too long for this book, and some examples will suffice. Among Rajputs, for instance, factions are based on the branches of each lineage; that is, the constituent units are branches A and B of the Chauhans (see p. 175), and two similar Solanki branches. In the past Chauhan A has sometimes been alone, opposed by Chauhan B together with Solanki A and B; and there have also been times when Chauhan A and B stood united against Solanki A and B. The shifts can be seen as reflexes of relations between the four headmen and other important men who headed these four branches. Indeed, the rival groups of Rajputs are known as *panthi*, the term used for a division of any whole (in this case the headmanship), rather than *thar*, the usual word for faction. Households of people linked to kin of any branch support them, unless their allegiance is estranged by living in the same ward as another branch.

[1] Anglo-Hindu law does not, in fact, recognize this as the basis for any claim.

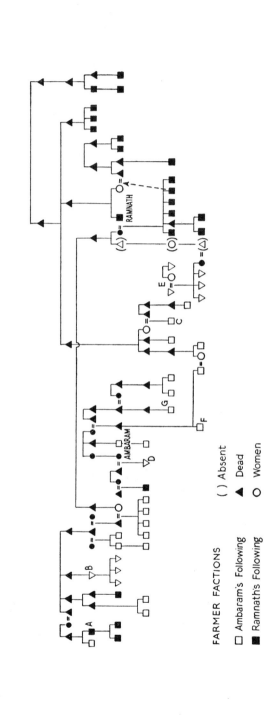

FARMER FACTIONS

☐ Ambaram's Following
■ Ramnath's Following
▽ Waverers

( ) Absent
▲ Dead
○ Women
● Dead Women
- - - ▶ Adoption

Again, quarrels among Bhilalas tend to divide the subcaste into the two clan groups, each with its linked households (see p. 173). Since these two clans comprise almost the entire population, there is not only a simple kinship, but also a fairly clear factional pattern.

The Farmers present a different picture. Here there has been a lot of recent immigration, and the diagram on p. 174 will have shown that the subcaste contains small numbers of agnates, linked by marriage in this or preceding generations. Alliances over disputes tend to be of a more shifting nature; for the alternative may exist of whether to support an agnate, or another type of kinsman. To illustrate this, I give the allegiance of the population over a series of disputes which have taken place between two important men— Ramnath and Ambaram. Here, allegiances within extended families vary. In the case of A-, this has coincided with a move from Ambaram's to Ramnath's ward; yet ward neighbourliness does not always make for conformity, for B- is said to support Ramnath at least covertly and yet lives an Ambaram's ward. The division can even come between brothers, as with A- and his sibling. Again, men like C- do not support the man to whom they are more closely allied; and the waverers like E- are those who have no very close tie with either protagonist, and so change with the self-interest of the moment.

The diagram shows that factional support tends to follow agnatic links wherever these are available to followers within the village context of kinship. A variety of cognatic and affinal alternatives makes for less predictable support, and may produce many waverers.

In questions involving property, on the other hand, agnates tend to be rivals or at least remain separate instead of co-operating. I have already dealt briefly with the incidence of the joint family and joint household (see pp. 181–2). There, I pointed out that the coparceners were usually from a small group of patrikin, rarely comprising more than two generations of adults, and that it was exceptional to find joint families existing after the joint household had divided. From this we can infer that there are frequent partitions of joint households and that the atmosphere is then such that nobody wishes to keep on holding land jointly, though joint farming is economically advantageous.

Partitions, in fact, are rarely amicable, and are usually the result of quarrels between the men or women of the joint household. The formal rule that the younger should obey the older does not always control members of a joint household. And the Mitakshara system of property holding, in which any member can claim his share without necessarily having the approval of the other coparceners, makes it easy for divisions to occur.[1] Though people will usually support each other against outsiders, bitterness born of partition may sometimes put brothers into opposed factions.

The division of property in this way is only part of the wider system of inheritance which involves a larger number of kin. Mostly it concerns land, for other property (money and movables) is usually divided by a person before his death, or is seized by the kin near him before others can assess it.

Inheritance concerns both self-acquired property and the share of the ancestral property held by a person after partition. According to the Banaras school of the Mitakshara system of inheritance followed in Dewas, the following are heirs in order of precedence: sons, sons' sons, sons' sons' sons, widow, daughters, daughters' sons, mother, father, brothers, brothers' sons, etc. The main feature is that, though inheritance is based on patrilineal principles, two women—the widow and the daughter—come very high in the scale of priority. One might expect that in a strongly patrilineal society the claims of the brother and other agnatic collaterals would be stronger. But the widow's claim stems from the notion that she is 'half the body of her husband' and this is shown by her membership of the husband's clan —for it will be recalled that she has made worship to his Clan Goddess—and the consequent power to perform *sraddh* to his and his ancestors' souls if there are no sons to do so.

The daughters are more closely connected to a dead man than the brothers because his 'blood particles' have been directly passed to them, whereas the brothers have in common only the 'blood particles' of the parents (and if this were accounted closer than the 'particles' of the dead person, then the brother would presumably also have priority over the son). The Mitakshara system is, subject to discordant authoritative texts, predominantly based on the priority of common 'blood particles,'[2] and this has given the inheritance scale a rather more diffuse aspect than it might otherwise have had.

The law may not prefer agnates from amongst near kin; but the ideas of the villagers are much more oriented towards them. Most informants in Ramkheri maintain that women had no priority at all in the days before the merger of States in 1948. If no sons were alive, they say, the estate went directly to the brothers and their sons. They assert that the present rules are new and view them with concern, saying that the increased powers of the daughter and widow mean more chance for the land to leave agnatic hands. Only a few men with legal knowledge support what I was told by a leading lawyer in Dewas, that the widow and daughter have always had priority. It

---

[1] I hope to analyse partitions in detail elsewhere.

[2] Kane 1941: 452 quoting the Commentary of Vijnaneswara on this subject.

may well be, of course, that both views are correct—for it is not unusual to have alternatives provided by customary law which override the formal legal code.[1]

The fact that daughters are said not to have claimed land in former times can thus be explained in two ways. One is that they were restrained by customary law from doing this (the restraint weakening with the merger of the Dewas States). The other is that they did not, for some reason, wish to assert the priority given them by the Mitakshara system. I suggest that this was because in those days there was plenty of land, and the daughters' husbands would not have wished to leave their villages. But now land is in short supply,[2] and any daughter inheriting it will try to gain possession. This may well mean a full application of Mitakshara priorities. The villagers realize that the situation has changed, and seek to connect it with a change in the law itself, which they assert has grown 'weak' in allowing so much power to women and affines.

The importance of women's inheritance is put into perspective by the following figures for registration of land in Ramkheri.

TABLE 1

Category	Number
Men registered who have inherited from father	121
Men registered who have inherited by adoption	8
Women registered	17
Total	146

The first category comprises men holding land singly and as coparceners. In the second are six men who were adopted by childless agnates or their widows (who inherited their husbands' lands), one who was adopted by a father's sister's husband, and one by an unrelated caste-mate. Adoption tends to be within the agnatic group, especially when property is involved; this is confirmed by considering all adoptions, with or without property considerations. Of fourteen adoptions, nine were by sonless agnates or their widows; this is a lower proportion than for adoptions with property interests.

Of the seventeen women holding land, three are sisters who have inherited from widowed and issueless brothers,[3] nine are widows of

[1] I regret that I did not find out whether such customary law existed.

[2] The last tract of moderately level open land was brought under the plough some twenty years ago in Ramkheri, and this seems to be a general trend.

[3] Sisters come very low in the order of heirs of the Banaras school, and their high priority here is presumably due to customary law. (See Rattigan 1929: 99 for similar cases in the Punjab.)

husbands without male issue, three are daughters inheriting from widowed fathers, two have land from a widowed mother. It is not surprising that widows comprise the largest category, for they have the highest Mitakshara priority. Three of these women have even already adopted agnates of their husbands as heirs; two others have young sons in whose names the property will be registered when they are old enough to be responsible for working it. Two have invited a daughter's husband to live with them and work the property, and his son or wife will later inherit; and the remaining two have no heirs living with them, but farm the land through labourers or tenants.

When widows inherit, the chances are that the land will remain with agnates, through an adoption if by no other means. Since this is often an adoption of a son of the dead husband's brother, the latter is not often hostile to the widow. Even if she does not adopt one of his sons, the brother has reasonable hopes of getting the land if she makes no other adoption. For she takes no more than a 'limited estate' which is inalienable save for the benefit of the estate or for pious acts for her husband's spiritual benefit. At her death, the estate reverts, usually to the husband's brother. Even during her lifetime, hope of getting the estate is not quite dead. Sometimes she can be proved to be incapable of farming adequately (i.e. cause 'waste' to the estate), sometimes she forfeits her claim by remarrying, and sometimes she is old, and can be expected to die soon. In all these cases the land will remain within the agnatic group, as long as she (or her dead husband) does not have a living daughter. And it is between the dead man's brother and his daughter that rivalries and tensions are most likely.

When the daughters inherit land, the agnates fear that this property will leave the descent group and never come to rest in the hands of collaterals, however remote. The daughter cannot herself sell it, but her son, if he inherits from her, becomes its full owner. It is not then classed as ancestral property for this man's son, and he can gift or sell the land, to the disadvantage of the agnates. This is the main reason for strenuous attempts by brothers and other collaterals to retain land and not allow sisters or daughters to inherit. Most land disputes have centred round this, some resulting in court cases and others in appeals to the revenue authorities who maintain the land registers. In some instances the brother has tried to show that he was unseparated at the death of his brother (when he would be the heir by survivorship); in other cases he has sought to maintain that the sister is wealthy enough to have no need of the land; in yet others, that she cannot adequately farm the land, since she is living with her husband in her conjugal village. The last case is now a strong one;

Government policy is against absentee farming, and the daughter may be torn between farming one or other of the lands available to her. In one recent case, a young Ramkheri Farmer died without issue or widow and his married sister inherited from him. She started farming through labourers, whilst living with her husband. The man's father's brother protested, and a compromise was reached whereby he farms the land and divides the crop with the sister. It is possible that the sister agreed to this (although this may eventually lead to the father's brother gaining complete control) because she feared that the land might otherwise be taken away entirely from her as an absentee owner.

The dislike of seeing land leave the control of agnates is clear in the few cases where an adoption of a non-agnate has been made. One man adopted his wife's brother's son, though he had a brother's son alive in the village. When he died, there were plenty of people who told the brother's son to claim the land, so that it should not pass to others. Their argument was that the adoption rite had not been properly performed. But the brother's son had some land of his own, just enough to support his fear of the law courts and make him deaf to the advice of his fellows.

Other occasions for quarrels occur when the male heir is young and under the care of his mother. One man told me, 'I was small when my father died, and there was a quarrel over the land certificate [of ownership] between my mother and my father's brother. Finally, my mother got it in her name, through the help of my sister's husband who was a clerk in the Government office. I do not know what he did, but we gave him a piece of the land in gratitude.' There are several instances where *legerdemain* has been used, either to support a rightful claim or to wrest land from the heirs.

What are the results of this pattern of inheritance and the attitudes of kin towards it? The main one is that affinal kin are getting more and more involved in property matters. Before, inheritance was almost entirely a matter for agnates; but now, the daughter (and her husband) claims rights as a person having a very high priority. Since the tenure laws now make it hard for the couple to farm at a distance, they will more and more come to live in the wife's parental village if the property is at all sizable; and this will exacerbate the hostility already aroused by the disposal of the property. It will also tend to change the residence pattern, of course, making the village caste group less of an extended agnatic kin-group and resulting in more splits of the extended household as men go to their conjugal villages. This is speculation, of course. But a man without male issue now tends to regard his son-in-law with suspicion, and makes arrangements to adopt an agnate. On the one hand, this makes for enmity between affines, and on the other, it may cause quarrels between agnates about who is to be adopted.

I have no evidence of very distant agnates claiming land (unless they live in the same village). But if pressure on land and other occupations becomes very intense this might start—for men would seize any opportunity to claim from distant intestate kin. Such a strengthening of extended agnatic ties would come just at a time when the rights of women (and through them affines) are being reinforced.[1] And these rights may create rivalry between brothers and sisters, in contrast to the close and emotionally binding tie I have noted.

Less common aspects of inheritance can affect relations within the household or small kin-group. Thus, the children of a man's remarriage have equal rights with his offspring by a full marriage. I have never heard of any dispute over their getting their shares. But I have noticed a certain condescension in the attitudes of their halfsiblings. These almost imply that the offspring of the remarriage have received shares through their kindness alone. This is not legally justified, but it may nevertheless colour relations between such kin.

Inheritance patterns provide an important factor in interpersonal kin relations, then. They do not directly affect the wider subcaste population; for neither do its members inherit the property, nor are they called to settle disputes, which generally go to the courts.

Most of my data on financial aid by kin concerns loans made by the mother's brother or the wife's father. They are given without interest, and it is not good manners to ask for the money back. The borrower, on the other hand, is impelled to return the money at the earliest possible moment, partly to avoid being obliged to these kin (especially his wife's father), and partly to keep his credit good—for it is after all quite possible for even these men to refuse to give loans. One man, for example, had borrowed money from his wife's father to buy some land. As soon as the Government started a programme of loans for well-digging, he borrowed money under it and repaid his father-in-law. Unfortunately, he omitted to do even the minimal work towards starting the well, and after a year the Government pressed him for the money, when they saw no results. At the time of my departure he was threatened with a summons. 'Of course,' he said, 'I could get enough money from my father-in-law to pay off the Government tomorrow. But I do not want to be always borrowing from him; for then, when I want it for an essential, he may only give grudgingly and my honour (*ijjat*) will be lowered.'

A man getting into such difficulties (financial, factional, etc.) that

[1] e.g. An unmarried daughter can now claim a share of the estate equal to that of her brother, at the death of the father (Hindu Succession Act 1956).

he has to leave the village seldom goes to live with an agnate if he has one. In Ramkheri there are five men who have come to live in their mother's brother's village, nine men who are in the settlement of their wife's father, and two who are living in the village of the father's sister. Three other men have come to the village of a sister's husband, and one to that of his wife's sister's husband. In all cases the immigrants were offered some help to get settled, or had at least the assurance of moral support which, at least in some cases, was less strongly offered elsewhere. In contrast, I know of no case where a man has come to live with a collateral.

This distinction between agnates and others cannot be pressed too far, for there is variation in specific instances. To the question 'Who is most likely to give a man financial help?' one man will say that the mother's brother will do so, and contrasts this by pointing to two brothers in Ramkheri, one of whom managed to get the lion's share of their property when it was divided, and has never done anything to help the other. But another man will answer that the father's brother or one's own sibling is the most likely to lend assistance, and he will give an equally valid instance to support his opinion. I have stated my own feeling that the majority of cases favour the mother's brother and wife's father; but this is only a tentative conclusion. Exceptions occur, based on the financial circumstances of the people involved, their likes and dislikes, the distance between their villages or the influence of their wives on them—e.g. the mother's brother's wife is said often to try to stop her husband giving help to someone for whom she has no particular sentiment. The fact that there is no system of marriage alliance which would link people of these descent groups and their descendants after them makes it easier for the individual to take his own decisions.

SUMMARY

What does this account show is the extent and quality of kin ties? The demographic pattern of subcaste distribution makes for a wide spatial scatter of kin. Some subcastes are found in many villages but with only a small population in each settlement; here the rules of exogamy forbid repeated marriages between a pair of villages and force matchmakers to look further afield. Other subcastes have larger populations in each settlement, but are found in fewer and more scattered villages of the region. Though more matches may link these villages, the average distance between affinal households in the different subcastes remains more than ten miles.

These affinal ties do not, of course, apply to the village *as a whole*, but only to the specific subcaste. Malwi Weavers, for instance, may have relatives in village A-, but if there are no Gujarati Weavers living there, we cannot say that the Gujarati Weavers have any tie with this village. The table below shows the extent to which more than one Ramkheri subcaste has made marriages into the same village (from the survey of 446 matches):

TABLE 2

Number of Subcastes	Number of Villages
2	35
3	19
4	4
5	—
6	1
Total	59

In these (out of the 219 villages into which matches have been made) something of a truly inter-village feeling exists. Thus, when a man of subcaste A- goes to the village to fetch his daughter, he may take greetings and ask for news from the affines of subcaste B-, who live in this village too. But since this is exceptional, most inter-village kin ties exist at the subcaste level only. I have already said that most members of a village subcaste group can trace kinship with villages into which fellow-members have married, and we can, in fact, see relations between village subcaste populations as kinship relations as well as common membership of a status group. These kin relations are not always effective—i.e. they may only be ones of recognition and not co-operation. The kindred of co-operation is, in fact, a smaller body and is not common to the whole village subcaste group. Rather, it is reducible to the closer kin ties of the people of a single household.

It might then be thought that larger households would have a wider spread of kinsfolk who are actually co-operating on any given occasion, but this is only partly true. For there are so many rites in a large household at which gifts are necessary from kin who attend, that many people cannot afford to come each time. In the largest Farmer household, a marriage took place nearly every year. I was surprised to see the attendance at the marriage of the eldest daughter of the eldest son was of only average size. I was told that not all the affines of the other brothers came, for they had already made gifts at the marriages of the latter's children some years before. And few villagers gave *ban*, for most had already given on other occasions and were now waiting for a reciprocation.

In general, a man will ask people from the households of mother's brother, wife's father, father's sister and mother's sister at least, as well as the parents-in-law of children who are engaged or married, and this will usually add up to more than half a dozen households. He may also invite his wife's sister's husband, his sister's husband, etc., and this brings the number around a dozen households. Richer men invite far more—the wife's mother's brother for example, and large marriage invitations will spread to more than twenty villages.[1] The largest feast, the funerary *nukta*, may take in a great many more people than this, guests sometimes numbering thousands. The size of these groups of kin is not only significant for studying the kin-group; it is also a major basis for social control within many subcastes, as the next chapter will show.

The occasions which draw attendance from outside the village are subcaste affairs; occasions which are based on inter-caste activity (e.g. Holi, Naumi, etc.) are confined to the village's population.[2] In only one context do the village and the inter-village subcaste populations meet in a single activity—at the worship of the Smallpox Goddess held every twenty years or so. At that time there is worship by all women with children who have survived an attack of smallpox. This is made at the same time by all villagers from Brahman to Sweeper, and is an occasion on which they invite kin from outside, particularly the mother's brother who brings clothes for the woman worshipping and for her children. There were several thousand guests at the Smallpox Goddess worship held in Ramkheri in 1955. Every household had at least the minimum of visitors I have just mentioned for weddings, and others invited many more. Men with several children to be married in the near future invited few kinsmen, lest they present gifts now and have none for the weddings later; others, with many invitations to be repaid, had large numbers of kin for the ceremony. Again, the gathering was for the Rajputs an occasion to make merry with meat and liquor;[3] the Farmers, on the other hand, being vegetarians had less incentive to throw a large and often riotous party. The Smallpox Goddess worship marked the only occasion when even an approximation of the 'total effective village kin ties' with the outside could be seen.

[1] Cf. Lang 1946: 167 for the observation that rich people have more relatives than poor people in China. Thus kinship largely depends on wealth and ability to invite and 'keep kin from growing cold' as the Ramkheri people say.

[2] It is alleged that people of other villages used to come to the Holi fair in Ramkheri when it was a royal village, but this is no longer the case.

[3] Hitherto, a goat was sacrificed by each meat-eating family in its worship, and the head left at the shrine of the Goddess, to be collected later by the Weavers (as I saw in another village). In Ramkheri vegetarian offerings were substituted in 1955, under the new influences I have mentioned (see p. 103), but goats were privately killed by carnivorous households, most of whose members deplored the fact that the Goddess had not been properly propitiated.

This account has shown a clearly defined separation of roles for different kin. These are based on distinctions of age and sex, and on agnatic on the one hand and affinal-uterine kinship on the other. I have shown how these roles operate in the household, and between kin living in one and several villages. At the same time, there are factors which make variation possible from the ideal role. Quarrels in a household, or between heirs, will upset the expected pattern. Again, a mother's brother will always act 'as a mother's brother' in the sense that he will always bring *mamere* rather than *ban* to a wedding; but he may not always come (because of distance, lack of money, etc.), and in this sense will not be acting as his role dictates. Usually, of course, the real mother's brother adheres most closely to the duties required of him, classificatory and ritual mother's brothers less strictly. But in all classes of relationship there are instances where the relation has 'grown cold'. This is generally a mutual procedure. One man does less, so the other does less too, and exchanges, etc., are gradually watered down. Money and the self-respect and piety which bind people to their socio-religious duty are the main bases for kinship relations, where affection may or may not exist. A man's failure to meet his kinship obligations does not stick in the minds of his fellow-villagers especially those of different subcaste (unless it is particularly blatant), for these are themselves related to people in different settlements, and therefore do not hear about it from *their* kinsfolk. The same attitude of detachment which allows differences in commensal behaviour, so long as they are manifested in other villages or the towns, enables people to decide on their course of action as kin so long as this does not affect their fellow-villagers. And the pattern and spread of marriage ties means that this does not often happen.

XII

SOCIAL CONTROL IN THE SUBCASTE

TYPES OF SUBCASTE COUNCIL

An analysis of social control within the subcaste interests us for two reasons. In the first place, it enables us to see with greater precision the extent and personnel of effective subcaste groups; and in the second place, it gives us understanding of the ways in which subcastes manage their affairs as separate groups, and the ways in which their members enlist the aid of fellow-villagers of different subcastes.

There are several kinds of council controlling behaviour—I use 'council' in the way I have distinguished it from the committee-type body (see p. 122)—all of which generally concern the single subcaste. Thus, in Ramkheri the endogamous Gujarati and Malwi Weavers have their own councils; where, however, two subcastes are in the process of merging into a single subcaste (as with the Malwi and Mewari Oil-pressers), the council may include people of both subcastes since they belong to a single endogamous group.

The deliberations of the councils cover a wide range of subjects. They deal with infringements of the rules of inter-caste relations (eating, drinking or smoking with forbidden castes, or allowing them to enter one's house), infringements of the subcaste's dietary rules (eating meat or drinking liquor, etc.), contracting marriage or sex relations within forbidden degrees of kin or with forbidden castes, and the killing of certain animals (cows and bullocks, squirrels, peacocks, etc.). All these offences are ritual ones since they require a purification (a penitential pilgrimage, or the hearing of holy scriptures) as well as a punishment (a fine, or the feeding of fellow subcaste members).

Councils also concern themselves with secular offences which do not need to be reported to the authorities, e.g. disputes between men of the same subcaste over land, non-cognizable assaults, non-payment of debts by subcaste mates, the breaking of an engagement of marriage. In addition, councils may be held about matters of general importance—raising subscriptions for the construction of a subcaste temple in Ujjain, purchasing cooking utensils for use at large gatherings of the subcaste, and changing the subcaste's name or food habits so as to raise its status.

251

The council of smallest scale is made up of some or all of the subcaste population of a particular village. There is nothing formal about it, though one or two men will be generally acknowledged as leaders and will arbitrate disputes. The larger subcastes are able to settle matters themselves; but the smaller subcastes must clearly call in an outsider since their entire membership may be involved in the dispute. There are, for example, only two households of Sweepers in Ramkheri. During my stay, quarrels between the two came to a head, and the elder brother denied his brother drinking water from the well situated in his courtyard. The younger brother was forced to get water from a well in a field at some distance, and after a few days of this he invited their mother's brother to come and settle the dispute; and this was temporarily successful. On other occasions the brothers had called in a Ramkheri Cotton-carder to arbitrate. I would classify all such councils as village subcaste councils whether or not an arbiter of another caste is called in; for the affair is internal to the subcaste, and the main parties to it as well as the councillors in all but the smallest subcastes are villagers.

This kind of council is distinct from what I have loosely called the headman's council (see p. 97) in which the village's leaders dealt with matters of common concern to all subcastes in the settlement, or disputes in which the protagonists were men of different subcastes. The village subcaste council can be easily and inexpensively called; all that is needed is some tobacco for those who come. Any issue to be settled is usually given a hearing at once, though a decision may not be reached immediately. If the subcaste contains factions, the members of each may sit to judge their own adherents, though if the affair concerns the status of the entire subcaste group the other faction will also attend. Village subcaste councils may well be held when there is a ritual gathering. Thus, at the *gaurni* feast for a Rajput woman, the entire village subcaste group attended, and the misdemeanour of a member was considered.

Larger than the village subcaste council is that composed of men from a group of neighbouring settlements. In some subcastes there is a specific number of places represented on this council, and this I shall call a circle.[1] The Hindi word is *pankhera*, literally meaning a group of five villages, though the size of circles may vary greatly. The circle council meets to decide cases which concern any member: if there is a dispute between men of different circles, the respective circle councils will judge their own members, or there may be a meeting between people of both circles. A circle can split into two or more smaller bodies. I have never heard of the amalgamation of

[1] I do not mean by this word a number of villages endogamously or hypergamously defined (cf. Naik 1957: 173).

several circles, but I presume that this is possible. The constituent unit of the circle is the entire village subcaste population; it was said to be impossible for one party in a village to belong to one, and another to a different circle. A deep split of this kind within a village subcaste group would result rather in one of the parties withdrawing from the deliberations of the circle, having instead its own informal council of arbitration organized along kinship rather than local lines.

The size of circles varied from five to thirty villages, and they were reported from twelve subcastes in Ramkheri. But I am by no means sure that all of these are 'real' circles, that is to say corporate groups of village subcaste populations. One criterion is that member villages should take part in deliberations for these to be valid. And this feature was reported by only two of these subcastes. The Rajputs have a circle of five villages, all of which lie within about four miles from the centre settlement, and my data on the pattern of invitation suggest that people of all villages have indeed been present at circle council meetings. The Gujarati Weavers have a circle of fifteen villages, some of which lie perhaps six or seven miles from the centre; here, it was said, there need not be attendance from all villages, but in three of them hereditary leaders existed and the presence of at least these men was necessary to have a proper decision made.

The second criterion for a circle is the presence of a leader (*mandloi*, or *jat patel*). This man occupies a hereditary post, and his main power is a ritual one. For it is his duty to eat first at any feast given by a man who has been put out of the subcaste; by his eating he signifies that the subcaste has again accepted the culprit as member. Mostly such feasts are given by men who have been ritually impure (e.g. who have killed cows, or have gone to jail and thus eaten impure food) and nobody wants to be the first to take their food. The *mandloi* takes this odium on himself, and absorbs what impurity remains; his prestige as leader means that he alone can do this and still have people following him rather than putting him out of the caste for eating with a boycotted man. For this work he may be paid token sums of money.

The *mandloi* does not appear to have any other hereditary power. As the ritual leader he has considerable standing which may overflow into the sphere of arbitration and make his voice the most respected in the circle council. But this depends on his personal ability, and there does not seem to be any rule that he should have the deciding voice on any case. The present *mandloi* of the Rajput circle, in fact, is said not to be the real authority in the circle council. I recorded four subcastes possessing *mandloi* with the status and duties I have described.

Both of the above criteria were met in only two of the twelve subcastes whose members said they had a circle. The remainder presented various inconsistencies. In some the number of villages in the circle varied from informant to informant; in others there was said to be a *mandloi*, but he lived in a village or town outside the circle and was said to serve other villages as well. Nor did he in all cases have the ritual responsibilities I have noted; instead of the *mandloi*, close kin of the culprits might be the first to eat, or there might be no distinction about who should lead. Further investigation might have shown that some of these subcastes had a formally corporate unit after all; but in a few cases at least, I think that a circle's existence was made up for my benefit, partly because my informants felt that it was proper to have a circle (for the Rajputs have a strong one), and partly because I was known to be asking about circles, and it would obviously please me to have one reported! Another explanation would be that the word *pankhera* was used by informants to mean villages which generally come together to decide issues, but which do not *have* to do so, as in the truly corporate circles. Since circles meet only occasionally, this is not the kind of data that can be checked during a year's stay.

The people of eleven subcastes said they had no circles. In some cases they told of circles in previous generations, but said that the authority of the *mandloi* no longer existed, neither was there any group of villages to decide matters, and that each man now tended to settle issues in his own way. 'Before, one headman; now, one hundred headmen' was a common saying; we have seen this trend in the village's pattern of authority and it exists in the subcaste too. In other cases there was no history of a circle, and this form of organization may not ever have been universal.

Such subcastes managed their affairs at any large meeting—usually at the assembly of subcaste mates for a marriage or a *nukta*. I have already indicated the size of these gatherings; they took in people of from between five and twenty-five villages (many more for large *nuktas*) and included kin of all members of the host's household. Very often people from other subcastes in the village were also asked, and these had equal rights to be heard in any deliberations though they were not implicated in the decisions themselves. Indeed, in one case where a Dairyman widow was brought before a subcaste council her main spokesman was a Rajput who was her contract labourer at the time. I shall call this kind of council a kindred council, since the main criterion of participation is the kin tie which has caused the host to give people invitations to that particular function (only the richest invite whole village subcaste groups, and even here there is usually a more or less tenuous relationship). The term 'kindred' does not exactly describe the composition of the gathering, for there may be people of the host's co-operating kindred who cannot accept the invitation; but it is indicative of the basis of this kind of council.

The circle and the kindred councils are, in fact, similar in the numbers of people attending, apart from those with a duty to be there in circle councils. For most meetings of the circle councils are also held at *nuktas* and weddings. Any man can call a council meeting if he is prepared to feed those who come from the prescribed villages, but there are few men wealthy enough, and few occasions pressing enough, to justify such expense. Most people wait until there is a gathering of the subcaste, and the opportunity is then taken to settle anything outstanding. Only one matter demands an urgent meeting of the council, and that is the killing of a cow or bullock (*gau hatya*). For a man who is judged to have done this is put out of the subcaste at once, and not readmitted until he has both made penance and fed a subcaste council. This feast of admission must be a separate affair from a marriage feast, etc., and is done as soon as possible, so that the culprit can resume normal life. He is said either to invite the villagers of his circle, or will ask the major subcaste leaders of the locality and his more important kinsfolk if he has no circle. The feast is never very large, for people do not like eating food which was cooked whilst the culprit was an outcaste.

The third type of council is what I call the provincial council. Again, there is a wide variation between subcastes with well-organized provincial councils and those with the possibility of some sort of loosely convened gathering on this scale. For most subcastes, the provincial council hinges on the subcaste temple at Ujjain. Perhaps three-quarters of the subcastes living in the part of Malwa around Dewas, Ujjain and Indore have their own temples there. In them Brahman and Bairagi priests perform rites to the deities enshrined; these rites are in no way subcaste rites and others can come to worship there or to fulfil vows made to the deity. But the temple is operated by the subcaste, the land on which it stands is in the subcaste's name and the priest is paid by it. The variation lies in the amount of participation by the general subcaste population. Some temples (e.g. that of the Malwi Oil-presser) appear to be entirely under the control of the subcaste's population in Ujjain; in other cases (e.g. the Farmer) the temple is controlled by a committee on which sit representatives from villages up to fifty miles from Ujjain. One of the main factors in this difference seems to be whether the temple possesses a lodge for pilgrims. If it does, then people from the country will stay there whilst on their way to worship in the large Ujjain temples, or to perform the obsequies of the *kriya karam* at the Bheru Ghat, some two miles from the city. If it does not, then villagers will rarely feel any need to visit the subcaste temple for, as I have said, there is no rite or deity specific to the subcaste.[1]

The men on the temple committees (they are committees, rather than councils) may act as initiators of general subcaste policies. They do this at the very large annual gatherings at Ujjain—notably for the bathing festival on the full-moon day of Kartik month. At that time crowds of villagers collect, and the committee itself meets to administer the temple. It is then easy to pass resolutions relating to the population of the area from whence this attendance comes. Thus, two resolutions were passed at a meeting at the Gujarati Barber temple by a body entitling itself The Main Council of the Barbers (*Sri Sakhopanc Nai*); that there should be a fine of Rs. 51 and the outcasting of any barber who steals a client from a fellow subcaste member before the client has paid his arrears to the former barber; and that a maximum of Rs. 51 should be set for the payment to a matchmaker who arranges a remarriage.[2] People could not tell how completely these resolutions had been obeyed, but they give an illustration of the kinds of matters put before the provincial council. In theory, the temple committee may in some subcastes act as a court of appeal from the local councils. But nobody was able to give me examples of cases which the committee had decided. As in the smaller councils, anyone present can talk during these meetings.

Some subcastes do not have provincial councils at Ujjain. The main temple of the Bhilalas is at Ongkeshwar on the Narmada river, the site of an ancient Bhil kingdom. The Dairymen of Ramkheri have their temple in Indore. And some other subcastes have local temples—at Dewas, etc.—as well as one at Ujjain. But the focus on the temple is the same. The Rajputs alone are organized differently. They have no temples at Ujjain, and the provincial meetings I recorded are instead based on the authority of some of the important Rajput nobles and landlords. Thus, there was a provincial meeting in a village near Ramkheri which considered the readmission to the main body of the small 'outcaste subcaste' of Pancholi Rajputs. Three important landlords attended, who took charge of the meeting. People are said to have come from villages up to twenty-five miles away to discuss the question (which was left in abeyance). The difference between Rajputs and other subcastes fits the dominant political position of the caste in this part of Malwa. Other subcastes do not have such landlords to adjudicate their affairs.

[1] There are exceptions. One such would be the deity Vishvakarma at the temple of the Mewara Carpenters; for he is specifically the patron deity of carpenters.

[2] The matchmaker in marriage negotiations receives no such payment.

PROCEDURE OF THE COUNCILS

The procedure in all these kinds of council is similar. In the first place, both sides to a dispute must be present, or the accused if it is a case of a man's breaking a subcaste rule. In the second place, there must be general consensus over the verdict; if not, the decision will be postponed. In the words of a leader in another part of India, the principle is 'to induce a spirit of compromise by repeated adjournments' [1] rather than to force a division of the council to get quicker action. Only when one or two individuals stand out against a decision which has the force of long precedent might a decision be considered justifiable without the consent of all present. A meeting is a debate on the issue by everyone, and the beginning is largely a display of the eloquence and perhaps the anger of the plaintiff and defendant. The more influential men say nothing at first. But when things have quietened down they start to question and to guide the council into some compromise or course of action. Here lies the value of oratory and a firm temper and character, so that these are said to be the main attributes of an arbiter, more than hereditary position or wealth. The leaders size up the feeling of the council and reckon whether they can get a consensus or not. If it is unlikely, they say less and less until the meeting peters out and it is understood that the matter will be taken up again later—there is not, in my experience, any formal postponement made.[2]

The composition of the council which will hear the issues on the second occasion may be different; and this, as much as the changing attitudes of the parties involved, may help to settle the case. But there are, of course, common values held by the people of both councils which enable them to make more or less the same judgment; the differences come in the different evaluation of evidence and extenuating circumstances. In matters of fairly simple fact, from which flow automatic penalties (whether a man ate with a forbidden caste, for example), there is usually no great difficulty in reaching a decision. But where the multiplexity of the relations between plaintiff and defendant are relevant, and where the issues are complex and without witnesses (e.g. in cases of recovery of debts), there is room for differences of opinion. And in a situation where there is nobody with the power to make judgment, these differences are sometimes hard to resolve.

There is no expectation of appeal from village to circle council and from the circle to the province. Issues which cannot be solved by the village council may later be placed before a village council

[1] Miller 1955: 47.

[2] For a lengthy description of a council's operation, see Fuchs 1950: 34–7.

augmented by a few important men from outside; but it appears rare for them to be opened anew at a circle or kindred council. As one man put it, 'if we fine a man in the village, the money he pays will give us a good penalty feast; but the more men we bring in, the less feasting will each person get. So we like to keep our affairs inside the village.' This may not be the entire reason, but it shows a facet of the general reluctance to let disputes spread which I return to later. An analysis of the cases for which I have data shows that slightly more are brought before the circle or kindred councils than the village council. But this, I will suggest, is because their content is less appropriate to the latter body; it does not mitigate the desire to keep in the village cases which have been started there.

The ideal pattern, then, is of a council reaching unanimous agreement on its verdict (whether at the first attempt or after several sittings), whereupon the culprit pays his fine, etc., or is boycotted. The latter eventuality is effected by circulating a notice (*terij*) to all the villages of the region (not only of the circle, if this exists) asking them to deny the culprit all facilities of subcaste membership. That is, nobody should eat, drink or smoke with him, marry their children to his, or help him in any way.

In practice, things do not always work out like this. In the first place, disagreement over the matter at issue may not mean a postponement of the council until a consensus can be reached, but may result in a split of the council itself. Take, for example, a kindred council of the Gujarati Barber subcaste, which sat during the *nukta* of one of its members in village B-. A man of village A- had been asked to collect subscriptions to purchase large cooking vessels for use at feasts by any subcaste members of the area. He died, and his son disclaimed any knowledge of the money already collected, as well as the responsibility to refund it. The council thereupon met to decide what should be done. Some people, including the host of village B-, called on the rule that a son is responsible for his father's debts, and alleged that he had 'eaten' the money and should be condemned. The other party maintained that because the money was in the form of subscriptions and was not technically a debt to the subscribers, no liability accrued to the son. The argument became warmer and warmer, and finally the men of village A- and some half a dozen neighbouring settlements got up and walked out without eating. Their opponents were doubly angered at this; not only did it show up the disagreement, but they held it to be an insult to their host and a waste of his food. This had happened several years before, but the villages still formed separate councils and did not, it was said, come to eat publicly with each other.

One man commented about this, 'Parties may be formed over this kind of quarrel. And the split may last five or ten years before there is an understanding. Some splits are complete and others only affect public occasions, for members of each side will eat together in private.' I would suspect that the latter situation is the more common. For there are many kin ties between two such groups of villages, and I doubt that these would be so easily severed. It is interesting that the split involves groups of villages, which are then self-sufficient in having enough people to man their councils. I never heard of a single village seceding in this way. It is this sort of split of a subcaste circle which may eventually harden into separate circles. Ramkheri's five-village circle of Rajputs, for example, was formerly part of a much larger circle of sixty villages. People knew that there had been some disagreement which had led to the division, though they could not (or would not) tell me what it was. There is now no bar to invitations with the villages of the other part of the circle. Separate 'outcaste' subcastes (like the Pancholi Rajput) apparently result from splits with some kind of underlying ritual pollution, on the other hand. In such cases the split is both public and private, and is of a much more permanent nature.

This kind of fission goes counter to the ideal pattern for subcaste councils. A second variation of desired procedure concerns the casting out of a culprit. This should be done through the *terij*, but such notices are rarely sent.[1] Several men in Ramkheri had been put out of the village subcaste group, and I was usually at first told that notices had been sent out. But after cross-checking had revealed inconsistencies it was admitted that this had not actually been done. The feeling was that it would serve no useful purpose. Those of other villages who had something to do with Ramkheri would know about the man, and would boycott him; and the rest would seldom see him in any case. This attitude is part of a general desire to limit any dispute. Leaders try to settle quarrels before they embitter people and involve others; and the behaviour of people in one village is, wherever possible, isolated from their contacts with people in other settlements. An instance is the boycott of the Oil-presser (see p. 124) where craftsmen of other villages continued to serve him without opposition from his Ramkheri opponents. Again, a Gujarati Weaver was put out of the village subcaste group for having taken his elder brother's widow in a leviritic marriage which is considered incestuous. He died before he had paid the fine demanded; his subcaste mates in the

[1] Recent legislation forbids discrimination in eating or drinking; it is aimed at the disabilities of the Harijans, but also hits at all public boycotts. Outcasting must now be done in private, but people say that the law will make no difference, for anyone has the choice of whom he invites to his house as a private citizen. The data I have refer to the times before this development.

village stood apart (including agnates) and the funerary rites were performed by kin from other settlements. These were allowed to do so because 'he was only put out of the village, not the subcaste (*biradari*)'.[1]

There is a similar dislike of spreading disputes within the village. On one occasion a Rajput woman set up house with her Brahman lover. Though the village expressed strong disapproval, and some people refused to have anything to do with the couple, no formal judgment was made and the village craftsmen's services were not withdrawn. When I asked one of the leading Rajputs why this was, he replied, 'If the woman's family (*kutumb*) do not do anything, then how can the subcaste or the village do anything?' Since the family had thought it enough to sever relations with the woman, but not demand her boycott, the rest of the population was content to leave things as they were. (It is, of course, likely that much stronger action would have been taken had she allied herself with a man of lower caste.) This attitude, I suggest, stems from a society containing many groups, each with its own variations of major custom, and each allowing the others freedom in their internal affairs. A subcaste can adopt almost any behaviour without remonstrance from others; these may change their own behaviour towards it (e.g. a subcaste taking up meat-eating might find its commensal circle more restricted) but they will not try to stop it unless it is held to pollute the whole village (no subcaste could take up butchery of cattle, for example), or unless it threatens the position of other castes in some way (e.g. as in the Oil-pressers' demand to eat in one line with the Rajputs).

CASES CONSIDERED BY EACH COUNCIL

Having discussed the procedures of the councils, I now set out the kinds of cases with which they are concerned. In Table 1 I give details of forty-five cases involving the people of Ramkheri in one or more sessions of deliberation. In the rare instances of a case being transferred to a higher level, each deliberation is marked separately.

Though small in number, these figures suggest that the main issues brought before the circle or kindred council are those of forbidden marriages or liaisons, and cases of cow-killing.[2] The village council,

[1] In the rare cases where a man dies having been put out of the entire circle or kindred, his kin will burn him, and will pay a token fine to the circle for their purification. If he has no kin, his subcaste mates must cremate him—'for you cannot leave a corpse to rot'. But none of the other rites will be performed.

[2] Killing of squirrels, etc., is a minor matter, needing purification at Ujjain but no large subcaste meeting.

Social Control in the Subcaste

TABLE 1

Subject of Case	Decided by:		
	Village	Circle/Kindred	Province
Cow-killing	—	3	—
Extra-subcaste sex liaison	2	7	—
Intra-subcaste sex liaison and prohibited degree of marriage	1	2	—
Purification of house*	1	2	—
Prohibited commensal relations	7	1	—
Disputes between affines	4	2	—
Economic matters (e.g. subscriptions)	2	3	2
Wider subcaste policies	—	—	2
Others	2	2	—
Total	19	22	4

* E.g. if a house is burgled, there should be a general purification, the earthern vessels being destroyed, lest the burglar was of a lower caste. Sometimes people do not bother to do this, and it is a matter for a council.

on the other hand, is the place to deal with breaches of commensal rules and disputes between affines. Sometimes these live in the same village, but even when they do not it is often thought better for a village rather than a circle council to settle their quarrels—usually at the village of the defendant, where the only outsiders are the plaintiff and perhaps a friend or two. Lastly, matters of general importance to the subcaste are discussed at provincial councils.

The circle or kindred council thus deals with affairs which are of consequence to the entire local subcaste group, and which are most easily apprehended and over which there is unanimity as to the appropriate punishment. Thus, the gravity of killing a cow is not a matter for discussion, nor is there room for argument over a man's guilt, for this is resolved by the drawing of lots: and a guilty man's penance follows as a matter of course (see p. 264). Similarly, liaisons with people of lower subcastes are important; for many people are related to the culprit, and his or her action will cast a slur upon them all, and make it harder for them to contract good marriages for their children. Again, a liaison or a marriage within the prohibited degree of kin will touch all members. Such actions are comparatively easy of proof, since they persist over a period and must eventually be more or less open, and the penalties are also generally agreed upon.

The cases dealt with by the village council, on the other hand, tend to be those which are harder to prove, over whose seriousness there can be varying opinions, and over which there is not such unanimous

261

feeling about the correct punishment. Breaches of commensal rules are no longer so grave, and some liberal people are inclined to wink at them, or advocate merely nominal fines. But the orthodox will insist on heavier punishments and there may be differences in the council over this. Further, a commensal offence often involves a single incident only; witnesses must then be produced, with all the pressure which both sides can exert on them to change their tale. The one case noted where a commensal breach was tried by the kindred council was, in fact, a continuous affair, where a youth lived with a man of low caste.

Again, disputes between affines are seen as private affairs, and since conflicting evidence may be hard to assess, they usually admit of shades of opinion and thereby lead to postponements or even the defiance of the council's decision. Just as I have said that in the circle council there may be a split between parties, so the decision of the majority in the village council may be unenforceable; partly this is because a minority genuinely believes that the council is wrong, and partly because it is in their interests to side with the culprit. There is a difference from the division I have described in the Barbers' kindred council; for an initial open split rarely occurs in the village council. What happens is that an overtly unanimous decision is taken to condemn a man. If he accepts, well and good; if he resists, a boycott is begun. But this boycott will slowly erode, until there are a number of covert supporters of the boycotted person, and the council has, in fact, divided into two parties. We have seen that this is also the process in the all-village Comprehensive Committee; it will be recalled that the Oil-presser was originally boycotted by the entire village, but that little by little he gathered people to his side. The same thing happens within the subcaste group, though the two are distinguished by villagers who call the subcaste factions by the Hindi word *thar*, whereas the inter-caste divisions are called *palti* (a derivation from the English word 'party').

I cite as an example of a village subcaste council's boycott the case of a Farmer (G- on the chart on p. 240) who started to live with a widow of his subcaste and village. The original dispute was over the right to cultivate the widow's land, and was between her former tenants and G- whom she had taken on later. This was brought before the Comprehensive Committee (then in its short-lived heyday of influence), and opinion there was that the widow should keep her former tenants since these had lived up to their agreements. G- then stood up and said that the owner was living with him and should thus give him the land to cultivate for their household. The way in which he said this, with the implication that it was none of the Comprehensive Committee's business, enraged its leaders and they ordered a village-wide boycott of G- forthwith. As I have already stressed, such boycotts were quite new to the villagers and after a few days G-, having no particular enmity towards the Comprehensive Committee leaders or his fellow-villagers (unlike the Oil-presser cited on p. 123), apologized to the Committee and was reinstated. Only after this did his Farmer rivals take steps for a subcaste boycott, and in this the rest of the village has taken no part. People say it is a matter for each subcaste to decide what to do about such unofficial liaisons, and that they were satisfied with G-'s apology over the tenancy issue.

The main instigators of the subcaste boycott were the widow's affines in the village, classificatory brothers of her dead husband, of whom Ramnath was most prominent. These arraigned the lover in a subcaste village council. Their main accusation related to the rule that the agnates of a first husband should not meet the man whom a divorced or widowed woman has remarried. Usually the villages of these two households differ, and avoidance is easy. But the presence of the lover in Ramkheri itself set up an intolerable position, made worse because these agnates of the dead man expected to have gained control of the widow's land had the lover not been there—for she had no children or parents. They therefore ordered the couple to go and live elsewhere, or to stop their liaison. This position was formally adopted by a meeting of the village subcaste council, and the pair put under a boycott by Ramkheri Farmers when they refused to separate.

But the boycott is 'going bad', as it is said. This is partly because of the issues involved, and partly because other villages have kept aloof. These outsiders said that it was none of their business, adding that the rule of avoidance applied only to the husband of a remarried woman, and not to her lover. This is a debatable point, and it is unlikely that such people would have taken the same view were the affair to have occurred in their own villages; but it supplied the pretext for their dissociation with the boycott. The boycotted man was thus able to get help from relatives in other settlements and so had no need to capitulate to his own village's subcaste group. He himself maintained that his close kin (he used the word *kutumb*) would have continued to help him even had the boycott extended to other villages.

Because the man was able to resist the boycott, a few people in Ramkheri started to weaken. These were men who had no advantage in breaking with him, were not closely tied by kinship to his opponents, and were in fact named as his main allies at the time the boycott was decided. They were marked as D, E and F on the chart at p. 240. Now, D and F are related more nearly to G- than to Ramnath, and they and E are either waverers in the main faction between

Ramnath and Ambaram or support the latter. One sees how ties of kinship combine with other factors to sway support in any controversy. These men have, it is said, either started to smoke privately with the boycotted man or would have no objection to doing so. This is enough to shake the effectiveness of the boycott, for now others are starting to think that perhaps G- could be reinstated without having to apologize to the village subcaste group. The case shows the elements of doubt in the verdict, and the lack of importance to the wider subcaste, which I have said are ingredients of many village subcaste council matters.

If it is true that the village council tends to deal with cases admitting dispute and differing interpretations, whereas the circle or kindred council is more concerned with issues over which people are agreed as to the need and severity of punishment and over which the subcaste in general is concerned, then it follows that more and more work will be given to the village subcaste council. For the rules of conduct of the subcaste are starting to be challenged in the 'new air' that blows. I have already said that people of different castes may now eat together privately, and commensal rules are no longer accepted unthinkingly. Even what one might call the stronghold of subcaste sanction—over cow-killing—is no longer as formidable as it was. To kill a cow is just as serious, but the expiation is no longer such a public act nor such a concern of the subcaste, as this example shows.

A Potter was accused of having beaten a cow which intruded into his backyard. The cow leapt over the wall to escape his blows and suffered internal injuries from which it was said she died two days later. A witness asserted that he had seen the Potter beat the animal; the Potter himself denied this, and a council was convened of the village leaders (not the subcaste). About a dozen people went to the main temple; two lots were placed in a pot, and a small child told to choose one. He chose the lot marked 'sin (*pap*)' rather than that of 'merit (*punya*)' and the man was judged to be guilty. He himself continued to say that he was innocent. Forced to admit the validity of the procedure, he nevertheless maintained that God was punishing him in this way for some *other* sin; but he had to bow to the divine verdict.

One should note that the village leaders took the first action. This was because the Potter population in Ramkheri consists of two brothers only; hence there was no subcaste elder immediately available to decide the guilt of the culprit (the Farmers, for example, decided a similar case at a subcaste meeting a few years previously). And there could be no waiting until a meeting of Potter representatives took place. For the man, if guilty, would have polluted the entire village in the meantime. In some matters, then, there must be immediate action by neighbours in their own interests (beef-eating would evoke the same response). Only the later stages of purification can be left to the subcaste. This is overt control, of course, but is at the same time so automatic that it can equally well be seen as a self-regulation.

I had previously been told of the complex procedure which had to be followed in such cases. When guilt had been established, it was said, the culprit was banished to the village boundary, a 'no man's land' where he would pollute no settlement. There he lived for several weeks in a roughly built lean-to, brought food but speaking to nobody. Afterwards he was allowed by the subcaste council to go for his purificatory bath to Gautamji, some 150 miles to the west. On his return he was shaved by the Sweeper, since no Barber would undertake such polluting work, and then sat before a small thatch hut. After rites, this was lit and he crawled through it, and ended the programme by feasting his assembled subcaste mates. The first food offered was never accepted, and the Sweeper took it; only afterwards would people eat a little with him to demonstrate his return to full subcaste membership.

But little of this procedure was followed by the guilty Potter. He did not go to the village boundary, but spent one night outside a shed which he used as a pottery at the edge of the village, maintaining that he was technically outside the settlement. People were reluctant to admit to me that he was not in the fields, and said that they did not know where he had gone; but I finally found him there. Passers-by took little notice of him, it is true, but on one occasion a man stopped to talk to me, and the Potter offered him a cigarette. He hesitated and then accepted it, saying that times had changed and he supposed it was all right to take the gift; but the two men did not smoke off the single cigarette, which they would normally have done. After only one day's wait, the Potter went for his purification, returning in three or four days. And only about a week after that he invited some twenty subcaste mates from nine villages, fed them and paid a Rs. 50 fine to be spent on maintenance of the subcaste temple in Dewas and on any public work of the subcaste. There was no ceremony of the burning hut, and the Sweeper complained that the first offering of food was not rejected and given to him.

It is significant that there was a rumour in the village that the Potter had not been readmitted to the subcaste because he had gone to Gautamji without the permission of the subcaste elders. For this emphasizes a major aspect of the incident—that the culprit took the steps he thought necessary, and the council later endorsed them. Formerly, the existence of a timetable and a set of elaborate expiatory rites meant that the leaders of the circle or kindred had to be consulted lest the procedure be improperly followed.[1] But now they have merely the role of confirming the culprit's acts, and it is clear that so long as he goes to Gautamji, they will do this.

In comparing their various activities, I have treated the village, circle and kindred councils of each subcaste as the same. But this is clearly a simplification, for the size of the local subcaste and the pattern of its distribution in the surrounding villages will obviously make a difference to its problems of social control. A small, scattered subcaste, like the Rajguri Nath, will seldom have the need for subcaste councils, for with so few members appropriate issues will rarely arise. And the councils which *do* meet will tend to have people from many villages. They will, I suggest, tend to be kindred rather than circle councils. For the villages in a formal circle council would be very scattered; the difficulties and expense of having to attend a meeting would sometimes be great, and it would be much easier to require only the attendance of kin who were in any case gathered on an occasion when subcaste matters could be discussed.

The Weaver subcastes, or the Rajputs or Farmers, on the other hand, have a large population within a smaller area (either spread evenly in almost all villages, or concentrated in a few settlements). One would expect more councils to occur, and for these councils to be as easily operated on a formal circle basis as on a kindred basis —though one would also look for more cases to be settled within the village when there is a large enough subcaste population there to have an effective village council.

Most of my data about subcaste councils come from these larger subcastes, and here again there are variations. The Rajputs, for example, have the best-defined circle, whereas the Farmers, being of the same size and with the same pattern of distribution, have no formal circle in the locality of Ramkheri. The Farmers suggest that this is because they are recent arrivals in most of the villages of this neighbourhood, and so have not had time to organize a circle; the Rajputs, on the other hand, have been here much longer and constant intercourse has produced a more organized procedure. Again, the Rajputs tend to have larger social gatherings than Farmers. After funerals they have wherever possible the *nukta* feast separate from the *ganta*, and spend as much on it as they can afford. Farmers, on the contrary, always combine the *nukta* and *ganta*, and this means that numbers of people may not be able to come at short notice. Farmer councils will thus be based largely on the closer kin, with less stress on a certain number of villages being represented, whereas

[1] Cf. Fuchs 1950: 46 for a description of the elders' decision in a similar case before the culprit purified himself.

people from a wider area meet under the Rajput custom. (As it happens, the Rajput circle which includes Ramkheri is very small, and this may be a reason for its continued existence. For when I asked a Rajput from a forty-three-village circle whether people from all villages always came to meetings, he had to admit that this was not invariable, although it should be so.) Finally, since the Rajputs are headmen in almost all villages where they live whereas Farmers are headmen less often, the former caste may accept formal authority in circles more easily. For they are more used to fellow subcaste members in authority in their villages as well as possessing more men who are trained as leaders; the Rajput *mandloi*, in fact, may often also be a headman. Among the Farmers, as several men said, 'Nowadays nobody will listen to any leader—and nobody who wishes to be a leader has the ability (*takat*) to enforce his decisions.'

Though several subcastes may still have circles, the general trend is away from formal groups. The man who may still be called *mandloi* or *jat patel* is, on further investigation, often found to be an influential man of the region, rather than a person with definite duties and a definite area of jurisdiction. This has two likely consequences. In the first place, it means that the subcaste populations of each village may be more isolated from one another, since there is no rule that men from nearby villages should attend council meetings. Second, co-operation will take place more between the kindred, for kin provide the alternative source of aid in handling matters for which people outside the village are needed. When the kindred occupies adjacent villages the pattern of inter-village contact may not greatly change. Thus, the Farmers have quite a large representation in two of the six villages which border on Ramkheri, and are linked to these by marriage. Whenever there is an important problem which Ramkheri Farmers cannot solve, the people of these villages will be invited, possibly with men of other settlements. This prompted one Farmer to tell me that there was, in fact, a Farmer circle comprising Ramkheri and these two villages as well as village X- about four miles off. I asked him, 'Why is not village Y- included, it is only three miles away, nearer than X-?' And he replied, 'We have no relatives (*ristedar*) there, so we would not ask them for any of our work.' But other Farmers present included Y- in the circle, and one maintained, 'I have my father's sister's relatives there.' This shows that the composition of councils varies according to the person who calls them, or according to the person who is giving the feast at which they are held; since the idea of the formal circle is still alive, such kindred councils tend to be described in terms of the circle. But one must remember that the circles were groups composed of entire village subcaste populations, into whose membership kinship did not in principle enter, though in practice it may have been an important integrative feature.

I have been talking about social control—i.e. the control of behaviour through punishments for deviance. But I must add a few words on the place of self-regulation [1]—the regulation of behaviour through the application of penalties, rather than punishments. In general, this form of sanction is rare at the village level, though common within the subcaste. I have few instances of strong village self-regulation taking place without the previous judgment of a subcaste council. One occasion, that of the Potter who killed the cow, has been described; here the village ascertained his guilt and then boycotted him completely. But this is a very particular situation, as I have suggested (see p. 265), and I have other instances where a man had committed an offence also universally disapproved of, but not universally polluting in this way, where the village had not taken action because the subcaste had not done so. Thus, a major leader had had as his mistress the wife of a subcaste mate, and this was common knowledge; but nothing had been done by subcaste or village. One would expect that the people of a village with a strong self-regulatory mechanism would act over any breaches whatsoever of accepted behaviour. The fact that this does not happen bears out Nadel's statement that 'the regulative effects must vary inversely with the separation of social roles, with the specialization of offices and tasks, and, implicitly, with the size of groups . . .'.[2] For one could characterize this society as one having considerable separation of roles and tasks through the caste system.

If, however, one takes the subcaste group as the focus, there is much less internal differentiation and according to Nadel there should be more self-regulation. My data suggest that this is true. One example concerns the concept of ancestry. On ancestry depend the kind of marriages that can be made for one's offspring, and so the kind of economic status and general prestige they will have, as well as the kind of reputation one will leave to posterity. None of the difficulties which stem from a marriage which is 'unequal' are explicit sanctions, but they are so pervasive that they provide a powerful regulatory force in the selection of marriage partners. Again, there is no punishment for remarriage of a divorced [3] woman in many subcastes. But the regulatory pressures are great—in parti-

---

[1] Nadel 1953: 266.   [2] Ibid.: 268.

[3] I hope to discuss elsewhere the way in which the term 'divorce' can be defined, and also remarriage.

cular the barring of certain villages from the second husband's social horizon, and the lowering of his future family's ancestry as well as his present reputation. Self-regulation, then, exists primarily within the subcaste; and the degree to which it operates at the village level is largely an extension of specific subcaste sanctions.

I have said that people generally have the idea that villagers should be as far as possible 'autonomous', making their own decisions and not taking quarrels with them to the outside. We have seen this feeling in the commensal and occupational sphere as well (see pp. 49 and 70). On the other hand, there is the feeling that the major unit is the local subcaste, i.e. the population of a particular region coinciding roughly with the kindred of recognition. Individuals put their subcaste membership on this local basis when they say, for instance, that a stranger belonging to the subcaste will not have commensal rights until he has shown his *bona fides*, determined in terms of links with people known to the villagers. The local subcaste group is the *effective* endogamous group (see p. 4), and in consequence it is held that matters affecting the subcaste should be decided by the entire population of the region, or as large a proportion as is convenient to gather in a circle or kindred council. If the village were autonomous and made all the decisions about its members, the wider subcaste councils would have little more than the occasional inter-village dispute to occupy them. Similarly, the village would not exist as a centre of social control if all matters were referred to wider councils. I suggest that a compromise has been reached. The village deals with cases in which the personalities of members are important and in which there are overflows of rivalries in other spheres of village life; the wider subcaste group deals with more cut-and-dried issues in which principles are more, and personalities less, at stake.

The village is a significant unit of social control at the subcaste level as well as at the inter-caste level. The latter rests on the headmanship and the statutory powers of the Village Committee. There is not a separate village subcaste control group *by definition*; and the village subcaste council is rather defined in terms of the activities in which it engages because it is the group most fitted to handle them. The disputes it deals with have so far tended to be internal matters rather than cases in which the external reputation and relations of the subcaste rest. But the present trend is reducing more and more subcaste matters from the kindred to the village subcaste group. This is working in the opposite direction to inter-caste affairs which are increasingly becoming matters for inter-village action (through both Village and Central Committees). The difference between these trends supports my major theme that we must view intra- and inter-caste affairs separately.

XIII

CONCLUSION

IT is worthwhile re-examining the main aim of this book, which has been to enquire into the nature of the caste and subcaste. In general, I have agreed with the position held by Ghurye and already quoted: ' . . . though it is the caste that is recognized by the society at large, it is the subcaste that is regarded by the particular caste and the individual'. With few exceptions, people outside it regard the caste as an undifferentiated population, and behave in the same way towards all its members.

What I have tried to do is to push this distinction further, and see what it means in terms of the social universe of the people of Ramkheri—which comprises a region of a few hundred villages, out of the many thousands which are inhabited by most of the castes and subcastes represented in the settlement. When we talk at this level, 'caste' and 'subcaste' become inverted, the caste group being smaller and the subcaste group larger. For people see the whole of a caste largely in terms of its representatives in their village. They may meet other members of the same caste when they go as guests to the villages of their kin, but their behaviour towards them conforms to that shown by the hosts and is, in a sense, only an extension of the village-based behaviour of the latter.

Thus caste, in this context, defines a *village* group, based on traditional occupation, commensal regulations and a particular status and mode of behaviour in the village. The caste of Rajputs means to the people of Ramkheri primarily the Rajputs of Ramkheri, with their custom of remarriage and their history of martial exploits, with their rules about eating with allied castes but not with Farmers, and their interest in public events. But Rajputs in another village may forbid remarriage, eat with Farmers and even (in one case near Ramkheri) contain many eminent vegetarians. Ramkheri people are of course aware that there are Rajputs in many villages, but they do not have to act as if these had any different customs from the Rajputs of their own settlement.

Again, Farmers in Ramkheri are a somewhat exclusive group, paying less attention to public works and more to their own domestic affairs. I do not know if there is any village where Farmers have a full Rajput-type of 'extrovert' character; but they certainly show powers

270

of leadership, and possibly a more relaxed standard of inter-caste contact, in the villages where they are headmen. There are several ways in which one can show that the two kinds of Rajputs and Farmers belong to the same caste—the common name, the legendary traditions of occupation and caste origins, perhaps diacritical marks of dress, etc., but not always kin ties (save in the case of 'unitary' castes). This is why I have called caste a rather shadowy category outside the village; it need not encompass a group of inter-acting members as does the subcaste.

The subcaste, applied to the situation on the ground, means the kindred of co-operation, with a 'halo' of the kindred of recognition, whose members can at once be transformed into those who co-operate because their status as genuine members of the subcaste is already accepted. These kindreds constitute the region of a village subcaste group. In some cases the subcaste has a more organized attribute in the shape of the circle and its leader and council. And in a few cases there is also a rather vague provincial overtone founded on the subcaste temple at Ujjain or elsewhere. As with the caste, the subcaste is distinguished by name, perhaps occupation and endogamy.

If we see the caste and subcaste as having this limited size, it is reasonable to expect variations over wide areas. Such differences in customs are not bewildering but natural if the whole named caste or subcaste is made up of at least hundreds of largely autonomous groups. Even within Malwa it is quite possible that amongst, say, the Bundela Tanners there is variation in customs and relations with other subcastes. And it may well be that little more than a common name links these people with subcaste mates in Bundelkhand, hundreds of miles to the northeast. In short, the terms 'caste' and 'subcaste' can mean either the whole or the effective part, that is, they have both a formal and an operational sense. I do not think it is right to forget the formal definition of the subcaste, and see it solely as a local group; nor, on the other hand, do I think it is wise to see caste only in its formal frame, and not consider that it has an operational connotation in which it exists in a small locality.

A point which flows from this is the importance of kinship in defining territorial units. For the subcaste's region is an area based on kin ties. These change constantly, and vary from person to person, so that it is impossible to map out definite regions for any particular group of subcaste members. The regions of individuals, and of subcaste groups, are a series of interlocking areas, covering eventually the whole subcaste population. This makes the region a fluid and rather unsatisfactory structural concept. Yet, I think, it corresponds to the villager's ideas of the extent of his effective subcaste population. The problem has already been discussed. Even when

271

dealing with a comparatively compact subcaste, Dumont found that for any person the territory of the subcaste was defined in terms of his kin links:[1] and he concludes that there can be no single delineation or definition of the territory of the Pramalai Kallar subcaste because there is no single kinship structure which corresponds to this. The entire subcaste may, in the last analysis, be a kin-group; but this is the anthropologist's abstraction, and would only in exceptional cases be a kin-group recognized as such by any single member. The 'territory' of a Ramkheri subcaste group is a variable kinship-territory, being the sum of the kin ties of the whole inter-related village subcaste group: but, if pressed wider than this, it attenuates into a mere connection through a common subcaste name.

A feature of this pattern of kin-based local organization is the absence of any extended structure of unilineal descent groups. Once lineage members put any distance between each other both the ritual and secular ties which linked them seem to fade quite quickly into a mere recognition without any requirement of action in common worship at the Bheru or Clan Goddess shrines, or in co-operation in matters of economic or jural importance.

This is especially significant for the Rajput population. For accounts from other areas tell of a strong agnatic structure over quite considerable areas. Thus, the Rajputs described by Cohn (1955) and those mentioned by Majumdar (1955) are all very conscious of their clan links, and in each case a lineage of considerable depth extends over fifty or more villages. Again, Blunt says that the council for social control is in the Rajput case based on the clan rather than the subcaste.[2] But in Ramkheri the clan does not have this structural importance for Rajputs. There is some notion of higher and lower clans (or branches), though no comprehensive hierarchy was ever listed for me. But beyond this the branch is mainly operative in marriage regulation.

The difference between the region around Ramkheri and those in the Uttar Pradesh described by the above writers may be historical in origin. Cohn's and Majumdar's Rajput branch cluster originated from conquest of a tract by a single Rajput, whose domain was progressively divided among descendants until each of the fifty villages is held by a different man, who is related to the others. Rajputs may have come to Malwa under the same conditions; but one may conclude that in the turbulent times which lasted until barely more than a century ago, the hold of any one man or group over a tract was impossible to sustain. Even the former Paramara kings of Malwa were forced from their thrones. Migration and continued internecine wars appears to have broken up any such territories, and thereby this

[1] Dumont 1957*a*: 13.   [2] Blunt 1931: 129.

structural role of the branch for the Rajputs. And the other castes had less political power and thus correspondingly fewer possibilities for establishing such domains. For all, the village or the region rather than the descent group has become the significant unit of internal structure. And only *within* the village is agnatic descent for the most part important.

Economic factors lie behind the patterning of the various kin-groups making up the subcaste, as well as the degree to which members keep in touch with each other. For the scattering of many kin-groups, which has helped to produce a weak unilineal structure, has been partly for economic reasons. In the old days, when there was plenty of land, the prices of crops were often so low as to make it hard for many to pay their land tax. So defaulters used to leave their villages. If they went to another settlement in the same State, their new headman would defend them against the attempts of the old headmen to recover the arrears; for if he did not, they would default on the land tax *he* was collecting. But a better idea was to cross one of the numerous State boundaries,[1] and thereby put a complex procedure of extradition between themselves and the tax collector. At the present time, movement from villages to towns is increasing since land is scarce; but the largest number of people leaving Ramkheri in the past decade have still been those going to another village to take up inherited land there. And I have shown how shortage of land has led to the assertion of the claims of women, and so to some of this movement being of sisters and daughters to their parental villages.

Both past and present factors make for a situation in which kinsmen are scattered. And under such conditions the economic ability to invite kin to weddings, mortuary feasts, etc., is important, as is the inclination to do so. It would indeed be difficult to resist kinship obligations if one's kin were in the same or adjacent villages. But when they live far away it is easier both to invite fewer, and for those invited to decline if they do not want to spend money on gifts, etc. Neither wealth nor inclination appears to be prior—for rich men do not always invite as many people as they could, and poor men are not bound to invite a number beyond their means. But on these gatherings rests the continuance of the kin tie, and people identify kin ties with invitations and so with money.

In the political sphere the chain of authority formerly passed from

[1] There was no law of nationality for Dewas Senior before 1947. Any person coming to take up residence in the State, or having immovable property there, was treated as the Maharaja's subject. In 1947 the Constitution Act was passed, in which certain criteria for nationality were laid down—among them a six-year period of residence in the State.

Maharaja to headman, and had little inter-village extension. But this has altered since 1948. I have shown the changing role of the headman after the abolition of the Maharaja's rule, and the emergence of new leadership roles sponsored by the present Government. These roles stem from elected committees (the Village and the Central Committee) composed of several villages. The following example shows how the Committees may influence the caste or subcaste structure. Though the Rajputs of Malwa keep apart from the subcaste of Eastern Rajputs, not eating or marrying with them, the Rajput candidate for the Central Committee chairmanship (see p. 130) canvassed the support of the Eastern Rajputs. When he won, an Eastern Rajput was rewarded with a seat on the District Committee. Politically, Rajputs of different villages closed their ranks, though socially they were still separate. But this sort of co-operation may well lead to greater social unification.

Though the village may be less autonomous as a political unit than it was, it appears to be gaining in importance as the unit of social control in the subcaste. I have suggested that disputes over which there is no agreed pattern of penalties, as well as those between people with complex relationships, are best handled by village rather than inter-village subcaste councils. For the people in the village council know the factors behind the case, and can be flexible in interpreting evidence and allocating punishment.[1] My hypothesis is that as changed modes of behaviour enter the village from the towns, so there is less unanimity over the sanctions and judgments to be made, and a greater tendency to keep discussion within the village subcaste population.

This book expresses in its way a present trend in studies of Indian peasantry. This is towards taking a larger canvas than the single village. Thus, Dumont talks of studying a single subcaste in order to abstract institutions which are part of the morphology of the culture area or civilization in which the subcaste exists.[2] Again, Marriott (1955a) has considered the ways in which the village is or is not an isolable whole, and suggests that villages cannot be studied as systems on their own. What, then, are to be the objects of future research? A subcaste as territorially compact as that studied by Dumont is probably rare; and it is in any case by no means certain that the subcaste should always be considered alone. Yet, if the region is the proper field, the difficulties of research in its hundreds of villages and dozens of castes appear great. How is the intensive work of the

[1] Srinivas (1955a: 19) observes that it is often more risky to take a case to an inter-village caste court than to have it adjudicated in the village—even if by members of another caste.

[2] Dumont 1957a: III.

Conclusion

anthropologists to be adapted to these conditions? This must happen if there is to be a systematic development of work on the nature of the local caste and subcaste group. And similar problems exist when the scale is widened, and we consider the nature of the caste as a whole. This book is an attempt to lay the foundations for continuing research, by analysing from data gathered in a single village, the nature of caste and kinship in that village and its region.

REFERENCES

AIYAPPAN, A. 1944. *Iravas and Culture Change*. Bull. Madras Govt. Mus., N.S. Gen. Sect. V.1. Madras.

ANONYMOUS (L. L. B.). 1955. 'Vikas Mandal' in *Kurukshetra, a Symposium of Community Development in India (1952–55)*. New Delhi. Pp. 264–70.

BAILEY, F. G. 1957. *Caste and the Economic Frontier*. Manchester.

BLUNT, E. A. H. 1931. *The Caste System of Northern India*. Oxford.

1946. Chap. II in Blunt ed., *Social Service in India*. London.

BOUGLÉ, C. 1908. *Essais sur le Régime des Castes* (Travaux de l'Année Sociologique). Paris.

BROUGH, J. 1953. *The Early Brahmanical System of Gotra and Pravara*. Cambridge.

BÜHLER, G. 1882. *The Sacred Laws of the Aryas* in Muller ed., *Sacred Books of the East*, Vol. XIV. Oxford.

1886. *The Laws of Manu* in Muller ed., *Sacred Books of the East*, Vol. XXV. Oxford.

CARSTAIRS, G. M. 1957. *The Twice-Born*. London.

Census of India. 1931. Vol. XX. Pt. II.

1951a. Vol. XV. Pt. I—A.

1951b. Vol. XV. Pt. I—B.

COHN, B. S. 1955. 'The Changing Status of a Depressed Caste' in Marriott ed., *Village India*. Chicago. Pp. 53–77.

COLE, B. L. 1932. 'The Rajput Clans of Rajputana' in *Census of India*, Vol. XXVII. Meerut. Pp. 134–41.

DAVE, T. N. 1951. 'The Institution of Bards in Western India', *Eastern Anthropologist*, IV. 3 and 4. Pp. 166–71.

DUBE, S. C. 1955. *Indian Village*. London.

DUMONT, L. 1957a. *Une Sous-Caste de l'Inde du Sud*. Paris.

1957b. *Hierarchy and Marriage Alliance in South Indian Kinship*. Occ. Papers of the Royal Anthrop. Instit. 12. London.

DUMONT, L. and POCOCK, D. F. 1957. *Contributions to Indian Sociology*, No. 1. Paris.

FORSTER, E. M. 1953. *The Hill of Devi*. London.

FUCHS, S. 1950. *The Children of Hari*. Vienna.

FÜRER-HAIMENDORF, C. VON. 1948. *The Raj Gonds of Adilabad*. London.

GHURYE, G. S. 1950. *Caste and Class in India*. Bombay.

GOUGH, E. K. 1956. 'Brahman Kinship in a Tamil Village', *American Anthropologist*, LVIII. 5. Pp. 826–53.

HOCART, A. M. 1950. *Caste*. London.

HU, C. T. 1956. 'Marriage-by-Exchange among the Tharus', *Eastern Anthropologist*, X. 2. Pp. 116–29.

HUTTON, J. H. 1946. *Caste in India*. Cambridge.

IBBETSON, D. 1916. *Punjab Castes*. Lahore.

References

KANE, P. V. 1941. *History of Dharmasastra*. Vol. II. Pt. I. Poona.
1953. *History of Dharmasastra*. Vol. IV. Poona.
KAPADIA, K. M. 1947. *Hindu Kinship*. Bombay.
KARVE, 1953. *Kinship Organisation in India*. Poona.
LANG, O. 1946. *Chinese Family and Society*. New Haven.
MAJUMDAR, D. N. 1955. 'Rural Analysis—Problems and Prospects', *Eastern Anthropologist*, IX. 2. Pp. 92–103.
MALCOLM, J. 1824. *A Memoir of Central India*. Vol. I. London.
MARRIOTT, McK. 1955a. 'Little Communities in an Indigenous Civilisation', in Marriott ed., *Village India*. Chicago. Pp. 171–222.
1955b. 'Social Structure and Change in a U.P. Village' in Srinivas ed., *India's Villages*. Calcutta. Pp. 96–109.
MAYER, A. C. 1952a. *Land and Society in Malabar*. Bombay.
1952b. 'The Holi Festival among the Indians of Fiji', *Eastern Anthropologist*, VI. 1. Pp. 3–17.
1955. 'Change in a Malwa Village', *Economic Weekly*, VII. 39. Pp. 1147–9.
1956a. 'Some Hierarchical Aspects of Caste', *Southwestern Journal of Anthropology*, XII. 2. Pp. 117–44.
1956b. 'Development Projects in an Indian Village', *Pacific Affairs*, XXIX. 1. Pp. 37–45.
1957. 'An Indian Community Development Block Revisited', *Pacific Affairs*, XXX. 1. Pp. 35–46.
1958. 'The Dominant Caste in a Region of Central India', *Southwestern Journal of Anthropology*, XIV. 4. Pp. 407–27.
MILLER, E. J. 1955. 'Village Structure in North Kerala', in Srinivas ed., *India's Villages*. Calcutta. Pp. 39–50.
NADEL, S. F. 1953. 'Social Control and Self-Regulation', *Social Forces*, XXXI. 3. Pp. 265–73.
NAIK, T. B. 1957. 'Social Status in Gujarat', *Eastern Anthropologist*, X. 3 and 4. Pp. 173–81.
OKADA, F. E. 1957. 'Ritual Brotherhood, a Cohesive Factor in Nepalese Society', *Southwestern Journal of Anthropology*, XIII. 3. Pp. 212–22.
RATTIGAN, W. H. 1929. *A Digest of Civil Law for the Punjab* (11th Edn.). Lahore.
ROSE, H. A. 1919. *A Glossary of Tribes and Castes of the Punjab and North-west Frontier Province*. Vol. I. Lahore.
RUSSELL, R. V. 1916. *Tribes and Castes of the Central Provinces of India*. Vols. II and IV. London.
SINH, R. 1936. *Malwa in Transition*. Bombay.
SRINIVAS, M. N. 1952. *Religion and Society among the Coorgs of South India*. Oxford.
1954. 'A Caste Dispute among Washermen of Mysore', *Eastern Anthropologist*, VII. 3 and 4. Pp. 149–68.
1955a. 'The Social System of a Mysore Village' in Marriott ed., *Village India*. Chicago. Pp. 1–35.
1955b. 'The Social Structure of a Mysore Village' in Srinivas ed., *India's Villages*. Calcutta. Pp. 19–32.

References

1957. 'Caste in Modern India', *Journal of Asian Studies*, XVI. 4. Pp. 529–48.

STEVENSON, H. N. C. 1954. 'Status Evaluation in the Hindu Caste System', *Journal of the Royal Anthropological Institute*, LXXXIV. Pp. 45–65.

TELANG, K. T. 1882. *The Anugita*, in Muller ed., *Sacred Books of the East*, Vol. VIII. Oxford.

TOD, J. 1829. *Annals and Antiquities of Rajast'han*. Vol. I. London (1950 edn. used).

TREVELYAN, E. J. 1929. *Hindu Law as Administered in British India*. Calcutta.

VENKATACHAR, C. S. 1933. 'Migration of Castes and Tribes into Central India and their Distribution' in *Census of India*, 1931, Vol XX. Pt. I. Delhi. Pp. 267–79.

GLOSSARY

ādivāsī   original inhabitant
ādmī   man, adult
aib   defect
amāvāsyā   day before new moon appears
ānā or *gaunā*   rite in the marriage cycle

bā   father's elder brother, father-in-law or any older man of his generation
bahin   sister
baiṭhak   sitting-place
bākal   ward of a village
bān   money given to spouse's father at wedding
bānā baiṭhānā   installation of spouse before wedding
bānā jhelnā   entertainment of spouse before wedding
bāṇṭedār   share-cropper
barābar   equal (of good ancestry)
barāt   groom's wedding party
baṛsās   wife's elder sister
barvā   genealogist
baṭāī   share-cropping tenure
battandār   patron of a genealogist
begār   compulsory labour
bhābhī   elder brother's wife
bhāī   brother
bhāībandh   clan or lineage
bhānej   sister's son or daughter
bhāṭ   genealogist
bhatijā   brother's son
bhauṅrā   physical defect, relevant in match-making
bidā   departure from a wedding
bidāgarī   gift made at departure of genealogist
birādarī   local subcaste group
byāhī   men related through the marriage of their offspring
byāhin   women related through marriage of their offspring

cāraṇ   bard
cauk   avenue, square; auspicious place for rite
caukīdār   watchman
cauṅrī   rite at wedding
cauṛā   calfskin used at Divali festival
cīrā   stone dividing village segments
coro   small boy

dādā   elder brother, or other person of own generation

dahej dowry
dalāl middle-man taking commission
dānā-pānī fate
darvājā door
devar husband's younger brother
devarānī husband's younger brother's wife
dharam religious duty
dharam kā bāp ritual father
dhol drum played by village drummer
dillagī joke
dokro old man

gaḍḍegāl stone commemorating treaty between villagers and marauders
gal swing
gangagaur genealogist at Ganges pilgrimage place
gāntā mortuary rite
gānv devatā village deity
gānv gotra clan affiliations (known to villagers)
gānv kā riṣtā village kin
gau hatyā killing of cow or bullock
gaurnī mortuary rite
geriyā song party at Holi festival
ghar house
gharjamāī husband living in his wife's household
gharsarī rite for protection of house
gharviyāh day before wedding
ghī clarified butter
gorā fair colour
gotra clan
gulli ḍaṇḍā game played in village
guṇ a quality
guru teacher
gurubhāī, gurubahin ritual brother, sister

hak authority, right
haldī lagānā rite of purification with turmeric
hīr songs sung at Divali festival
hukkā hubble-bubble pipe

ijjat reputation, honour
imlī tamarind
inām gift, rent-free land
istamurdār landlord

jāgīr grant of land
jāgīrdār landlord
jajmān patron
jamāī son-in-law
jāt species, caste

Glossary

jāt paṭel   caste headman
jāydād   inherited property
jeṭh   husband's elder brother
jeṭhānī   husband's elder brother's wife
jiyājī   sister's husband
juār   sorghum

kaccā   food cooked with water and/or salt
kākā   father's younger brother
kālā   black, dark-coloured
kāmīn   craftsmen
kaṇḍāriyā   grain-heap on threshing-floor
kāṅkṛā   type of wood found in village
karam (Skt. *karma*)   destiny
kavālī   songs sung at Holi festival
khālā   threshing-floor
khalsā   landlord-free village
khāndān   clan, lineage, genealogy
khās   main, chief, real
kheṛā   village, hamlet
khvāṅsā, khvāṅsī   real and classificatory brothers, sisters of spouse acting
      as aides at wedding
kriyā karam   mortuary rite
kṛṣak   farmer
kul   clan, lineage
kunku   red powder used in rites
kuṭumb   family

lagan   auspicious time, a wedding rite
lāṛī   son's wife, younger brother's wife

māc   drama played in villages
madadgār   go-between
madhyam   middle-range
majdūr   day labourer
makān   house
māmā, māmī   mother's brother, mother's brother's wife
māmere   gifts from mother's natal clan mates or others in this category
maṇḍap   wedding booth
maṅḍloī   leader of subcaste group
maṅgat   beggar, ascetic
manikum   model of parrot used in wedding
māsī, māsā   mother's sister, mother's sister's husband
mausāl   uterine kin
modī   storekeeper, wealthy man
mukām   residence
mukhātī   important man of Khati (Farmer) caste

nām   name, reputation for posterity

namūnā   a copy
nanand   husband's elder or younger sister
nātedār   relative
nāthrā   remarriage
naukar   contract labourer
nayī havā   new air (i.e. new customs)
nīc   low
nihaṅgī   naked; a celibate ascetic
nīm   margosa tree
nuktā   funerary feast
nyautā (Skt. *nimantraṇa*) invitation

pagṛī   turban, a mortuary rite
paharāvanī   gifts from bride's to groom's relatives
pakkā   food cooked in *ghi*
pakkā kṛṣak   owner of land
pāliyā   monument to man dying violent death
pālṭī   inter-caste division (Engl. party)
pañc   member of council
pañcāṅg   almanack
pañcāyat   council; local administrative committee
paṇḍā   spirit medium
paṅgat (Skt. *paṅkti*)   line of persons at a meal
paṅkheṛā   circle of villages
pāṅthī   division
pāp   sin
parausī   neighbour
pariṣad   council
parivār   family
parsād   food offered to deity, later distributed
parsāī   village priest
paṭel   headman
pāṭlī   wooden platform on which Clan Goddess is placed
paṭṭā   certificate of ownership
paṭṭedāṛ   landholder
patvārī   village accountant
pherā or *cauṅrī*   rite at wedding
phuā, phuphā   father's sister, father's sister's husband
pīhar   woman's parental household
piṇḍ   offering to ancestors at propitiatory rite
pīpal   sacred tree
pīrbhāī, pīrbahin   ritual brother, sister (Muslim)
pravara   exogamous unit
pūkarī   former name for Harijan castes
pūnam (Skt. *pūrṇimā*)   day of full moon
puṇya   meritorious

rākhī   thread of protection tied at Raksha Bandhan festival
rāojī   genealogist

Glossary

ristedār relative
roṭī dry flour pancake
ṛṣi gotra exogamous units mainly known to genealogists

sabhā council or committee
sagāī pre-marital engagement
śākhā branch, division
sālā, sālī wife's brother, wife's younger sister
sāmān baggage, farmer's equipment
samiti committee
saṁskāra rites in life cycle
sanad badge of office
sañjaholi mortuary rite observed in village
sansārī worldly; non-celibate branch of ascetic castes
sapiṇḍa kin with whom no intermarriage is allowed
sārkārī official, belonging to government
śarm shame, modesty
sarpañc head of council
sāṛū bhāī wife's sister's husband
sasur, sās wife's or husband's father, mother
sasurāl man's or woman's conjugal household
satī woman immolating herself on husband's funeral pyre
sevan type of tree found in village
śikmī type of tenancy
sivcaunī gifts made to bride at wedding
somvatī amāvāsyā new-moon falling on a Monday
śrāddh rite of propitiation to ancestors
śramdān voluntary contribution of labour
strīdhan woman's personal possessions

tablā drum
tāḳat ability
ṭānā rite observed by villagers in cattle epidemic
tānej nephew or niece in second descending generation
tāziyā element in Muslim festival of Muharram
terij notice of outcasting
ṭhākur Rajput landlord; title given to all Rajputs in courtesy
thaṛ faction
thūnī founding stone of village
tilak mark made with coloured earth or unguents on forehead
toraṇ wooden frame used during wedding

ujle clear, white; used to denote superiority
uttam high

vaṅś (Skt. *vaṃśa*) dynasty, line
vāris heir
varṇ classical division of Hindu society
vivāh marriage

285

INDEX

Index

288

Index

289

Index

Farmer headmen, 17
  subcastes, 153, 154, 155, 241
  weddings, 225–6
Farmers, genealogists of the, 195–7
  land ownership of, 71
  Ramkheri, kinship chart of, 174
  ritual kin ties of, 142
  social expenses of, 88
Farmers and commensality, 35, 36, 39
  and the Village Committee, 115, 116
  and village leadership, 127
  as moneylenders, 86
  See also Occupations and Subcastes
Father, ritual, 143–4
Feasts, expenses of, 87, 237, 255, 273
  expiatory, 251, 255, 258, 265
  funerary, 67, 87–8, 168, 200. *See also* Rites
    (*Nukta*)
  selection of guests for, 41–3, 168, 248–9,
    273
Festivals, 99–112, 113, 128
  Akhatij, 22
  Bathing, 256
  Colour Fifth, 109
  Dasahra, 13, 96, 99n., 184
  Divali, 100n., 104–6, 191, 226
  Gangaur, 139–40
  Gokulashtami, 57n.
  Holi, 67, 106–10, 123, 225, 226, 238, 249
  Maka Sankrant, 72, 111
  Moharram, 72
  Naumi, 67, 71, 99–103, 249
  Nine Nights, 99n., 104, 184n., 226
  Raksha Bandhan, 17, 140, 143, 219, 225, 226
Fines, 114, 115, 118, 251, 256, 258, 265
Five-Year Plan, 118
Food, *Kacca* and *Pacca*, 33, 34, 37, 38–41, 50,
  195
Forster, E. M., xiii, 13n., 57n.
Fuchs, S., 3, 26, 100n., 140, 187n., 257n.,
  266n.
Funerary rites, 71, 87–8. *See also* Rites (*Nukta*)
Fürer-Haimendorf, Professor C. von, xv, 192n.

Ganges, 200–1, 235
Gaur, Sri G. D., **xvi**
Genealogists, 162, 164, 165, 166, 187, 190, 203
  functions of the, 194–201
Genealogy and worship, 189, 190
Ghurye, G., 9, 270
Gifts, exchanges of, 139–40, 143, 223, 225, 237,
  248
  wedding, 225–6, 228, 229, 231–5, 249
Goats, sacrificial, 101, 103, 238, 249n.
Gods. *See* Deities
Gough, E. K., 3–4n., 4
Government, borrowing from the, 246
  local, 128–31
  policy of, for crops, 138
    of, for farming, 245
    of, for land, 79
    of, for liquor, 87, 104
    of, for Village Committee, 119, 120, 274
  relations of with village, 95, 97, 115
  village representative of, 93
Government camps, commensality at, 50, 51
  officials, 95, 96, 129
Grants (of land), 68, 72, 73
Grazing land, cultivation of, 123–4
  rights, payment for, 103

Gwalior territory, 194
  villages, 115n.

Harvests, 23, 137
Headman, village, caste group of the, 92, 96–7,
  99, 131n.
  official duties of the, 93–7
  unofficial duties of: non-secular, 99–111,
    191
  unofficial duties of: secular, 97–9
Headman's Council, 97, 121, 252
Headmen, village, 17, 18, 19, 73, 74, 92, 112–14,
  114, 128
  numbers of, 93
  powers of, 96–7, 103, 110, 112–13, 115,
    115–16, 138, 274
  relations with leaders of caste groups, 97,
    112
  rivalry among, 94
  wives of, 108, 109, 111
  and the Village Committee, 115–16, 118
Health, and marriage, 205, 207
Hierarchy, commensal, 34, 36 (Table), 37–40,
  41–3, 52
  of occupations, 74–8
Hindi caste names, 35–6
Hindu castes, 34–5
  Pollution Concept, 33
  Succession Act, 246n.
History. *See* Records
Hocart, A. M., 53, 75n.
Horoscopes, 229, 231, 233
House, purification of the, 261
House building, conditions governing, 16–17
  rite, 16–17
  sites, allocation of, 115
  tax, 115
Household, the joint, 181–2, 218, 241
Household composition, 21, 177–83
  relations, 214–22, 246
Households, joint, partition of, 241–2
Houses, design of, in Ramkheri, 15–16, 56, 178
  rules for entering, 56
Hu, C. T., 204n.
Hutton, J. H., 6n., 33n., 153n., 156n.
Hypergamy, 24n., 25n., 29, 156, 163, 165, 206

Ibbetson, D., 37
Image, of Bheru, 189, 190
  of Clan Goddess, 187–8
Immigrants, caste preferences concerning, 154,
  210–11
Immolation, 18, 193–4, 221
Individual, effect on of caste membership, 24, 89
  independent decision by an, 265–6
  obligations of, to kindred, 182–3, 247, 250
  role of within caste and subcaste, 6, 9, 49, 160,
    269
Individuals, relations between, in agricultural
  castes, 84
Indore, xiii, 14, 103, 159, 255, 256
Industry, movement into, 78
Inheritance, 25, 198, 222, 239, 242–7
  patrilineal system of, 179
Inter-caste discrimination, legislation against,
  48, 50, 58n., 259n.
  relations, 44–7, 87, 92, 127, 141–2, 144, 151,
    158, 249
  control of, 251
Inter-subcaste relations, 158–60, 249

290

Index

Intra-caste relations, 8, 151
Islam, 34n.
  conversion to, 26n.

Jokes, 221, 226, 229
Justice, administration of, 95, 114–15, 117, 120
Justice Committee, 129

Kane, P. V., 235n., 242n.
Kapadia, K. M., 228n.
Karam, doctrine of, 89
Karve, 1, 5n., 164n., 184n., 203n., 209n.
Ketkar, S. V., 6
Khandan, 167–9, 207
Kin, affinal. *See* Affines
  behaviour of, at mortuary rites, 235–9
    of, at weddings, 227–35
    of, in secular matters, 239–49
  circle of, 203
  individual, 231
  inheritance rights of, 242–7
  ties of, 28, 140, 146, 172, 212, 235, 247–50, 259, 271–2, 273
  uterine, 173, 222, 224, 229, 232, 237, 241, 250
Kin-group, household constitution of a, 214–22
  loans within the, 86, 91, 246–7
Kin-groups, 5, 6, 151, 167, 170, 172–7, 182–3. *See also* Agnatic Groups
  bilateral, 170
  scattering of, 273
  size of, and social control, 249
Kin relations, interpersonal, 214–50
  terms (modes of address), 144–5, 146, 216, 234
  ties, inter-village, 248–9
Kindred, 5, 5n., 212, 231–3, 267–8
  Councils, 254–5, 258, 260, 261, 262, 266, 267. *See also* Subcaste Councils
  gatherings, 235, 254–5
  of co-operation, 4, 161, 170, 171, 212, 236, 248, 255, 271
  of recognition, 4, 161, 171–2, 207, 212, 248, 269, 271
Kinship, agnatic, in village, 6, 9, 29. *See also* Agnates
  uterine-affinal, in region, 6, 9
  village, 144–6, 247–9
Kinship roles and village intrigue, 224
  ties, inter-village, 130, 212, 248–9
Kinsmen, duties of, 222–4, 250
Kolhapur, Maharaja of, xiv
Kutumb, 167, 170–2, 263

Labour, compulsory, 95, 113
  Government demand for, 97
  'voluntary', 115, 120–1
Labourers, 75, 78, 79, 83 (Table), 124, 137
Land, bequeathing of, 79
  disputes over, 73, 98, 138–9, 194, 244, 251, 262–3
  distribution of, 80–2
  foreclosure on, 79, 85
  gift of, 79, 244
  inheritance of, 242–7
  ownership of, 78, 79, 80 (Table), 81–2, 181, 182, 228
  rent-free, 68, 72, 73, 95
  sale of, 79, 244
  scarcity of, 19, 88, 103, 243, 243n., 273
  size of holdings, 79, 80

Land registers, 244
  tax, 18n., 19, 78, 79, 94, 96, 115, 138, 273
Landlord, royal, advantages of, 19, 96
Landlords, 18n., 19, 96, 107, 109, 114, 115n., 128, 256
  absentee, 82, 245
  non-cultivating, 80n., 81, 82
Landowner, 78, 78–9, 98, 137
  cultivating, 75, 79, 80, 81
Lang, O., 249n.
Law, customary, 243
Law enforcement, 95, 97, 112, 114–15
Leach, Dr. E. R., xv
Leaders, village, 253, 254, 257, 259, 264, 267, 268
Leadership, village, 92–3, 93–4, 96–7, 98–9, 112–13, 113, 119, 121, 124, 127, 128–9, 253, 273–4
Leprosy, 102, 205, 206, 235
Levirate, 221
Lineage, analysis of, 167–9, 171–2, 173–7, 182–3, 190–1, 200
  charts of, 174, 175
  decline in ties of, 272
Lines, clan, 164–5
Livestock, trading in, 85
Loans, 85, 86, 91, 246. *See also* Moneylending
Local government, 128–31

Madhya Bharat, Chief Minister of, xv
  Government of, 115
  Government, Officials of, xv
  State, xiii, 13, 21n., 48
Madhya Pradesh State, 13
Maharaja. *See* Dewas
Majumdar, D. N., 272
Malabar, 160
Malcolm, J., 11n., 14
Malwa, xiii, 5, 14, 19, 28, 99, 100n., 110n., 160, 192, 211, 213, 221, 255
  castes of, 13, 272
  geographical position of, 11
  history of, 11–14, 272–3
  subcastes of, 153–4, 271
Malwi villages, headmen in, 93
Marriage, demographic aspects of, 208–13, 247–9
  expenses of, 43, 205, 206, 225, 225n., 233–4
  inter-caste, 25, 155
  inter-clan, 166, 202–3
  inter-village, 248
  intra-village, 209
  leviritic, 221, 259
  reciprocal, 24n., 156
  rules of, 29, 198, 202
  significance of, 227–8
  the pattern of, 202–13
  virilocal, 179, 222
  when contracted, 215
Marriage chains, 210–11, 212
  direction, 210, 211 (Table), 212–13
  parties, 225–6
Marriages, broken, 227
  forbidden, 260–1
  irregular, 198, 203, 205, 206
  when held, 42–3, 230. *See also* Remarriage, Rites and Weddings
Marriott, McK., 99n., 234n., 274
Match-maker, 206, 206–7, 256

291

Index

Mathur, Sri K. S., xv, 3n., 49n., 156n., 162n., 216n.
Matrilineal descent tie, 204. *See also* Marriage
Mayer, A. C., 36n., 37n., 61n., 80n., 110n., 122n., 127n., 129n., 231n.
Meat-eating. *See* Vegetarianism
Mediums, 99–100, 106
Memorials, 102, 191, 193–4
Migration. *See* Caste, Subcastes *and* Clan
Millar, E. J., 257n.
Mitakshara system, the, 241, 242, 243, 244
Money, loans of. *See* Loans *and* Moneylending
Moneylenders, protection against, 79
Moneylending, 85, 90
Mortgage of land, 79
Mothers, unmarried, 26n.
Muslim castes, 34–5. *See also* Castes
Mysore villages, 126, 160

Nadel, Prof. S. F., xv, 268n.
Naik, T. B., 252n.
National Extension Service, 115
Nationality, in Dewas Senior, 273n.
Nine Nights. *See* Festivals (Naumi)
    Women. *See* Festivals (Naumi)

Occupations:
  Accountant, village, 21, 73, 74, 76, 91, 94, 125, 127, 129, 231
  Barber, 63–4, 67, 69–70, 75, 101
  Beggar, 63, 71–2, 75–6
  Blacksmith, 65, 67, 75
  Carpenter, 64–5, 67, 70, 75
  Cotton-carder, 72
  Dairyman, 72
  Drummer, 66, 67, 74, 101
  Farmer, 72, 75, 76, 137–8. *See also* Farmer in main index
  Goatherd, 72, 75, 103
  Grain broker, 72–3
  Market gardener, 72
  Oil-presser, 75
  Potter, 65, 67, 75, 101
  Priest, 71, 72, 75, 101, 229, 235, 236, 255–6
  Schoolmaster, village, 74, 76, 114, 115
  Storekeeper, 72–3
  Sweeper, 66–7, 70, 74
  Tailor, 72
  Tanner, 66, 67, 74
  Tobacco-curer, 72
  Trader, 72
  See also Castes *and* Subcastes
Occupations, and subcaste classification, 156
  hierarchy of, 74–8, 88
  payment for, 67 (Table), 71, 72
  traditional, and caste, 35, 61–3, 76–8, 88, 89, 90
Offences, ritual, 251
  secular, 251
Officials. *See* Government
Okada, F. E., 141n.
Outcasting, 154–5, 163, 253, 255, 256, 259–60

Pande, Sri M. C., xv
Parenthood, 215
Patrikin, 182, 194, 233, 241
Patrilineal affiliation, 25, 28–9, 145, 161
Payment for agricultural labour, 79–80, 80n.
  for genealogy, 196, 198, 199
  for purchases, 72–3
  for work, 63, 67 (Table), 68, 71, 72, 73

Pilgrimages, 200–1, 251
Pocock, D. F., 126n.
Police, 73, 95
Pollution, 45, 52, 57, 62, 74–5, 90, 124, 260, 264–5
Prestation. *See* Gifts
Prestige, 200
Processions, village, 99, 100, 104–5, 107–8, 110–11, 111–12
Procreation, theories of, 204, 217
Property, ancestral, partition of, 242, 243–4
  disputes over, 117, 241–2
  inheritance of, 198, 222, 242
  joint, 181–2, 241
Provincial Councils, 255–6, 261
Public works, 94, 97, 200, 265
Punishment, 95, 251, 262–6, 268. *See also* Boycott
Purification, 58, 87–8, 228, 230, 235–6, 251, 260n., 261, 265

Rajasthan, 11, 13, 166, 211n.
Rajput, *nukta* of a, 87–8
Rajput branch names, 162–3
  caste, internal structure of, 164–6
  caste group, ritual kin ties of, 142
  circles, 253, 259, 266–7
  clan groups, 93, 187–8, 272, 274
  dominance, 131, 267
    in Ramkheri, 92, 97, 110, 111, 113, 116, 123, 125–7
  genealogists, 195
  headmen, 17, 18, 82, 92, 97, 110, 267
  landlords, 256
  marriages, 205, 206–7, 209, 210, 211, 234
  occupations, 36
  subcaste, lineage of a, 173–6
  subcastes, 153–4, 236, 256, 259, 266–7
Rajputs, distribution of, 130
  factions among, 113, 126–7, 239
  Kshatriya status of, 63
  land ownership of, 71, 81–2, 83, 90
  social expenses of, 87–8, 91
  traditional origin of the, 164–5
  variations in customs among, 270
  wealth of, 86
Rajputs and allied castes, 37n., 60, 88, 131
  and commensality, 35, 37–40, 43, 49, 60
  and moneylending, 86–7
  and the Central Committee, 131
  and the Village Committee, 115–16, 123
  as arbitrators, 98, 125
Ramkheri Village:
  administrative action in, 119–23
  age distribution in, 20–1
  agriculture in, 22–23, 80
  boundaries of, 21, 102, 110
  caste composition of, 19–20, 24, 28, 34, 35 (Table), 60, 159
    councils of, 49. *See also* Caste Councils
  distribution in, 54–5 (diagrams), 56
  cemeteries in, 237n.
  changes in voting strength of, 127
  climate in, 11
  clothes washing in, 53
  commensal hierarchy in, 34–40, 41–3, 47–8, 52
  description of, 15
  emergence of new leaders in, 127
  external contacts of, 128

292

Index

Index

Subcaste Councils, procedure of, 257–60
  types of, 251–6
    Village, 252, 257, 260–1, 261–2, 263–4, 266, 269, 274
  group, expulsion by the, 124, 253, 255, 259–260, 262–6
  region of a village, 161, 212–13, 271
  groups, 151, 212–13, 224, 248–9, 251–2, 261, 263–4, 269, 271. *See also* Kin-Groups
  factions among, 239–42, 252, 262, 264
  membership, significance of, 5, 24n.
  policies, initiation of, 256
  Provincial Councils, 255–6, 261
  region, as field for research, 274–5
  temple, Dewas, 265
    Ujjain. 251, 255–6, 271
  temple committees, 256
  ties between villages, 91, 151, 208, 247–8, 248 (Table)
Subcastes:
  Bhilala, 210, 241
  Deshvali Mina, 158
  Farmer, 156, 208, 210, 240 (Table), 241, 263, 266–7. *See also* Farmer in main index
  Goalbans Dairyman, 38, 153, 156
  Gujarati, 4, 13, 153, 156
  Gujarati Barber, 256, 258
  Gujarati Blacksmith, 156
  Gujarati Gardener, 156, 208
  Gujarati Tailor, 156
  Gujarati Weaver, 5, 152, 158, 253
  Jadavbans Dairyman, 38, 159
  Kanauji Brahman, 153, 159
  Malwi, 4, 38, 153, 156, 157
  Malwi Carpenter, 156
  Malwi Goatherd, 156
  Malwi Oil-presser, 156
  Malwi Potter, 156
  Malwi Weaver, 210
  Maru Kumavat, 153
  Mewara Carpenter, 256n.
  Mewara Oil-pressers, 156–7
  Mochi, 156, 160
  Nababansi Drummer, 153, 156
  Pancholi Rajputs, 154–5, 256, 259
  Pramalai Kallar, 272
  Purviya Tanner, 153, 156
  Rajgeria Farmer, 155
  Rajguri Nath, 153, 156, 266
  Rajput, 156, 208, 210, 266–7. *See also* Rajput in main index
  Rajput, 'Eastern', 154
  Rathor Oil-presser, 153, 157
  Sanodiya Brahman, 153, 156, 159
  Saticuri Sweeper, 153, 156
  Srigaur Brahman, 153
  Ujle Goatherd, 38
  Ujle Mina, 153, 156, 158
Subcastes, differences between within one caste, 159–60
  distribution of, 159, 208, 12–13, 247–8, 271–2
  endogamous, 90, 155–6, 160. *See also* Endogamous Group
  genesis of, 4–5, 154–5, 155n.
  immigrant, 154, 157–8, 159, 190
  isolation of, 182–3
  kin composition of, 172–7, 271–2
  merging of, 157–8
  number of clans in, 208

Subcastes, ranking of, 156–7
  records of the, 196
  variations of behaviour in, 154
Sub-clans, 166

Tax, arrears of, 79, 273
  land. *See* Land Tax
Tax collection, commission on, 94–5
Taxes, collection of, 94–5, 112
Telang, K. T., 62n.
Temples, 101–2. *See also* Subcaste Temples
Tenants, 75, 76, 78, 79, 82, 83, 98
Territory, subcaste. *See* Region
Theft, privileged, 107
Threshing-places, village, 137–9
Tod, J., 164n.
Town, economic ties with the, 91
Towns, movement from villages into, 273
Trade, 84–5
Transvestite, 140n.
Trevelyan, E. J., 203n.
Turban, white, 235, 236–7, 239
Tutelary spirits, 100, 140, 167, 192n.

Ujjain, 11, 12, 13, 103, 105, 235, 236, 239
  subcaste temples at, 251, 255–6, 271
Unilineal descent group, 99, 101, 167, 169, 184–201, 230–1, 235, 236, 272. *See also* Kin-Groups *and* Marriage
Unions, informal, 25, 154, 205, 207, 260, 261, 262–3. *See also* Marriage
Untouchability, 57–9
Untouchables, 40. *See also* Castes (Harijan)
Uterine kin. *See* Kin
  links, 170
Uttar Pradesh, 211, 272

Varn, *Kshatriya*, 44, 61–3, 162–3
  Sudra, 61, 62
  Vaisya, 61, 62
Vegetarianism, 44–5, 48n., 87, 103, 238, 249
Venkatachar, C. S., 13, 158n.
Village, boundaries of, 9, 21, 95, 102, 110, 265
  conditions for starting a, 17
  conjugal, 140–1, 144, 179
  external contacts of the, 128–31
  foundation stone of a, 17, 102
  pollution of a, 260, 264–5, 268
  Ramkheri. *See* Ramkheri Village
  region of a, 212–13, 271
  the, as administrative unit, 128, 273
  the, as discrete social unit, 93, 95, 146–7, 269
  typical, characteristics of a, xiii
Village activities, corporate, 101, 106, 110, 113, 249
  autonomy, 268–9, 274
  Committee, the, 15, 57, 64, 73, 93, 94, 95, 113, 120–3, 123–7, 274. *See also* Comprehensive Committee
  caste representation on the, 115–16
  chairman of the, 98, 111, 115, 116, 117, 118 121, 127, 128–9
  elections to the, 119–20
  foundation of the, 114
  income of the, 115
  powers of the, 114–15
  statutory authority of the, 114, 269
  Committees and inter-village relations, 129

294

Index